PLACE NAMES
OF SAN ANTONIO

plus
BEXAR
and
SURROUNDING COUNTIES

David P. Green

THIRD EDITION

MAVERICK BOOKS
Trinity University Press
San Antonio

Published by Maverick Books, an imprint of
Trinity University Press
San Antonio, Texas 78212

Third Edition

Cover design by Elms Wyatt

978-1-59534-674-2 paperback

Trinity University Press strives to produce its books using methods and
materials in an environmentally sensitive manner. We favor working with
manufacturers that practice sustainable management of all natural resources,
produce paper using recycled stock, and manage forests with the best
possible practices for people, biodiversity, and sustainability. The press is
a member of the Green Press Initiative, a nonprofit program dedicated to
supporting publishers in their efforts to reduce their impacts on endangered
forests, climate change, and forest-dependent communities.

The paper used in this publication meets the minimum requirements of the
American National Standard for Information Sciences—Permanence of
Paper for Printed Library Materials, ansi 39.48–1992.

CIP Data on file at the Library of Congress

26 25 24 23   5 4 3 2

Contents

Foreword

Some years ago, I read that there were 15,000 streets in San Antonio—a figure that must have increased exponentially during the last decade or so of explosive development, particularly in far northern San Antonio.

Developers have no doubt been kept busy by the need to come up with previously unused, attractive-sounding names for their plats of Lanes, Ways, Crescents and Courts.

But that wasn't how San Antonio's older streets were named. Main-traveled roads were known by the places they led to; streets got their names from what people called them—after how they looked, or who lived on them or what had happened there. Later, civic worthies named streets after each other, or after people who were considered to be admirable at the time. They extended these naming practices to parks, schools and other institutions.

Even the names of early suburbs, made possible by ever-extending streetcar lines, tell us something about what it was like to live here in other times. Neighborhoods named "Heights" or "Hill" told prospective buyers that this land was less likely to flood in the spring and fall, and better situated to receive cool breezes in the summers before air conditioning.

Every name—in English or Spanish—meant something about who had lived in San Antonio and what their values were. With the names they gave places they had in common, our predecessors showed us whom they respected, which communities they had connections with, what their streets were used for and how their physical world was configured before growth and progress changed the city's streetscape almost beyond recognition.

Less casual but still significant ways of naming followed. Some names given in the late 19th and early 20th centuries were arbitrary systems meant to tell those in the know where a street was: states on the east side, American cities north of the city center and so on. There were letters and numbers, Alamo heroes, trees and vines, Mexican cities—a hodgepodge of systems picked up from other cities that probably confused more than they helped. Now, these seemingly unrelated names preserve a sampler of naming practices of the era—and, perhaps, the ambition of San Antonio's leaders to be as organized and progressive as other cities to the north and east.

Just like public statuary, names are all too easily overlooked monuments to what the community has considered important. Each tells a story, but until this book was compiled the history signified by our community's names was scattered. The city's research libraries all hold information on street names, in vertical files and chapters or brief references in books on San Antonio history. But those who were curious about namesakes had to know where to look, and the search could be time-consuming.

Since 1992, I've written a question-and-answer column on local history for the San Antonio Express-News. I've also led downtown history tours and taught a community-education course on San Antonio geography. If there is any one category of question I've been asked most often, it's namesakes: Who's it named for? Why did it used to be called something else? Is this naming story just a legend or is it true?

Some of the answers to queries like these are well documented, while others are lost in conjecture and alternate explanations. In Place Names of San Antonio, plus Bexar and Surrounding Counties, Dr. David Green has been careful to separate fact from legend, while assembling a well-organized key to names both traditional and contemporary.

Use it as a reference or browse it for the stories—either way, it's a valuable guide to San Antonio's past that will deepen our understanding of the present city.

Paula Allen

PREFACE TO THE THIRD EDITION

Eponym: The person for whom
something is or is believed to be named.

This book is about eponyms. It is about the names that we live with in San Antonio. The aim of this book is to put faces and stories with those names. In this city and its satellite communities, we are surrounded by people's names—on streets, buildings, businesses, towns, parks, schools and so on. In this third edition, the stories behind nearly 1,000 of these people are revealed, providing tiny glimpses into the lives of those persons as well as suggesting how the names came about.

In the 1970s, before beginning my career as a surgeon, I was a mem-ber of the faculty at the University of Texas Health Science Center at San Antonio. My address was on Floyd Curl Drive, but no one seemed to know who Floyd Curl was. My curiosity over the naming of this street led to an ever-widening search for stories behind the names of San Antonio. But I realize that no matter how many editions of his book are written, it will never be "finished."

There will always be new streets added to our community, and the stories behind names of many long established streets and places will remain obscure. Through a combination of dedicated research, seren-dipity, coincidence and pure luck, I have managed to stumble across some older names, but many more are unknown. More than once I have followed what I thought was a path to the identity of a mystery name, only to have it slam into a dead end or peter out with insufficient documentation.

Although every effort has been made to verify the validity of what is in this book, I have no illusion that every bit of information is totally correct. Much material was gleaned from oral communication, word of mouth stories and handwritten family histories. No doubt some truths have been shaded by misinterpretation, bias and incomplete informa-tion, but history becomes how we remember it or how it is told. Several entries in the first and second editions were found to be inaccurate and were rewritten, usually thanks to feedback from readers.

Thus I earnestly solicit feedback from readers, either to correct something that is wrong or to contribute information about a new name.

And, by the way, thanks for reading this book.

David P. Green, MD

· 1 ·
EARLY SPANISH NAMES

In early 1691, an expedition set out from Mexico to establish missions among indigenous people living in the Spanish province of Texas. Leading the expedition were Domingo Terán de los Ríos, the first Spanish governor of the province, and Damian Massanet, a Franciscan priest in charge of missionary work in East Texas.

During the era of Spanish exploration, it was customary for Franciscans to name a place after the saint on whose feast day they encountered the site. On this particular expedition both men kept diaries. Terán recorded that on June 13, 1691 they encountered a stream which he named for San Antonio de Padua, because that was the feast day of Saint Anthony. Father Massanet's diary says he named this place San Antonio de Padua for the same reason. After the first Spanish settlers arrived in 1718, San Antonio developed as three separate communities: church-controlled missions with their Indian converts; the military garrison, based on Military Plaza; and the civilian community, centered on Main Plaza.

St. Anthony de Padua   Saint Anthony was born in Portugal in 1195 to a family of nobility. His name was Fernando. He entered the religious order of St. Augustine at age 15, but his life took a crucial turn 11 years later when he was inspired by the deaths of five Franciscan missionaries who had been tortured and beheaded by the sultan of Morocco. Desperately wishing to be sent to Morocco to be a witness for Christ and desiring martyrdom for himself, Fernando left the Augustinians and joined the Franciscan order, at which time he changed his name to Anthony.

The Franciscans did send him to Morocco, but he became seriously ill and

Portugal donated this statue of St. Anthony, a native son, to his namesake city in 1968 for Hemisfair '68, which marked San Antonio's 250th anniversary.

had to return home. Storms in the Mediterranean forced his ship to land on the east coast of Sicily, where he was taken in by friars at Messina. Described as frail and sickly, he was initially assigned to be a kitchen helper, which allowed him to spend most of his time in prayer, contemplation and study. He is said to have had an unusually retentive memory that enabled him to acquire an extraordinary knowledge of the Bible.

Anthony was content to live in obscurity, immersing himself in the monastic life, until fate changed the course of his life. At a gathering of friars in the town of Forli, he was forced to address the assembly because no one else in his order was prepared to speak. Anthony begged to be excused, but his superior told him to say whatever words the Holy Ghost should put in his mouth. The eloquence of his sermon that day astonished the whole company. For the rest of his life he traveled throughout France, Spain and Italy as the Church's most acclaimed preacher and gifted teacher of theology. Although he preached to crowds of 30,000 and was revered by the masses, Anthony is said to have never lost touch with poor and common people.

His last home convent was in Padua, where he died on June 13, 1231 at the age of 36. There were many stories of miracles performed by Anthony during his lifetime, and within a year he was canonized by Pope Gregory IX.

Three decades later, a magnificent basilica was built in Padua for his order, and his remains were transferred to a burial crypt there. It was discovered that the flesh had entirely decayed except the tongue, which was said to have been as incorrupt and fresh as it was when he was living. The tongue has been preserved in a costly case in the church since then.

In addition to being the patron saint of Portugal, American Indians, travelers and many other groups, St. Anthony is also the patron saint of lost or stolen items. Pope Pius XII proclaimed St. Anthony as Patron Saint of the City of San Antonio. For HemisFair, San Antonio's world's fair that also celebrated the city's 250th anniversary in 1968, Portugal donated a statue of Saint Anthony, now tucked among shrubs and palms on the north bank of the River Walk extension near Rivercenter Mall. Another life size statue of St. Anthony, donated to the city in 1955 by the Order of Alhambra, was recently moved to a more visible location in the renovated Main Plaza.

It is interesting to speculate about what San Antonio might have been named if those Spanish travelers had arrived a little earlier or a bit later. The saints with feast days closest to St. Anthony's are St. Ephrem, on June 9, and St. Romuald, on June 19. Shortly after publication of the second edition of this book, Brother Edward Loch, archivist for the Archdiocese of San Antonio, informed me that if the expedition had arrived one day later San Antonio would likely have been named Corpus Christi, as that is a movable feast day and in 1691 happened to have fallen on June 14.

El Duque de Béxar   In 1718, under orders from the Viceroy of Mexico, the Marquis de Valero, Don Martín de Alarcón was leading an expedition to establish Spanish colonies in Texas. The viceroy's older brother was the Spanish war hero Don Manuel, eleventh Duque de Béxar, who had died leading Spanish troops against the Turks near Budapest in 1686. On May 5, 1718, Alarcón picked the name of the viceroy's late brother for a new settlement on the San Antonio River—the Villa de Béxar. He also established a military installation, the Presidio of San Antonio de Béxar.

A picturesque town named Béxar already existed in Spain, 100 miles west of Madrid and 50 miles south of Salamanca. Béxar straddles both sides of a mountain range with rivers flowing through rugged lands. A current tourist attraction there is the Ducal Palace, an old castle rebuilt in the 16th century and home of the current Duque de Bexar.

The letter "x" in Old Spanish was the phonetic equivalent of "j" in so-called Modern Spanish. Thus "Béxar" is the Old Spanish spelling of Modern Spanish Béjar. The correct pronunciation for both is BAYhar. Why and when did the "x" become silent? The most likely answer is that Anglo settlers in Texas had trouble pronouncing the harsh Spanish "j." Linguists refer to such speech patterns as "phonetic drift," but it is not clear when the transition to the current pronunciation of "Bear" took place.

San Fernando de Béxar   With the Spanish army's Presidio de San Antonio de Béxar established on what became downtown's Military Plaza, or Plaza de Armas, the King of Spain sought a civilian community as a buffer between Spanish Mexico and French Louisiana, so he imported Spanish settlers from the Canary Islands.

In 1731, some 56 persons arrived to settle in the area previously designated by Alarcon as the Villa de Béxar. Many say the new settlement was renamed San Fernando de Béxar in honor of the heir to the Spanish throne, the future Fernando VI. Fernando VI, however, was not a saint. A more likely candidate is Fernando III, a 13th-century Spanish king who fought against Muslims in Spain for 27 years. He was canonized—but not until 1671, only 60 years before the Canary Islanders arrived in Texas.

For a century the community was called simply Béxar, but was renamed San Antonio in 1837. Following the War of Independence from Mexico, the Congress of the new Republic of Texas in January 1837 passed an act incorporating the "town of Bexar." That December, the congress approved a charter authorizing the City of San Antonio in the County of Bexar.

SPANISH MISSIONS

San Antonio de Valero/ The Alamo   With the military component established as the Presidio of San Antonio de Béxar and civilians organized under the Villa of San Fernando de Béxar, Native Americans were gathered into missions of the Catholic Church. The first in the San Antonio area was Mission San Antonio de Valero, established in 1718. Why it was nicknamed the Alamo is not clear, but there are some good guesses. In Spanish, Alamo means "poplar," a tree including the cottonwood. Cottonwoods flourished along the river around the mission. The eastward extension of what is now Commerce Street was called the Alameda—"poplar grove" in Spanish. At the time of the battle in 1836 it was described as broad and irregularly shaped, flanked on both sides by huge cottonwood trees.

There is a more likely explanation. In the early nineteenth century, as Spain fortified its northern territories against French expansion, Spain created light, mobile troops called "flying companies." One company of 100 mounted lancers was recruited in the Coahuilan town of San José y Santiago del Alamo de Parras, a village known for grapevines ("las parras") and cottonwood trees ("los alamos"). This unit arrived in 1803 to bolster the San Antonio garrison stationed at the Mission San Antonio de Valero. For the next 25 years or so the names Valero and Alamo were apparently used interchangeably, but eventually the name Alamo predominated.

Concepción Mission Nuestra Senora de la Purisima Concepción de Acuña, Our Lady of the Pure Concepción de Acuña originally had the suffix "de los Hainais," after the East Texas Indians the mission was to serve when originally founded in 1716 near Nacogdoches. After the move to San Antonio in 1731 that was changed to honor the viceroy Juan de Acuña, Marques de Casafuerte, who had authorized the move.

Espada Mission San Francisco de la Espada was Mission San Francisco de los Tejas when it was the first Spanish mission established in east Texas in 1690. Four moves later, in San Antonio in 1731, it was still named after St. Francis, but the reason for the ending "de la Espada"—Spanish for "of the sword"—is unknown.

San José Mission San José y San Miguel de Aguayo combines the names of St. Joseph and the Marques de San Miguel de Aguayo, who in 1720 authorized founding the mission.

San Juan Mission San Juan Capistrano, founded in 1716 in East Texas as San José de los Nazonis, was moved in 1731 to San Antonio, where there were no Nazoni Indians to serve but where there was already a mission named for St. Joseph. So the new arrival was renamed to honor a recently canonized saint, Italian-born John of Capistrano, a theologian and inquisitor who rallied peasants for a critical victory over the Turks at Belgrade in 1456.

· 2 ·
STREETS

Some San Antonio street names are obvious. For others it seems impossible to identify the precise person(s) for whom a street was named, particularly when an old family name may represent the patriarch—or matriarch—or a later descendant. Origins of many street names outside Loop 410 are likewise difficult to trace, for so many streets originally led to farms and ranches, and often little is known about the original residents.

San Antonio city limits for some two centuries formed a square of six miles on each side. When the limits were outlined in 1731, the city's center was established as the front door of the original San Fernando Cathedral, a point now marked by a plaque in the floor of the enlarged church. During this period, an official plan was established for naming streets. In 1906, when San Antonio was divided into wards, the city council under Mayor Bryan Callaghan passed an ordinance specifying how streets were to be named: Wards 1, 2, 3 (downtown, southwest and northwest)—old Spanish names to be retained; Ward 4 (north central)—names of trees, shrubs and plants; Ward 5 (around the Alamo)—Texas heroes; Ward 6 (northeast)—U.S. presidents and others of national repute; Wards 7 and 8 (southeast)—states, cities or territories.

In 1911 a new street naming system was established, with results evident today. Streets running north and southwest of Santa Rosa Avenue were to be named for Texas rivers, and many were: Comal, San Marcos, Brazos, San Saba, Nueces, Medina, Salado, among others. South of Commerce Street, streets running east and west were to be named for cities in Mexico, giving us Monterrey, Matamoros, Durango, Torreon, Juarez, Chihuahua, Vera Cruz, Tampico.

This plaque in the floor of San Fernando Cathedral marks the spot of the church's original front door, the historic geographical center of San Antonio.

During research for this book, more reasons emerged for naming a street, park or building:
• To honor a distinguished citizen—war hero, civic leader, politician, successful businessperson, or famous American.
• To honor a courageous act, as a segment of Houston Street was named for Rosa Parks (p. 67).
• For assassination, accident or disease victims, especially those who die at a relatively young age. When a famous person dies or is martyred by assassination, there is often a scramble to find the appropriate street or building to rename in his or her honor, a process often contentious and prolonged (p. 66).
• Landowner. Especially in areas outside Loop 410, roads were often named for the farms and ranches they led to or passed through, such as Poss, Rittiman and Weidner roads. Several hyphenated names, such as Jones-Maltsberger and Perrin-Beitel, were named for the property owners on either side of the road.
• Land donor. Some landowners deeded segments of their property to the city or county for roads, such as Wurzbach Road and Kyle Seale Parkway. When railroad construction reached San Antonio in 1877, many small towns along the route were named for the person who enticed the rail builders to pass through, usually by donating land for the right-of-way.
• Developer's choice. When plans are laid out for a new subdivision, it is the developer's responsibility to submit a list of street names, according to procedures added to the city code by city council under Mayor Howard Peak in 1998. Procedures are also outlined for changing the names of existing streets.

Although final approval is given by the Post Office Department, proposals for new streets seem limited only by the developer's imagination. Some areas include the subdivision's name in virtually every street (as in Whispering Oaks, Forest Oaks, Bluff View, Hunter's Creek) while others have such themes as movie stars. Many developers not only name a street for themselves, but include family members, friends, even pets.

City Center

Arciniega Street In 1811, Gregorio Arciniega was granted land along what is now South Alamo Street south of Nueva. In 1841, his son Miguel mortgaged the property to John Riddle, losing it a few years later when Riddle foreclosed. Miguel Arciniega was important in both the Mexican and Texas republics. Appointed by Mexico to lay out the Austin colony, he founded the town of Bastrop. In 1830 he was alcalde (mayor) of Béxar and an interpreter when General Cos surrendered in 1835 after the siege of Béxar (p. 77). Texas named him judge of the Municipality of San Antonio, so it appears that this street honors Miguel rather than his father.

Bonham Street   Although often referred to as "Colonel," James Butler Bonham (1807–36) was actually a second lieutenant, and had no standing in the Alamo's chain of command. In his home state of South Carolina, he served briefly as a lieutenant colonel in the militia. Expelled from the University of South Carolina for leading student protests, he later helped organize rallies and volunteer companies to support the Texas cause. Almost immediately upon arriving in Texas in 1835 he became directly involved. About three weeks before the Battle of the Alamo, he was sent to obtain aid. He returned three days before the battle with a letter from Robert M. Williamson assuring Travis that help was on its way and urging him to hold out. Help never came.

Bowie Street   James Bowie (1796–1836) was a "born leader," apparently a gracious, well-mannered gentleman, though with a violent temper. In a single fight with a large hunting knife brother Rezin had given him, James gained instant notoriety, creating the Bowie knife legend. A slave trader, land speculator and gambler, he married into the prominent Veramendi family of Béxar (p. 20). His wife Ursula and both of her parents died of cholera two years after their marriage. He and Travis shared command at the Alamo, Bowie leading the volunteers and Travis the regulars. But by the time of the battle, Bowie was gravely ill. He urged his men to follow Travis and, legend has it, was killed in his sick bed.

Buena Vista Street   Buena Vista in Spanish means "good view." Although located in an area with many streets named for cities in Mexico, this street has special historical significance. The Battle of Buena Vista, fought just south of Saltillo on February 23, 1847, was the last major battle in northern Mexico during the Mexican War. Santa Anna had four times as many troops facing Major General Zachary Taylor ("Old Rough and Ready"), who overcame the deficit by effective use of artillery and won the battle, and parlayed his military fame into a successful presidential bid in 1848. Taylor's troops were mainly a collection of state volunteer militias, so locations in several states became named Buena Vista in honor of the battle. The present route of this street is unique in having three names. It begins at the Convention Center as Market Street, connects to the west near the Bexar County Courthouse to Dolorosa Street and then, as it passes under IH-10, becomes Buena Vista Street.

Callaghan Avenue   Bryan Callaghan Jr. (1852–1912) was one of the most powerful and colorful characters on the San Antonio scene. His father, mayor in 1846, was an Irish immigrant, and his mother a descendant of original families from the Canary Islands. Part of his early education was in France. He married the daughter of one of the city's leading French citizens and spoke fluent English, Spanish, French and

"King" Bryan Callaghan Jr. was an immensely popular mayor who was elected three times.

German. Elected mayor on three separate occasions, he served in that office a total of 17 years from 1885 until his death in 1912. Often called "King" Bryan, Callaghan was a classic political boss, but did not benefit financially from the power he wielded and died without a personal fortune. Loved by people from all walks of life, his funeral was the largest in the history of San Antonio until perhaps that of Henry B. Gonzalez in 2000. The street named for him is very short, running diagonally off South Presa Street east of the King William area. The longer and better-known Callaghan Road was probably named for Bryan's son Alfred, also a mayor (p. 36).

Camaron Street   Camarón means "shrimp" in Spanish. This street, which parallels part of San Pedro Creek, is said to have been named for the abundance of shrimp that once flourished in the creek.

College Street   St. Mary's College began in 1852 behind St. Mary's Catholic Church between the river and what became known as College Street. Boarders began moving to a new campus in near western San Antonio in 1894, where St. Louis College had been established. St.

College Street is named for St. Mary's College, predecessor of St. Mary's University. Original buildings beside the San Antonio River are now part of the Omni La Mansion Hotel.

San Antonio's original main business street was named Commerce Street and is shown looking east from Main Plaza about 1905.

Louis and St. Mary's colleges were combined there in 1923 as St. Mary's University. The College Street campus was used as the law school until the 1960s, when the buildings were sold to become what is now the Omni Mansion del Rio Hotel. It is not to be confused with College Boulevard in Alamo Heights (p. 23).

Commerce Street   In the late nineteenth century, this was the main thoroughfare in the city and was sometimes called Main Street. Prior to this, it had three or four different names. The east end was called **Calle de la Alameda**, alameda meaning a grove of poplar trees. From the San Antonio River to Main Plaza the street was called **Calle del Potreto**, meaning Pasture Street. The west end was **Calle Real**—Royal Street or Presidio Street, after the adjacent old fortress of Bexar.

Convent Street   In 1851, Ursuline nuns built a complex of buildings for their school and convent in this location (p. 135). Although the school moved and later closed, and the buildings are now the Southwest School of Art, the street named in honor of the Ursulines is unchanged.

Crockett Street   Although a Texan for less than two months of his 49 years, David Crockett (1786–1836) was the most renowned of the Alamo defenders. Most of his life was spent in Tennessee, which he represented in the U.S. Congress and where he gained a reputation as a frontiersman, sharpshooter and Indian fighter. Originally aligned with his former militia commander and then President Andrew Jackson, Crockett eventually lost his congressional seat by incurring the enmity

Convent Street is named for the convent of the Ursuline Academy, its campus now part of the Southwest School of Art and Craft.

of the president. He left Tennessee with the memorable parting shot, "You may all go to hell and I will go to Texas." Although Crockett apparently did not intend to become involved in the Texas War of Independence, he was sworn into the Volunteer Auxiliary Corps of Texas in Nacogdoches and traveled with this group to Bexar. At the Alamo he held no rank other than private, usually being referred to as "Colonel" as a title of respect rather than of authority.

Dolorosa Street   Dolorosa means "painful" in Spanish. Historians have stretched that to mean "sadness" or "sorrow." The most popular story about why the street has that name is that following the 1813 Battle of Medina on the Medina River some 12 miles south of San Antonio, victorious Mexican General Joaquin Arredondo ordered the arrest of several hundred women from the city's best families. Held in confinement in a large enclosure near the present day courthouse and forced to cook and serve the conquering Mexican army under oppressive conditions, some women died. In memory of the sufferings endured by those women, the street on which they were held is said to have been named Via Dolorosa. Such stories may be myths, however, as Via Dolorosa appeared on city maps as early as 1790, long before the Battle of Medina. Thus the name may have been either a tribute to the Via Dolorosa in Jerusalem, revered by Christians as the path traversed by Jesus Christ on the way to his crucifixion, or a tribute to Our Lady of Sorrows.

Dwyer Avenue There were many Dwyers of Irish heritage in early San Antonio, but this street is probably named for Edward Dwyer (1808–54), mayor of the city in 1844–46 and owner of property on Main Plaza where the courthouse now stands. His brother Thomas was a judge. Edward died young, and Francois Guilbeau (p. 12) was appointed guardian for his son Joseph E. Dwyer (1841–84), who became a major in the Civil War and then a local and state politician. An earlier name of this street was Calle de los Curbelos, honoring one of the original Canary Island families that owned a land grant on the east side of this street. Juan Curbelo was the second alcalde of the settlement, San Fernando de Bexar. It was

In this portrait David Crockett looks more congressman and less "King of the Wild Frontier."

also known as **Quinta Street** from La Quinta, a home that served as the city's post office during the Republic of Texas, which stood on the riverbank near the present courthouse.

Flores Street This street may have been called **Calle de Flores** (Spanish for "flowers") since in Spanish times houses along it were fragrant with jasmine, vanilla, roses and wild honeysuckle that grew in irrigated gardens. Or it could have been named for one of the several Flores families who owned property on the street. Nicolas Flores de Valdez, who died in 1731, came to San Antonio with a supply expedition in 1693 and later was captain of the presidio of San Antonio de Bexar, his main job rebuilding the presidio to protect the garrison from Apache raiders. Or it could have been named for Jesus V. Flores, born to Canary Island settlers in 1834 and said to have built the first house on the street. It seems unlikely that the true story will ever be known.

Giraud Street Although mayor from 1872 to 1875, Francois P. Giraud (1818–77) is best known for his work as an architect. Among his projects were original buildings of St. Mary's College on the river, the Ursuline Academy and the renovated facade of San Fernando Cathedral. His name is also preserved in Club Giraud, a private club in an old Ursuline building.

Guenther Street Like so many other Germans in the mid-nineteenth century, Carl Hilmar Guenther (1826–1902) in 1851 walked from Indianola on the Gulf coast to San Antonio, going on to Fredericksburg to build a gristmill. He moved his operation to San Antonio in 1859, where it has grown into Pioneer Flour Mills and the food products con-

C. H. Guenther's milling company has grown into a national food conglomerate.

glomerate known as C. H. Guenther & Son Inc., still owned by Guenther's descendants. Guenther's enlarged stone homestead on the west bank of the San Antonio River beside the mill has been renovated as the Guenther House, a charming restaurant, gift shop and museum. Built east of the river, the house has overlooked the west bank since the river's original course around the mill was straightened in 1968.

Guilbeau Street This short street just north of Durango Boulevard is named for a family that moved to San Antonio and opened a bakery in 1839. Francois Guilbeau Jr. (1813–79) served as French consul from 1855 through the Civil War, and his elegant home was the French consulate. Sadly, this landmark mansion was torn down and replaced with a postal substation in 1952. His wife was a descendant of the Canary Islanders, and his daughter Adele married her cousin Bryan V. Callaghan Jr. (p. 7). Guilbeau is credited with having saved the French wine industry, decimated from phylloxera in the 1860s and 1870s. A highly regarded horticulturist, Guilbeau collaborated with Thomas Munson, a viticulturalist, to ship tons of disease-resistant Texas mustang grapevine cuttings to France.

Hardberger Way It is appropriate that this short street running off Haven for Hope Way is named for Phil Hardberger, the mayor who was a driving force in initiating this endeavor (p. 83).

Haven for Hope Way Formerly Salado Street, this was renamed to commemorate San Antonio's daring $100 million social services project to combat homelessness. Haven for Hope coordinates more than 60 non-governmental organizations, among them San Antonio Metropolitan Ministries, which has sheltered homeless people for more than 25 years, and the Food Bank, which has assumed responsibility for feeding several hundred residents at the Haven for Hope complex on a daily basis. Bill Greehey (p. 177) was the major driving force from the private sector for the project.

Herff Street Ferdinand Charles (or Ludwig) von Herff (1820–1912) was born into an aristocratic family in Germany. After completing his medical education in Germany, he was a surgeon in the Hessian army. In the mid-nineteenth century Herff helped organize a group of mainly university-educated professionals who tried to establish a commune called

Bettina on the Llano River. It failed, and Herff returned briefly to Germany before settling permanently in Texas, dropping "von" from his name. At that time San Antonio had no hospitals, nurses or medical facilities. He struggled to establish a medical practice in San Antonio until the opportunity arose to operate on a Texas Ranger. In full view of eager spectators, including other rangers, a lithotomy (removal of bladder stones) was performed in the Veramendi House (p. 20). Herff is given credit for many firsts in Texas surgery, including the first eye cataract operation. His sons and grandsons followed him into the surgical profession.

Dr. Ferdinand Herff, far left, is shown in an operation at Santa Rosa Hospital with his son Dr. Adolph Herff, center, with the dark beard.

Houston Street   Had defenders of the Alamo heeded the orders of Sam Houston (1793–1863) there likely would have been no Alamo legend. As commander of the Texas Army, Sam Houston thought it a bad idea to defend this poorly fortified old mission against Santa Anna's overwhelmingly superior force. He sent Bowie with 30 men to demolish its fortifications and withdraw its detachment further east, where he thought they would stand a better chance. But Houston's orders were disobeyed, and Santa Anna's troops killed the Alamo's defenders. (Fort Sam Houston, p. 186)

Indianola Street   The street is named for the Matagorda Bay port selected by Prince Carl of Solms-Braunfels (p. 205). Indianola became the chief port through which European and American immigrants entered western and south central Texas, including the predominantly German towns in the Hill Country. Little is left of Indianola but a dot on the map. With a population of more than 5,000, the port was at the peak of its prosperity when the 1875 hurricane struck. The town was rebuilt on a smaller scale, but it was virtually obliterated by a second hurricane in 1886 and was abandoned.

Jack White Street   This short street is named for Arthur Cleveland (Jack) White, manager of the then prestigious 12-story Plaza Hotel (now Granada Homes) overlooking the river. The street was originally on private property owned by the hotel, unnamed and used simply as turnaround space for cabs. It was difficult to give directions to a street without a name, so White had the street named for himself. White was instrumental in gaining funding to adopt Robert Hugman's design for the River Walk. As chairman of the river project board, he broke ground for the River Walk with a golden shovel on March 29, 1939. He served as mayor from 1949 to 1952.

Jones Avenue   This short street intersecting Broadway at Maverick Park was named for Enoch Jones (1802–36). His early engineering projects including, in 1832, the dam at Johnstown, Pennsylvania gave way under torrential rains in 1889 and killed more than 10 percent of the 21,000 inhabitants. Selling businesses in Detroit and St. Louis, Jones came to San Antonio in 1835 and became a business partner of John W. Smith, the first mayor (p. 90), and a financier of the Republic of Texas. He also owned a quarry on the site of Brackenridge Park's Sunken Gardens. The street alongside was named Jones Avenue but was changed to St. Mary's Street. He began a mansion on the Medina River south of town but died before it was finished. It was bought by a European nobleman and became known as the Von Ormy Castle (p. 196). This street was previously named **Grand Avenue**, since it was intended to become an impressive entry into town from the first Southern Pacific railroad depot a few blocks east.

King William Street   The first home on this street is thought to have been built in 1867 by Ernst Hermann Altgelt (1832–78), a German-born lawyer and real estate investor who named the street after Wilhelm I, made King of Prussia in 1861 and German emperor when Bismarck unified the country ten years later. The street was originally called **Kaiser Wilhelmstrasse**, but because of anti-German sentiment during World War I it was renamed for General John J. ("Black Jack") Pershing, commander of American troops in that war (p. 30). In 1921, city council approved requests to restore the original name, Anglicized as King William.

Josephine Street   This street may have been named for Josephine Smith Tobin (p. 52), wife of Sheriff William G. Tobin and mother of Mayor John Wallace Tobin. The Tobin Hill neighborhood (p. 198) takes its unofficial name from this family.

Laredo Street   Before trains arrived in San Antonio, the main road leading south from the city was this thoroughfare, over which ox carts headed for the Rio Grande River to where the city of Laredo is now located.

Losoya Street   Across from the Hyatt Hotel stands a statue of Toribio Losoya, one of many Tejano defenders of the Alamo. The occupation of Bexar by the Mexican Army in 1835 forced Losoya and his family from their home in the southwest corner of the Alamo mission. He enlisted as a private in Juan Seguin's Tejano forces and died in the battle, but his wife and three children, who had sought refuge in the Alamo, survived. Despite all this, the street was probably named not after him but after his brothers, Miguel and Cipriano, who in 1773 received a land grant on the east side of the San Antonio River, including the area later designated as Losoya Street. The street apparently did not have an official name until it was designated Losoya in 1858, at which time the breakup of the Losoya property (where the main downtown post office now stands) sparked growth in the area. Ownership of this property was long disputed and finally settled by the U.S. Supreme Court in 1877.

Main Avenue   This street was first named Acequia Street since it followed the San Pedro Acequia from San Pedro Springs to Main Plaza. It was chosen as the north-south dividing street for separation of cross streets into designations of east and west, but was never the "main street" of San Antonio. When acequias began falling out of use in the 1890s, the street was renamed for its destination, Main Plaza. Main Avenue

Acequia Street was renamed Main Avenue since it led to Main Plaza,
above. The low buildings at far right center were later removed for
the extension of Main Avenue south past the courthouse.

was extended south from Main Plaza past the courthouse and bisected the U.S. Arsenal in 1929. The city's first high school was built on the street in 1882 and named San Antonio High School until 1917, when the second high school, Brackenridge, was opened. The original high school was renamed Main Avenue High until the name was changed again in 1961 to honor Louis W. Fox (Fox Tech, p. 122).

Martin Street Although no unequivocal documentation could be found to make the connection, a Martin died in the Battle of the Alamo. Albert Martin (1805–36), born in Providence, Rhode Island, moved to Gonzales, Texas, where he ran a general store. At the outbreak of the Texas Revolution, he was a defender of the "Come and Take It" cannon and later part of the force that besieged San Antonio de Béxar in 1835. The following year he was back in San Antonio, and on February 23 was sent by Alamo commander William B. Travis as an emissary to invite General Santa Anna to meet with Travis. That offer was rejected, and the following day, Martin carried Travis's famous "To the People of Texas" letter to Gonzales. He returned to the Alamo on March 1 with a small relief force and died in the ensuing battle on March 6.

Milam Street When Santa Anna sent an army under Gen. Martín Perfecto de Cós (p. 77) to subdue revolutionary settlers in San Antonio, Benjamin Rush Milam (1788–1835) is credited with lifting the Mexican siege after shouting, "Who will go with old Ben Milam into San Antonio?" Milam did not live to see the success of his charge, being killed by a sniper's bullet two days before Cós surrendered.

Navarro Street José Antonio Navarro (1795–1871) was one of three Mexican signers of the Texas Declaration of Independence, the others being his uncle José Francisco Ruiz and Lorenzo de Zavala. He served various roles in the new Texas government and strongly supported annexation of Texas into the United States (Casa Navarro State Historical Park, p. 72). In 1846, in recognition of his contributions to Texas, Navarro County was named in his honor. Its county seat was called Corsicana because his father was a native of Corsica.

José Antonio Navarro is remembered in a street, a county and a state park.

Presa Street Presa is Spanish for dam. This street actually ran from dam to dam. It originated beside the Pajalache Dam on the San Antonio River, where South Presa Street passes over. The Pajalache, or Concepción, Acequia, part of the city's network of irrigation ditches from the Spanish era, was created by the dam here to divert water from the San Antonio River down to Mission Concepción lands two miles south. Presa Street leads south to Espada Dam, part of the oldest continually operating irrigation system in the nation. In 1745, San Francisco de la Espada Mission was established (p. 4) and the Espada dam on the San Antonio River was begun to divert water into the mission's acequia.

Richter Street   In 1877, 19-year-old William L. Richter opened a bakery in Fredericksburg. His venture failed because thrifty housewives baked their own bread, so Richter hitched a ride on top of a load of cowhides to San Antonio. After a stint as a pastry cook at the Menger Hotel he went to work for his future father-in-law, Henry Solcher, who owned a bakery where the Gunter Hotel now stands. This became Butter Krust Bakeries, a family-owned business until sold to a Georgia-based company in 1994.

St. Mary's Street   St. Mary's Catholic Church, designed by the noted architect Francois Giraud and completed in 1857, gave its name to this street. The church was damaged in the flood of 1921 and replaced by the present building. St. Mary's University began in buildings still standing to the rear on College Street (p. 8) and incorporated into the Omni Mansion del Rio.

St. Mary's Street gained its name for passing by St. Mary's Catholic Church, shown as it appeared from 1857 until being replaced after the flood of 1921.

Soledad Street   Soledad means "solitude" in Spanish. When Don Fernando, patriarch of the Veramendi family (p. 20), was killed by Apaches in 1783, he left his heirs a residence called Soledad. It was renamed the Veramendi Palace when Don Fernando's son Don Martin became vice governor of the province Bexar in 1830. The landmark was razed to widen Soledad Street in 1910.

Stumberg Street   Herman Dietrich Stumberg (1818–87) came to San Antonio in 1846 from Hanover, Germany. As a young man he fought in the Mexican War, and in 1870 he and his son George Rudolph (1848–1914) built a two-story stone building which became not only the leading general mercantile store in the growing city but also a center of community life. The pair also built a camp yard adjacent to the store. Catering mainly to farmers and ranchers from out of town, their stock included groceries, hardware and a wide variety of incidentals. The building, just north of Stumberg Street on South Flores Street, is now the Cadillac Bar. Herman's daughter Lena Stumberg McAllister was the mother of San Antonio mayor Walter W. McAllister (p. 63).

Sweet Street   James R. Sweet (1818–80) was born in Nova Scotia. He moved to San Antonio, where he prospered in business with his brother-in-law John James (p. 76. He was mayor from 1859 until 1862, when he resigned to become a cavalry officer in the Confederate army. He is best remembered as the man who owned the property and built the first home on land at the head of the San Antonio River, now within the City of Alamo Heights on the University of the Incarnate Word campus (p. 133).

Toudouze Street   Gustave Toudouze (1819–1902), patriarch of the family for whom this street is named, came from France in 1848 and settled with his wife Josephine in southeast Bexar County, where a **Toudouze Road** went through family property. A taxidermist and

*In 1941 Toudouze Supermart became San Antonio's
first store to provide onsite customer parking.*

naturalist by trade, Gustave operated a combination gift shop/museum on the second floor of Honore Grenet's store adjacent to the Alamo. In 1913, Gustave's grandson A. C. (Augustus Charles, 1881–1965) bought a tiny store in Cassin, south of San Antonio. Three years later he opened a new store at what was then the hub of San Antonio commerce, at the confluence of Pleasanton Road and South Flores, from which Toudouze Street now emerges. He sold lumber and general merchandise and is said to have had the city's first customer parking lot. A. C.'s son Charles ventured into other lines, especially furniture, and endured difficult times during the Depression and World War II. Unable to compete with national furniture chains, the company reverted to what it had sold best—groceries. It developed the state's original "cash and carry" grocery warehouse, open to the general public with no membership fees. Though primarily a wholesale firm, Toudouze Market remains open to the public and is run by Gustave's great-great grandsons Chuck and Wilson Toudouze.

Travis Street At the age of 26, William Barret Travis (1809–36) was in command of the Alamo garrison. When Santa Anna arrived in San Antonio on February 23, 1836, Travis gathered his troops inside the walls of the Alamo and prepared the former mission for battle as best he could. His letter addressed to "the People of Texas and All Americans in the World" the following day eloquently described the plight of Alamo defenders. Travis is said to have died early in the battle by a single shot to the head.

William Barret Travis commanded the Alamo garrison in 1836.

Treviño Street This one-block street between San Fernando Cathedral and the old Frost National Bank building that now contains City Council Chambers appears on few city maps. Alejandro Treviño was an officer in the Spanish army who bought this property for his home in 1831. He was popular in San Antonio and was eventually called "the General," though it is not clear if he ever officially attained that rank. He never married, and when he died in about 1834 his sister inherited the property.

Vance Street This short street running obliquely off South Presa Street just south of downtown is probably named for William Vance (1813–78), a business leader of San Antonio in the mid-nineteenth century. An Irishman, Vance settled in San Antonio after serving as a U.S. commissary agent in the Mexican War. He and brothers James and John built the first U.S. Army barracks in San Antonio adjacent to a two-story building housing army headquarters. Lt. Col. Robert E. Lee occupied the second-floor office when he commanded the U.S. Army's Department of Texas. The building was headquarters for local Confederate forces during the war. In 1872 it was converted into a hotel known as the Vance House, later becoming the Mahncke Hotel. It was replaced by the Gunter Hotel (p. 153). The James Vance home built in 1845 just south of the present courthouse was considered the finest antebellum house in Texas, but was torn down in 1952 so the site could be used for a Federal Reserve branch bank.

Veramendi Street At one time this block-long passageway was the shortest street in San Antonio. It has disappeared beneath a high-rise office building, though the street appeared on city maps just a few years ago. It led to the Veramendi House or "palace" on Soledad Street (p. 18). The first Veramendi in San Antonio was Don Fernando de Veramendi (1743–83). His son Juan Martin (1778–1833) was governor of Coahuila in 1832 and alcalde—mayor—of San Antonio in 1833. James Bowie (p. 7) befriended the family and married Juan's daughter Ursula, who died two years later of cholera.

NORTHEAST

Ashby Place The Street Renaming Committee appointed by city council sometime before 1915 changed the name of an existing street to Ashby Place in response to a petition signed by many local residents asking for this change in honor of "General Ashby." Although there is no record of a general named Ashby in Texas, it could have been the Confederate hero Brigadier General Turner Ashby (1824–62) whom southern-leaning San Antonians wanted to honor, though Ashby's life was spent in Virginia and he was killed fighting in the Shenandoah Valley.

Austin Highway The route from San Antonio to Austin was once a winding roadway from downtown, starting with Austin Street and heading east beside Fort Sam Houston along what is now, in whole or in part, Old Austin Road, Harry Wurzbach Highway and Corrine Drive. In 1935, hard-won State Highway 2 opened as the new road to Austin, following Broadway from downtown north to the center of Alamo Heights. There existing blocks were cut through diagonally and homes were removed so the new highway could extend northeast and meet the old route nearly three miles away at Salado Creek. Austin Highway flourished until IH-35 opened in 1964 as the new major thoroughfare to the state capital, named for colonizer and Texas patriot Stephen Fuller Austin (1793–1836).

Bartlett Place   This short street in Terrell Hills was probably named for Terrell Bartlett, an MIT graduate born in 1885, a respected engineer, and an originator of the Medina Dam project. He was not related to Dr. Frederick Terrell (p. 195), owner and developer of Terrell Hills.

Basse Road   Edgar A. Basse, son of a Fredericksburg merchant, saw opportunity in new self-service grocery stores. Starting with a single San Antonio store in 1918, he built a 32-store Texas chain that joined the national Piggly-Wiggly chain.

Edgar A. Basse

Belknap Place   Most selective of the volunteer militia groups formed by male members of society in the latter 1880s was the San Antonio Rifles, which excluded younger men, who, in 1884, formed the Belknap Rifles under Augustus Belknap (1841–89). A New Yorker who left the Civil War, wounded, as a captain, he had come to San Antonio in 1877 and founded the city's first streetcar system. The Belknap Rifles won most national drill company prizes, but disbanded when members went off to the Spanish-American War. The first captain was Robert B. Green (p. 150).

Brees Boulevard   Shortly after graduating from college, Herbert J. Brees (1877–1958) entered the Spanish-American War as a first lieutenant. He was decorated for valor in World War I, and in 1940 re-

The Belknap Rifles pose with a portrait of their patron, Col. Augustus Belknap, lower left. Future county judge and hospital namesake Robert B. Green is standing third from right.

tired as a three-star general. He served four tours of duty at Fort Sam Houston, and after his retirement was president of the National Bank of Fort Sam Houston.

Bushnell Avenue   The only clue uncovered for this name is in the obituary of Colonel John R. Shook (p. 32), which mentions that in his early law career Shook practiced in the office of Allen R. Bushnell, subsequently twice elected to Congress from Ohio. On this street was built the prestigious Bushnell Apartments, the first high-rise apartment complex in Texas.

The spelunker at left holds a candle as he prepares a group to enter "Robber Baron Cave."

Cave Lane   Just west of where this street meets Nacogdoches Road is the fenced-off opening of what is said to be the longest cave in Bexar County, with more than a mile of passageways. Called Robber Baron Cave by owners who invented the name to lure customers for guided tours, the cave was visited by about 300,000 people from 1926 until it was closed in 1933. Prohibition against entering the cave of course made it the perfect party and exploration spot for local teenagers. The site is now owned by the Texas Cave Management Association and is being upgraded to make it safer. Access will be limited to cavers and educational organizations.

Cheever Boulevard   This street, officially designated a boulevard although much of it is quite narrow, is between Broadway and Nacogdoches Road. It passes the Broadway National Bank, co-founded on Broadway in Alamo Heights in 1941 by Col. Charles E. Cheever and his wife, Elizabeth. When he was transferred to Europe in World War II, his wife ran the bank until he returned. Col. Cheever had a law degree, and the culmination of his service was as staff judge advocate for the Third Army under Gen. George S. Patton. Upon retiring from his military career in 1948, he was president of the growing USAA financial services conglomerate for 16 years.

Coker Loop Road   Soon after coming to San Antonio in 1834, South Carolina-born John "Jack" Coker (1789–1861) joined Sam Houston's army and served in Deaf Smith's group. He is credited with the idea of destroying Vince's Bridge near Pasadena during the Battle of San Jacinto, which kept Santa Anna's army from retreat or reinforcement. In recognition of his service, the Texas Legislature gave Coker nearly 2,000 acres in what is now northern Bexar County. With his brothers Joseph and James, he built a thriving community. Its school evolved into Coker Elementary in what became the North East Independent School District.

College Boulevard   In 1910, West Texas Military Academy moved from Grayson Street to become Texas Military Institute on a larger campus at the head of a broad street in the new suburb of Alamo Heights. Developers jumped to the conclusion that it would become a college, though it never has. TMI moved from Alamo Heights to far northwestern San Antonio in the 1980s and its old campus was subdivided for homes. College Boulevard is not to be confused with College Street in downtown San Antonio. (p. 8).

Contour Drive   This tortuous but beautiful drive forms the eastern and northern boundaries of the City of Olmos Park. It is said to have been so named because its contour maintains the same elevation as Olmos Dam, but this does not check out. The Texas State Historical Association reports the top of the dam is 728 feet above sea level, while the road is at 840 feet.

During World War II, Elizabeth Cheever, far left, took over the Broadway Bank while her husband, Col. Charles Cheever, second from right, served in Europe.

Craig Place   One Denver entrepreneur who invested in local real estate was the Rev. William Bayard Craig, who developed Laurel Heights with two of his prominent church members, Frank and Logan Russell (p. 32).

David Edwards Street   On November 15, 2003, David Edwards (1987–2008) was a junior safety on the Madison High School football team in a regional playoff game against Austin–Westlake. He tackled a Westlake wide receiver and fractured his cervical spine, rendering him immediately paralyzed from the neck down. After surgical treatment in Austin and extensive rehabilitation, he was able to return to Madison in his wheelchair the following semester, and graduated in 2005. Teammates, classmates, coaches and teachers described him as an inspiration for his indomitable spirit and strength of character. He delivered a commencement address in which he urged his peers to "enjoy every day and love your family." Edwards briefly attended classes at San Antonio College until illness forced him to withdraw. In February 2008, respiratory problems and pneumonia forced a readmission to the hospital, where he died three days before his 21st birthday.

Eisenhauer Road   This street is not named for general and president Dwight Eisenhower, but rather for a German immigrant farming family that settled east of San Antonio in the early 1840s. It is not clear whether it is named for William Eisenhauer, who came in 1844 from Hanover, Germany, or for Paul Eisenhauer, who came in 1842.

Elizabeth Road   This street appears to have been named for Elizabeth Cassin Bartlett, wife of Terrell Bartlett (p. 21) and the daughter of San Antonio's William Cassin, for whom the town of Cassin was named (p. 191. Her husband, Terrell Bartlett, and her father, William Cassin were engineers who worked on the Medina Valley irrigation project.

Evans Road   Robert B. Evans (1821–1905) left his native Tennessee and came to San Antonio in 1847. Two years later he left for the California Gold Rush by way of the Isthmus of Panama. He panned enough gold to buy 160 acres of land near the present-day intersection of Evans and Nacogdoches roads, where he built a stone homestead in 1882.

French Place   One might assume that this street was named for James Henry French (1835-93), reform mayor of San Antonio from 1875 to 1885. But this street was named for a Mr. French of Pittsburgh, who developed several blocks just south of Laurel Heights.

Funston Place   This street beside Mahncke Park (p. 79) is named for Maj. Gen. Frederick Funston (1865–1917), who won the Medal of

Honor during the Philippine Insurrection in 1899. In 1906 he organized and led relief and rescue efforts after the San Francisco earthquake. Camp Stanley in northwest Bexar County was originally called Camp Funston (p. 186). Funston was to command American troops in World War I, but he died unexpectedly and the job went to Gen. John J. Pershing (p. 30). In 1915–17 at Fort Sam Houston, General Funston commanded the Southern Department, the Army's largest and most important command.

Geneseo Road The grandest residential street in Terrell Hills, with its broad esplanade, was named after the hometown in western New York's Genesee Valley of retired Army officer and rancher John K. Burr. One of Geneseo Road's earliest residents, Burr was a friend of landowner Dr. Frederick Terrell, and his name appears on the parallel Burr Road. Geneseo and Genesee evolved from the Seneca Indian word jo-nis-hi-yuh, meaning pleasant or beautiful valley.

Gordon A. Blake Highway State Highway 78, also known as Seguin Road, runs along the northwest boundary of Randolph Air Force Base. The segment immediately adjacent to the base's main entrance is designated Gordon A. Blake Highway in honor of Lt. Gen. Gordon Aylesworth Blake (1910–97). Soon after graduation from West Point in 1931, Blake completed pilot training and ten years later (as a major) he was operations officer at Hickham Field in Hawaii on December 7. He was awarded the Silver Star for gallantry during the Japanese attack on his base that day, and at the end of the war was part of a task force preparing for an airborne invasion of Japan. Highly decorated for service in the Pacific, his later command positions included being director of the National Security Agency and, earlier, chief of the U.S. Air Force Security Service, headquartered in San Antonio, where he settled after his retirement in 1966. Other segments of Seguin Road are called **John E. Peterson Road**, but information regarding the origin of this name could not be found.

Harrington Court This Alamo Heights street is thought to have been named for himself by a developer named Louis Harrington who built homes in Alamo Heights during the 1920s.

Harry Wurzbach Highway A lawyer, county judge and the first native Texan elected to Congress, Harry McCleary Wurzbach (1874–1931) was already a practicing attorney when he enlisted as a private in the Texas Volunteer Infantry in the Spanish-American War. When he returned to his law practice in Seguin and, after being elected to Congress in 1920, Wurzbach did much for veterans of

that war. Veterans' wives and widows pushed to have this road named for him. Relatives of his brother William Wurzbach (p. 45) spoke against this because there was already a Wurzbach Road on the northwest side of town, and they thought it would be confusing to have a road on the northeast side with the same name. It is.

William Wurzbach, left, and his congress-man brother Harry, right, both had major roads named for them, creating some confusion for motorists.

Hildebrand Avenue At the turn of the twentieth century, two Hildebrand brothers were prominent in city affairs. According to descendants, this street was named not for attorney Ira Polk Hildebrand—later dean of the University of Texas Law School—but for his businessman brother, Henry Elbert Hildebrand, founder of Southern Transfer and Storage Company. H. E. Hildebrand was local chairman of the Democratic Party and was influential in bringing its state convention to San Antonio in 1906, as well as for helping acquire right-of-way for the Southern Pacific Railroad through San Antonio. A street with the unlikely name of North North Street was changed to Hildebrand by city council, which wished to honor members of their renaming committee, one of whom was H. E. Hildebrand.

Hubertus Road Wilhelm Hubertus and Anna Maria Kneuper were born in Germany and married in New Braunfels in 1853. They were farmers, and profits from selling cotton allowed Wilhelm to buy more land, one piece at a time. Ultimately he acquired over 200 acres, but quit buying land when it became prohibitively expensive—$10 per acre, around $200 in today's dollars. When he died the property was divided among his six children. The homestead was inherited by his youngest son, Wilhelm Jr. The land continued to be split up with each succeeding generation, and gradually all tracts were sold out of the family. The original homestead, razed in the 1960s when IH-35 replaced U.S. Highway 81, was located where the west side frontage road crosses Hubertus Road. Many other roads crossing IH-35 between San Antonio to New Braunfels—such as Engel, Ruekle, Schwab, Wiedner and Wiederstein—likewise refer to families who owned farms in the area.

Jackson-Keller Road This Jackson is the same landowner, Brig. General William H. Jackson, for whom Vance Jackson Road was named (p. 44). One assumes that land adjacent to the Jackson ranch was owned by Judge C. A. Keller (1851–1918) because of the custom of naming streets that divided property. A native of Mount Vernon, Illinois, Keller practiced law and served as a judge there until coming to San Antonio in search of better climate for his wife's health. Almost half of his obituary is devoted to his activities in the Independent Order of Odd Fellows. Keller was elected to many of the order's local, state and national offices, eventually becoming grand master of the international organization.

John Saunders Road   When the city created a Department of Aviation to oversee San Antonio's airports in 1952, John Saunders was named its first director. Three other short streets around the San Antonio International Airport were named for subsequent directors: John Cape, John Huth, and Paul Wilkins.

Jones-Maltsberger Road   Like many hyphenated street names, this denoted a right-of-way between the property of two families. Jerry Melvin Maltsberger owned a dairy north of what is now the San Antonio International Airport. A family named Jones also had a dairy in the vicinity. However, the names go back a good deal further than that, and there were apparently strong connections between the two families. The Coker cemetery holds about thirty Jones and twenty Maltsberger ancestors. Patriarchs of the Coker community were Jack, James and Joseph Coker (p. 23), who founded the community after the Texas War for Independence. Joseph's daughter Jane Maria married Amos Dickens Jones, which started the Jones clan in the area. Later an Annie Jones— probably Amos's daughter—married a Maltsberger.

Katherine Court   Katherine was apparently the daughter of developer Louis Harrington, who named this street running parallel to his own Harrington Court (p. 25) for her.

King's Highway   In the years following World War I, this name was given by developers seeking to show that this was the most luxurious and restrictive street in the city. It was—and is—lined with homes built by so-called cattle barons and cattle kings who ranched throughout South Texas. It is unrelated to the real "King's Highway," El Camino Real, which connected the far-flung outposts of the Spanish empire in the New World (p. 29).

Laurel Heights Place   Laurel Heights is a development now largely within the Monte Vista Historic District (p. 194).

Lookout Road   This road takes its name from the small promontory to which it leads, a landmark adjacent to and incorporated into the grounds of the Julia Yates Semmes Library (p. 138). From the center of Comanche Lookout Park—the fourth highest point in Bexar County, elevation 1340 feet—Native American tribes launched raids on Spanish and Mexican mule trains and pioneer travelers. A stone tower at the top of the peak was built by Edward Coppock, a retired U.S. Army colonel, who also preserved the ancient Comanche Council ring.

Comanche Lookout Park—the fourth highest point in Bexar County, elevation 1340 feet—Native American tribes launched raids on Spanish and Mexican mule trains and pioneer travelers. A stone tower at the top of the peak was built by Edward Coppock, a retired U.S. Army colonel, who also preserved the ancient Comanche Council ring.

Marion Road   When Dr. Frederick Terrell laid out the design for Terrell Hills, he named a street for his baby granddaughter Marion, who still resides in San Antonio as the wife of orthopedic hand surgeon Spencer Rowland. The street may have also been named in memory of Dr. Terrell's wife, Marion (Clement), who died in the influenza epidemic of 1918.

Mary D. Avenue   In 1909 Clifton George bought the struggling Alamo Heights Land and Development Company and became largely responsible for its successful development. According to a 1946 article by Frances Coleman Huff in the Alamo Heights News, George converted the partially completed Alamo Heights clubhouse on Lagos Avenue into his home and renamed that part of the street to honor his wife, Mary D. George. Other longtime Alamo Heights residents dispute this, saying it was named by developer Louis Harrington (p. 25) for one of his two daughters.

Maverick Street   One of the big early landholders in the Monte Vista area (p. 194) was William H. Maverick (1847–1923), fourth son of Samuel A. Maverick (p. 153). It is probably safe to assume that this short street just north of San Antonio College was either named for him or by him in honor of the Maverick family.

Presbyterian missionary John McCullough found San Antonio "overrun by a devilish set of men and gamblers."

McCullough Avenue   The first Protestant church services in San Antonio were held by Presbyterian missionary John McCullough (1805–70) and Methodist missionary John W. DeVilbiss in 1844. A bronze plaque marks the location on what is now the corner of West Commerce and Soledad streets, where the river bypass flows under Commerce Street. In 1845 McCullough accepted an assignment from the Presbyterian Board of Foreign Missions (Texas was not yet part of the United States) and returned to San Antonio. He found the town "overrun by a devilish set of men and gamblers," who occasionally took shots at him. In 1846 McCullough organized what became First Presbyterian Church and opened a day school for Mexican children, laying the foundation for the first free school system in the city. McCullough Avenue now passes the present First Presbyterian Church downtown and extends northward beyond Loop 410.

Nacogdoches Road This once led to the East Texas town of the same name, perhaps the oldest town in Texas. A legend is told of an old Caddo chief who lived near the Sabine river and had twin sons. When the brothers grew to manhood and were ready to become leaders of their own tribes, one—named Natchitoches—was sent to settle his tribe three days eastward toward the rising sun and the other—Nacogdoches—was sent three days westward with his tribe toward the setting sun. The brothers remained friendly, and the road between Nacogodoches, now in Texas, and Natchitoches, now in Louisiana, was well traveled. It became an important gateway for trade between the Spanish in Texas and the French in Louisiana, where the road became the eastern end of El Camino Real, "The King's Highway."

Oblate Drive The word oblate refers to a person serving and living in a monastery but not under monastic rule or full monastic vows. This person continues to live in the world while promising to dedicate himself or herself to the service of God and neighbor. The street takes its name from the Oblate School of Theology, founded in San Antonio in 1903 with the initial goal of educating young men to serve as Oblate missionaries. Its scope has since been broadly expanded, including a Ministry to Ministers program, a four-month spiritual and theological sabbatical experience for priests and others who have been in ministry for a number of years. In the 1980s, the school also created programs for laypersons. The school is part of the Missionary Oblates of Mary Immaculate, founded in 1815 by St. Eugene De Mazenod in France to serve the poorest populations of Provence. Missionaries were subsequently sent to many places throughout the world, including Texas, where they first came in 1849.

Ogden Lane In 1889, J. W. Ballantyne Patterson, R. H. Russell and Charles W. Ogden formed the Alamo Heights Land and Improvement Company, which bought the property that eventually became Alamo Heights. Several decades passed before the development became successful (Mary D Avenue, p. 28). Ogden, son of a San Antonio judge, never lived in Alamo Heights, but his son, Capt. C. W. Ogden, after retiring from the Army in 1928, lived on the street that bears the family name. At the turn of the century this street, earlier known as Hondondo and Corso, was the turning around point for the streetcar from downtown.

Pat Booker Road   This connects IH-35 with the main entrance of Randolph Air Force Base. When constructed and named in 1963, it was a cutoff from Austin Highway to Randolph and was named for a San Antonio native killed in a military training exercise. Capt. Francis P. Booker entered the Army during World War I and later joined the fledgling Air Corps. He served in the Panama Canal Zone in a squadron commanded by Capt. William M. Randolph (p. 188), and later was stationed at Randolph Field. His next assignment was the Air Corps Tactical School at Montgomery, Alabama, where he died when his plane crashed in 1936. Local writer Paula Allen reported that even though Booker had five crashes prior to his fatal flight and that doctors concluded he had a fear of flying, he was never grounded.

Patterson Avenue   This contoured drive in Alamo Heights, forming a loop at the west end of Terrell Road and passing the Argyle, honors J. W. Ballantyne Patterson, who helped convert that home to a hotel (p. 149).

Perrin-Beitel Road   This road was named long before the area was annexed to the city. Two families with those names had substantial land holdings in the area where Nacogdoches and Perrin-Beitel roads now intersect. During the 1870s, Alphonse Perrin, born in New York of Swiss immigrant parents, bought a tract between branches of Salado Creek northeast of San Antonio, where he established Hope Farm. Moses Campbell Judson (p. 98) married Martha Cornelia Perrin of the same family. Born in Germany, Joseph Beitel (1806–89) and his wife, Elizabeth, settled in San Antonio around 1830. He fought in the Plum Creek Battle against the Comanches and in the Battle of Salado against the Mexicans. In 1851, Beitel bought 565 acres on Salado Creek for $141.25. Five years later he was elected a Bexar County commissioner. His sons established a lumber business that prospered with the arrival of the Southern Pacific Railroad in 1877.

Pershing Avenue   Named in 1916 to lead an expedition into Mexico to pursue Pancho Villa, Gen. John J. Pershing (1860–1948) was also commander of the Army's Southern Department, headquartered at Fort Sam Houston. His nickname "Black Jack" derived from his service with a regiment of black troops early in his career, but it came to imply his stern bearing and rigid discipline. He was selected by President Wilson to organize and command American troops in World War I, the 3- million man American Expeditionary Force. Returning a hero, he was named General

Gen. John J. Pershing rode at the left of the back seat in the Battle of Flowers parade in 1917, shortly before he left to command American forces in France.

of the Armies—a rank previously held only by George Washington, though the five-star rank of General of the Army was created during World War II. Pershing, however, never wore more than four stars.

Peter Baque Road Many residents of the company town of Cementville (p. 158) were Roman Catholic Mexicans who had fled their homeland during the Mexican Revolution and found jobs with the San Antonio Portland Cement Company. But the nearest Catholic Church was St. Peter, Prince of the Apostles Church off Broadway, a very long walk for people without cars. In 1925, Father Peter Baque (1886–1938), a native of Catalonia, was appointed pastor of St. Peter's. Within two years he had the Shrine of St. Anthony built in Cementville to honor the patron saint of San Antonio. The sixty-seat church with its Alamo-shaped façade was dedicated on June 13, 1927, the feast day of St. Anthony of Padua (p. 1). It was succeeded nearby in 1957 by a much larger parish church, also with an Alamo façade. The old shrine fell into disrepair and was slated for demolition, but a major renovation restored the building and moved it 100 yards north, where it was dedicated in 2003 as St. Anthony Adoration Chapel. The current church, restored chapel and a retirement center for priests (Padua Place) are on Peter Baque Road.

Plumnelly Lane This short private road leading to only one home, that of the late bank president Reagan Houston, has a story too good to leave out of this book. When Mr. Houston built his home on this inherited strip of land in the middle of the Coker Ranch, a woman delivered some curtains and pillowcases she'd made. During the exchange she said, "Mister Houston, I didn't know you moved to plumnelly." When he asked what she meant, the seamstress replied, "Plum out of town and ne'lly out of the country." Houston's wife, Mary Jane, wanted to give the street the more dignified designation "Sir Winston Lane," because it's in the Churchill High School area, but he chose the more whimsical name.

Primera Drive   Taking its name from the Spanish for "first," this was the first street developed by H. C. Thorman when he began building the early homes of Olmos Park (p. 194).

Rittiman Road   Of many Rittimanns who lived in this area, this road is probably named for Anton, born in 1828. His German-born parents, Johannes and Anne Marie, arrived in Galveston 1846, apparently part of Henri Castro's Medina County colony, though they later moved to Guadalupe county. When Johannes died in 1865 without a will, the court decreed his property be sold to pay debts. Anton, the highest bidder, got for $1,000 what is likely the property for which the road is named. Walter John Rittimann, who died in 1993 at the age of 99, grew up on the ancestral ranch and was an auto mechanic for 69 years. His Rittiman Road business, Goll Automotive Service, survives in the name of his son-in-law. When the city named the road, the last letter of the family name was dropped.

Roy Richard Drive   This road is apparently named for a dentist who was the second mayor of Schertz.

Russell Place   Part of Laurel Heights/Monte Vista was developed by Denver investors Frank and Logan Russell.

Shook Avenue   This street is apparently named for one or both members of a distinguished family. Attorney Col. John R. Shook (1837–1913) was born in Ohio and came to Texas in 1858. After commanding troops in Civil War combat, he settled in Pleasanton, renewed his law practice and was Atascosa County district attorney before moving to San Antonio. His son Phil H. Shook (1869–1939 was in the Belknap Rifles (p. 21), ran unsuccessfully for mayor and was Bexar County Judge in 1906–12. He continued county road system development begun by his predecessor, Robert B. Green (p. 150).

Terrell Road   This Alamo Heights and Terrell Hills street honors Terrell Hills founder Dr. Frederick Terrell (p. 195), and passes his home at the northeast corner of Terrell Road and North New Braunfels Avenue.

Thorman Place   As a young man in Toledo, Ohio, Herman Charles Thorman learned construction as a carpenter and contractor. Arriving in San Antonio at 23, began building upscale homes with great success, including the San Antonio Country Club addition in the Mahncke Park area, Olmos Park and Olmos Park Estates.

Tuleta Drive   Dela White contracted measles prior to the birth of her daughter Tuleta, who was born profoundly deaf. In 1947 Mrs. White founded Sunshine Cottage School for Deaf Children (p. 129) in a former caretaker's building on the grounds of Landa Library at Shook and Bushnell avenues. In 1952 the school moved to a site across from Alamo Stadium. The street it faced, which

H. C. Thorman

ran from northwestern Brackenridge Park to Stadium Drive, was named Tuleta Drive in honor of the student responsible for establishing the school. In 2010 Sunshine Cottage moved to a 20-acre campus a half-mile to the northwest on the far side of Hildebrand Avenue.

Tuttle Street   This street at the southwest border of Randolph Air Force Base (p. 188) is probably named for San Antonio Public Service Company President Col. William Tuttle, who was chairman of the Chamber of Commerce Military Affairs Committee when it was competing for location of national aviation training center. His committee raised private funds, obtained creative city financing and on December 31, 1927—the day before the Congressional deadline—had the site available to the Air Corps as a gift. Also probably named in his honor is **Tuttle Road** in Terrell Hills, where Col. Tuttle lived.

Col. William Tuttle

Voelcker Lane   Along Salado Creek west of Blanco Road, this road is a survival of the 4,000-acre ranch of three Voelcker brothers—Max, Louis and George—where Max and his wife Minnie Alma operated a dairy farm for most of the twentieth century. Minnie (1905-2000) worked in every operation—administering to livestock, operating milking equipment, overseeing help and delivering milk to market from the farm, at that time many miles out in the country. After Max died in 1980, many developers tried to purchase the valuable property, but Minnie rejected all offers. In 2006 the estate sold 151 acres to KB homes and 311 acres to the city, at the urging of Mayor Phil Hardberger (Phil Hardberger Park, p. 83).

Walzem Road   A large dairy farm owned by the Walt Walzem family fronted on a dirt road everyone called Walzem Road. About 1960 the farm was sold to Murray and Barbee Winn as the final piece of property to create Windcrest (p. 196). This road now forms its southern boundary.

Weidner Road   The farmhouse on this road was the homestead of one of the pioneer families of the Cibolo area. Fred W. Weidner was born in that house in 1909, and he died in 1994 after having served as postmaster for Cibolo, Bracken and Converse for 23 years.

Wetmore Road   This once led to a town that is no longer on the map. Wetmore was founded in 1880 on the new Houston and Great Northern Railroad 11 miles northeast of downtown San Antonio. It was named for Jacob S. Wetmore, a director of the railroad. As San Antonio absorbed it the unincorporated community lost most of its separate identity.

Willim Street   W. B. Willim was prominent in the company succeeding the Alamo Heights Land and Development Company. Formerly called Lee, it was changed by Clifton George (see Mary D Avenue, p. 28) to honor his predecessor.

Northwest

Admirals Way   This short street is named for San Antonio's most famous non-admiral, San Antonio Spurs superstar David Robinson (p. 47). Although his rank was no higher than lieutenant, junior grade, when he served on active duty following his graduation from the U.S. Naval Academy, Robinson was dubbed "The Admiral" by the local media, and the nickname stuck.

Babcock Road   The naming tale reported about Babcock Road in the first edition of this book—that the road was named after a man who furnished cattle to Santa Anna—has turned out to be apocryphal. The true story was uncovered by local historian Catherine Meaney. Amos Babcock (1811–87) was a wealthy businessman and philanthropist who was born in Connecticut but, at 31, moved to Canton, Illinois. There he established a successful mercantile business and was an abolitionist. His obituary said that "his charities were extensive" and that "he gave liberally to the needy." The Canton Register reported that Babcock traveled to San Antonio in February 1877, the year the railroad arrived, and bought a 2511-acre ranch in northwest Bexar County. His property was conveniently located where cattle could be easily loaded from towns west of San Antonio onto trains, shipped to Chicago and sold for a handsome profit. Early maps show the ranch to be bordered by present-day Prue Road on the north, Huebner Road on the south and Leon Creek on the west. Part of the current Babcock Road probably ran through the middle of the ranch.

Bandera Road   Many roads in San Antonio were named for the towns to which they originally led (Bandera, p. 203).

Bitters Road   There is no shortage of possibilities for the naming of Bitters Road, but not one is supported by solid evidence. After researching its origin for nearly ten years through countless e-mails and other forms of communication, I've concluded the most likely candidate is John A. Bitter, county tax assessor in the 1920s. The next most plausible theory is that a rancher named Sam Bitter owned property adjacent to the Walker Ranch (p. 91), which became Hill Country Village. Or it could have been named for Clarence Bitter, who had a store and restaurant at the corner of Bitters Road and San Pedro Avenue (now US 281) in the 1950s. There were eight people with this fairly common German surname listed in the 1891 city directory. Most prominent was Charles Bitter (1863–1910), who owned a meat business facing Alamo Plaza said to be "the best market in the city." But for the time being, this road remains on the author's mystery list.

Bluemel Road   On the Fredericksburg Road end of this short street (BLEEmel) that runs at right angles to itself once stood Bluemel's Store. In 1895 Richard Bluemel, son of Austrian wool merchants, opened the Alamo Bar across from the Menger Hotel. In 1908, he sold the bar to purchase 300 acres between what is now Fredericksburg Road and IH-10, where he built a grocery and feed store. His children added a number of adjacent businesses, including a filling station, car repair shop and Club Petite, a favorite watering hole for soldiers training at Camp Stanley during World War I and later. Bluemel in German means "little flower."

Braun Road   For a long time this name was on the author's mystery list, primarily because there are so many Braun (pronounced BROWN) names on the west side of the city. But the mystery has been solved by local author Cynthia Leal Massey, who wrote a book about Helotes, and by Fred Wendt, a Braun descendant who has compiled a massive family tree of Brauns. The patriarch was Philip Braun (1810–87), who along with his wife, Mara Susanna (1812–1903), settled in the Helotes area in the 1860s. Originally from Bicken, Prussia, the couple and their five children arrived in Galveston by ship in 1855 After living in New Braunfels awhile they moved westward. Philip purchased 362 acres near Helotes in February 1862, and later acquired several thousand more along Helotes Creek. The Braun children married into other

German immigrant families, most had many children and by the third generation nearly everyone in the Helotes area was related by blood or marriage. Braun Station Elementary School on Tezel Road (p. 43) and Braun Hall were named for Theodore Braun, a grandson of Philip who owned a ranch where these buildings are now located. Several members of the Braun family were among the German settlers who formed Zion Lutheran Church of Helotes in 1906, the first church built in northwestern Bexar County. Many settlers and their descendants are buried in the church cemetery.

Callaghan Road Meandering from Vance Jackson Road west and south to Highway 90, this was named for Alfred Callaghan, the third Callaghan to be mayor of San Antonio. Alfred, son of the more flamboyant Bryan Callaghan Jr., was mayor from 1947 to 1949, and apparently was instrumental in planning Loop 410, crossed by this long road. A short street downtown was named for his father (p. 8).

Countess Adria Street The fourth mayor of Leon Valley was Richard C. Adair, who first developed the Castle Estates subdivision. Adair obviously liked to play with words. He named his daughter Adria (an anagram of Adair) and added the title "Countess" when he named the street for her.

De Zavala Road bears the family name of pioneer preservationist Ádina De Zavala.

De Zavala Road There at least three people for whom this busy street may have been named. The first is Lorenzo de Zavala (1788–1836), one of three Hispanic signers of the Texas Declaration of Independence and the first vice president of the Republic of Texas. He helped create a republic in Mexico after the break with Spain and served as Governor of the State of Mexico. When Santa Anna defied the 1824 Mexican constitution that de Zavala helped write, de Zavala resigned in protest and moved to Texas. The second candidate is Lorenzo's granddaughter, Adina De Zavala (1861–1955), a feisty and controversial schoolteacher who fought to preserve many of the state's historic sites, including the Alamo. She is best remembered for having barricaded herself for three days, in 1908, inside the so-called Long Barracks adjacent to the Alamo church to protest its being rented to a group of St. Louis investors. Later, she initiated the campaign to save the Spanish Governor's Palace. The third and least glamorous, but most likely, possibility for the naming is Lorenzo's son and

Adina's father, Augustin De Zavala, postmaster in 1881 of the **Shavano** stagecoach stop (p. 194). His home was across what was once part of Fredericksburg Road (now IH-10) from the old Locke Hill School, now Northside Alternative Middle School North.

Eckhert Road   This road in front of Marshall High School is named for a family that owned property in the area long before the school existed. Note that this street is spelled differently from and is named for a different family than Gus Eckert Lane (p. 38).

Evers Road   In 1874, Claus Hartwig Evers (1817–1900), an immigrant from Schleswig-Holstein, Germany, bought 211 acres near what is now the corner of Evers and Huebner roads for $3 per acre. His son Christian expanded the holdings to some 1,300 acres, part of which is now the Forest Oaks subdivision. In 1894, Christian donated two acres for the area's first school. It is thus reasonable to assume that this road is named for Christian Evers (1847–1900) rather than for his father. The original pronunciation—EEvers—has been lost over time, and most now pronounce it simply Evers.

Fredericksburg Road   Unlike wandering roads first used informally for ranch purposes, the initially arrow-straight Fredericksburg Road was surveyed in the 1840s as a military route to the frontier. In 1855 it was traversed by camels used in an Army transportation experiment based at Camp Verde in southern Kerr County. In the World War I era, Fredericksburg Road was the path for troops marching from Fort Sam Houston to maneuvers at Leon Springs Military Reservation, later camps Stanley and Bullis. One campsite en route was Nine Mile Point, nine miles from Fort Sam down Hildebrand Avenue and up Fredericksburg Road at the present-day intersection with Wurzbach Road. As development encroached, troops moved to a less-populated path, up present-day Harry Wurzbach Highway and out Military Highway to Leon Springs. In 1929 Fredericksburg Road became a link in the automotive cross-country Old Spanish Trail Highway from San Diego, California to St. Augustine, Florida that pioneered the route of IH-10. It is named for a major destination from San Antonio, the Hill Country town named for Prince Frederick of Prussia (1828–85). Frederick was a member of the colonizing Adelsverein, and was known as the Iron Prince for his exploits as field marshal during the Franco-Prussian War.

Galm Road   Samuel Henry Galm (1862–1944) was born in Pennsylvania to German immigrant parents. The family moved to Helotes in 1872 and established a farm where Galm Road (Hwy. 1560) now runs. A prominent local farmer, Galm was a founder of Zion Lutheran Church.

His son Clarence was an early board member of a public consolidated school district that eventually became Northside ISD. Clarence Galm Elementary School is named in his honor.

Gass Road   Susanna Braun (1852–1923) was three when her family landed in Galveston from Prussia (Braun Road, p. 35). In 1873 she married Karl Gass (1849–1935), a farmer and stonemason who owned 880 acres. In 1998 the Texas Family Land Heritage Program honored the Karl Gass Farm as a "continuous agricultural operation by the same family for 100 years or more."

Grissom Road   John Grissom (1879–1961) was born in Lavaca County, but as a teenager he and a friend set out on horseback for the southwest. After ranching in New Mexico and mining in Arizona he rode to El Paso, where he sold his horse and took the train back to San Antonio. The remainder of his life was spent in the land and cattle business in South Texas. He was by all accounts a very sound judge of cattle. His wife Marie Thompson Grissom (1894–1997) was born in Navasota. After college in Texas and graduate work at Columbia University she taught school in San Antonio, where she and John became business as well as marriage partners. Their premise was that any transaction should benefit both parties. They started many families in the ranching and dairy business by selling them cattle on credit and renting them land. Many prospered and became well-to-do thanks to their benefactors' generosity. John and Marie Grissom donated a right-of-way through their Bexar County ranch to create Grissom Road.

Guilbeau Road   This road is named for Francois Guilbeau Jr., for whom a downtown street is also named (p. 12), because the family owned property in this area.

Gus Eckert Lane   The homestead of Gustave Eckert (1854–1930) stood on the hill alongside Fredericksburg Road across from the USAA building and on the site of the Bent Tree Apartments. Some maps show this street as Cinnamon Hill, which it turns into a half-mile from Fredericksburg Road. Gus Eckert is not the same person for whom Eckhert Road (p. 36) was named. Eckert and his wife, Christine, are buried in the nearby Locke Hill Cemetery at Fredericksburg and Huebner roads.

Hamilton Wolfe Road   This street's name is different from most double-named roads which identify separate families who owned land on either side. In this case, Hamilton and Wolfe owned property not on either side but at either end of the road. Worthy Wolfe owned the property on the west end. On the corner of Fredericksburg and Wurzbach roads stood the family-owned Wolfe's Inn restaurant, far out of town when it was built. Fredericksburg Road was paved to the corner in 1934. A renowned horsewoman named Hamilton had a horse farm at the east end of the road, where it intersects with Babcock.

Hausman Road Fritz Hausman married Helen Evers, daughter of Christian Evers and granddaughter of Claus Hartwig Evers (p. 37). The Hausmans, farmers and ranchers, owned a large tract between Fredericksburg and Bandera roads. In time the property was divided by Loop 1604, which split the original road into West Hausman Road—an east–west road now connecting IH-10 and Loop 1604—and South Hausman Road, a north-south road connecting Loop 1604 with Prue Road where it joins Bandera Road.

Huebner Road Joseph Huebner (1824–82) arrived in the port of Galveston from Bohemia with his wife and two children in 1853 and settled in San Antonio. Known as "Doc" Huebner for his skills as a silversmith and watchmaker, he went to work at Bell Brothers Jewelers. In 1858, he began purchasing land in the area of present-day Huebner, Babcock and Bandera roads and eventually owned 850 acres, on which he raised mules and horses. His homestead on Bandera Road across from Leon Valley City Hall was a stagecoach stop on the San Antonio-Bandera route and is often referred to as the Onion House because the Onion family lived there from 1930 until 1983. It has been purchased by the city of Leon Valley in hopes of its restoration as a historic site. Huebner was a prominent member of San Antonio's German community and probably a founder of the San Antonio Schutzenverein, or Shooting Society. As a rancher and horse dealer, Huebner faced an occupational hazard in this part of Bexar County: Indian raids. In 1915, his heirs were awarded $1,098 by the U.S. government to settle a lawsuit filed for theft of horses by Comanches in 1869 and 1870.

Igo Drive About 1880, Napoleon Bonaparte Igo married Alice Taylor, who inherited land extending from what is now IH-10 to Vance Jackson Road and from Wurzbach Road halfway to Huebner Road. The family home stood on Wurzbach Road on the site formerly occupied by a supermarket. When the three Igo daughters and one son sold the property to developers, one stipulation was that new subdivisions have streets named for their parents. For Dad that was easy—Igo Drive—but Mom proved a bit more difficult. There were already streets in San Antonio named Alice and Taylor, so developers came up with a clever solution (Tioga, p. 44). Daughter Hattie married Grover Cleveland Crandall, who donated part of the property on Wurzbach Road that became the site of Oak Ridge Baptist Church. Hattie donated the site of St. Matthew's Catholic Church. Napoleon and Alice's great-grandson is John Igo (p. 137), a retired college professor and local historian who provided much information about names in this part of town, where he has lived since 1927.

Ingram Road   Hudson Ingram (1901–90) and his brothers founded Acme Wire and Iron Works, later Ingram Manufacturing Company. They made ornamental iron products, many still in use in homes in Monte Vista, Alamo Heights and Olmos Park. Ingram, who recognized the city's transportation needs long before others, worked in 1947 for passage of a bond issue to build the first expressway in San Antonio—the downtown section of IH-10—and later saw the need for a loop around the city. He donated land for a northwest segment of Loop 410 and for Ingram Road.

Kyle Seale Parkway   In 1941, Mid Seale bought his first ranch property in the area of what is now Loop 1604 at FM 1560 (Hausman Road, p. 38). In the same year, his son Kyle graduated from Jefferson High School and entered the University of Texas at Austin. The younger Seale volunteered for the Army in the fall of 1942, became a private and was sent to officer candidate school. He became a decorated combat infantry officer in the Southwest Pacific in World War II. After the war he earned a law degree at the University of Texas, returned to San Antonio and was given the original part of the ranch by his parents, Mid and Jewell Seale. He added most of the Loop 1604 frontage. Over the years the family donated land for the parkway that bears his name as well as rights-of-way for streets to access such facilities as the Cedar Creek Municipal Golf Course and several subdivisions.

Lee Hall Street   This street through Los Angeles Heights was probably named for a famous Texas Ranger, Jess Leigh Hall (1849–1911), who was born in North Carolina, moved to Texas in 1869 and changed the spelling of his middle name to Lee. Described by Ranger historian William King as "a man of daring and almost reckless physical courage, of fine physique and resistless energy," Hall served a short but distinguished career as a Ranger from 1876 to 1881. Most of his subsequent business ventures were failures. He later organized and led two regiments in the Spanish-American War, then was a leader of the Macabebe Scouts in the Philippines. William Sydney Porter (O. Henry), in an effort to find a healthier climate than his native North Carolina, lived on the Hall ranch for two years, and is said to have used Lee Hall as the model for the Ranger who appeared in many of his Texas stories.

Leslie Road   This road beside O'Connor High School takes a right angle to connect with Hausman Road. It was named for a Texan imprisoned in Mexico's Perote Prison, Andrew J. "Jack" Leslie (1819–85), who came to San Antonio from Arkansas and was a court deputy in 1842 when the Mexican Army under Gen. Adrian Woll suddenly appeared and captured the entire court. Fifty-two men were taken to Mexico and held in Perote Prison for 18 months. Upon their return, some received land grants. Leslie was awarded 1,280 acres just south of the confluence of Culebra Creek and Helotes Creek, where Culebra Road now intersects Loop 1604. Local author Mary Lee Gussen Sloan uncovered records showing that Leslie was entitled to this grant because he resided in the new Republic of Texas for three years and had been in military service from December 1836 until June 1838. Although Leslie received the land more than 25 years before Philip Braun and other German immigrants who settled to the north and west, Sloan did not move there until the 1870s. Leslie Road is believed to have been the route from his property to the neighboring ranches.

Lockhill-Selma Road Lockhill-Selma was a cross-country road linking northwest San Antonio with Austin Highway and with Selma. **Locke Hill** (also spelled Lock Hill and Lockhill) was bounded roughly by Bandera and Huebner roads, Northwest Military Highway, and IH-10. The founder was William Jackson Locke, who brought his family from Illinois in 1850. Son John's home was up the road from the De Zavala home (p. 36), about where the present-day Gunn Infiniti dealership is. Historians note that there was rivalry between Locke and Augustin De Zavala, who also owned property in the area and was the first postmaster of a stagecoach stop called Shavano. For years these men apparently argued about whether the area should be called Locke Hill or Shavano.

Merkens Drive In a neighborhood where almost all streets are named for movie stars (p. 196), it seems odd that there would be a street named for one of San Antonio's most prominent ministers. The Rev. Guido Merkens started Concordia Lutheran Church in a cinder block building at 1826 Basse Road in 1951. In large part due to the charisma and dynamic leadership of its pastor, the congregation grew to 4,000 in the 42½ years of his pastorate. Merkens was internationally known as an author of seven books, an inspirational speaker in the U.S. and 14 foreign

Concordia Lutheran pastor Guido Merkens preached in 49 states and 14 foreign countries.

countries and as a TV personality with separate spiritual programs for adults and children. The congregation finally outgrew the original site and moved in 1998 to a new location outside of Loop 1604. So why this name for a street far removed from either site? When Shepherd of the Hills Lutheran Church was built in 1969, one parishioner had connections with the developer of the property across Wurzbach, and suggested that the street alongside the church be named in honor of a man who had done much for Lutherans in San Antonio. Merkens was the father of three daughters and a son, Guido Jr., who played for nine seasons in the NFL as a corner back, wide receiver, quarterback, punter and kick/punt return specialist.

Mike Nesmith Drive Guitarist Mike Nesmith was a member of the 1960s pop-rock quartet called the Monkees, which had its own TV show in 1966–68. Nesmith was a nephew of the wife of Leon Valley's Castle Estates subdivision developer, Richard C. Adair (p. 36).

Northwest Military Highway The road that winds its way northwest from Loop 410 to Camp Bullis is a remnant of the road that once connected Fort Sam Houston with Camp Bullis. The original route included what is now Harry Wurzbach Road and a segment of Loop 410 across the north part of town.

Palmer Moe Drive This street on the grounds of Texas Military Institute near Camp Bullis Road is named for the managing director of the Kronkosky Charitable Foundation (p. 169), who as President of Valero Energy played an important role in rescuing TMI construction plans during a severe economic downturn that occurred just as the school was moving from its longtime Alamo Heights campus. Palmer Moe was raised in Montana and educated there and in Denver, and still escapes to the streams and mountains of his home state to fly fish in the summer. As a CPA with Arthur Andersen in Houston, he testified before the Texas Railroad Commission in the Coastal States-Lovaca energy litigation. One outcome of the trial was the spin-off of Valero Energy Corporation, to be headquartered in San Antonio (p. 172). Moe moved to San Antonio in 1978 to set up a satellite Arthur Andersen office, with Valero as one client. Valero CEO Bill Greehey (p. 177), created the position of COO and hired Moe for the job. Moe worked at Valero until 1992, and in 1997 became managing director of the Kronkosky Foundation.

Poss Road Heinrich Theodore "Henry" Poss (1870–1956), born in Bulverde, raised his family on a farm in Van Raub near present-day Fair Oaks Ranch (p. 43 but in 1922 bought 185 acres in the Leon Valley area. He and his wife Clara Voges Poss raised dairy cows, leased his fields to other dairymen for grazing and sold fresh butter and eggs. What is now Poss Road between Bandera and Evers roads was once part of Huebner Road (p. 39). In the early 1950s the county cut through the Poss property to straighten out this dogleg in Huebner Road. The short segment, now no longer in continuity with Huebner, was renamed Poss Road. Most of the Poss land was sold for development, but some Poss families still live on a small part of Henry's land, the fifth generation to do so.

Prue Road   Running between Fredericksburg and Bandera, this is another street with a confusing name origin. Henry Martin Prue, according to his grandson, bought property in Bexar County around 1918. Henry's son Floyd B. Prue (1903–59) had a ranch "on a dirt road off Fredericksburg Road." The family had moved to Texas from Prue, Oklahoma, a small town northwest of Tulsa that was also named for Henry. Although this is the most likely origin of the name, there is an intriguing coincidence. In 1837, a man named Anselmo Pru was awarded one league of land (4,428.4 acres) in this same area by virtue of his citizenship in the Republic of Texas prior to the signing of the Texas Declaration of Independence in 1836. He probably never set foot on the property, and sold the land shortly after acquiring it.

Ralph Fair Road   During the 1930s, oilman Ralph E. Fair bought several tracts that became the 5,000-acre Fair Oaks Ranch, which spilled over from Bexar County into surrounding Comal and Kendall counties. At first the main focus of the ranch was race horses, but when Texas laws on horse racing changed in the 1940s the emphasis shifted to raising registered cattle. The ranch became a pioneer in artificial insemination. After the death of Fair and his wife in the late 1960s, heirs opened the ranch for development. A golf and country club used the original 14,000-square-foot home as its center. The community eventually became the incorporated city of Fair Oaks Ranch, which now has a population of some 5,000.

Steubing Road   Hwy. 1560 in northwest Bexar County has two names, Galm Road (p. 37) and Steubing Road. Heinrich Steubing Sr. (1832–1915) was born in Germany and arrived in Texas at Indianola (p. 13) in 1848. He married Katherine Margarethe Wetz (1841–72), and they had six children, all born in New Braunfels. By 1885, he had moved and established one of the first farms in Leon Valley on Bandera Road at Leon Creek. Heinrich and two sons were charter members of Zion Lutheran Church.

Sunshine Drive   This formed the southern border of the Albert Maverick family's Sunshine Ranch, headquartered in a home no longer standing at the head of Sunshine Ranch Road off Babcock Road. Typical of family properties broken up for development, several streets on the former ranchland bear surnames of later family members—**McNeel, Crossette, Epler, Padgitt**. One nearby street, **Laddie Place**, is named for a family dog.

Tezel Road   In the mid-1870s, brothers William and Herman Tezel (TETzel) arrived from Germany and settled northwest of town. There were eventually four Tezel families in the area, all farming mainly corn, oats, and wheat. Spelling and pronunciation of the name probably relate to the original German spelling.

Tioga Drive   It would be logical to associate this name with the American Revolution, the source of many street names in this neighborhood, for Tioga County in upstate New York was crossed in 1779 by an American expeditionary force punishing the Seneca Indians for siding with the British. The real story, however, comes from local historian and writer John Igo (p. 137). He reports that this name was created to honor Alice Taylor Igo, wife of the owner of the property that would become the Summit of Colonies North and Shenandoah subdivisions (Igo Drive, p. 39). It was stipulated in the sale by the Igo children that both parents would have streets named for them. Igo Drive was named for the father, but both of the mother's names—Alice and Taylor—were already street names. The solution was to take their mother's initials and last name—A. T. Igo—and find an anagram containing only those letters. The result was Tioga.

Toutant Beauregard Road   There are two possibilities for the origin of this name. The more prominent Beauregard was Pierre Gustave Toutant (1818–93), a Confederate general from Louisiana who played a key role in the early stages of the Civil War. As commander of troops in Charleston, he gave the order to fire the war's first shots, against Fort Sumter, ironically commanded by Union Maj. Robert H. Anderson (Argyle, p. 149), who had been his artillery instructor at West Point. Pierre Gustave Toutant Beauregard also commanded Confederate troops in the first real battle of the Civil War, Bull Run (Manassas), where Union troops were commanded by Irvin McDowell, a former West Point classmate in the class of 1838. The other possibility for the source of the name is A. Toutant Beauregard, Pierre's brother, whose story is a bit closer to home. In 1856, Samuel Maverick sold his cattle and brand to A. Toutant Beauregard, who had to hunt for the animals. These so-called maverick cattle (p. 154) were originally allowed to wander freely, but in 1854 were rounded up and brought to San Antonio, where they were again allowed to roam freely over a wide area.

Vance Jackson Road   The first half of this name is for the family that owned the famous Vance House downtown (p. 19) and a ranch to the northwest, and that speculated in land. William Vance (1813–78) came to San Antonio in 1846 with his father and brothers James and John as commissary agents during the Mexican War. After the war they built the first U.S. Army barracks in San Antonio. Born in New York but raised in Kentucky, William Houston Jackson (1803–88) arrived in 1849 to establish a ranch on the Emanuel Leal grant of 640 acres, "about seven miles northwest [from downtown] as the crow flies." During the Civil War he saw much action and became a brigadier general. Afterward he was a Bexar County justice of the peace, but his major interest appears to have been raising cattle. Since it was customary to name a road for the properties it ran between, it is reasonable to assume that Vance and Jackson owned adjacent lands in this part of town.

Woller Road   Local historian John Igo's grandfather Frank Woller (1870–1925) was a farmer; he settled in the area southwest of what is now the University of Texas at San Antonio campus in the 1880s.

Wurzbach Road/Parkway   In 1904 William Wurzbach and his father-in-law, Gustav Schmeltzer, bought 1,400 acres in northwest San Antonio. Wurzbach, an attorney and county judge, built a home in a pasture now at IH-10 and Wurzbach Road, site of an H-E-B store. The family built a road so they could get around the farm, extending it up the hill as far as what is now Fredericksburg Road and later deeding the roadway to the county. When Wurzbach Parkway is completed across the city north of Loop 410, the name will extend far beyond the original family property. Stories about the Wurzbach brothers, William and Charles (p. 25), were passed on to the author by William's daughter, Emily Wurzbach Mickler, who died in 2007 at the age of 107.

EAST

Ackerman Road   Ackerman Road is named for a pioneer family that settled in the area during the wave of German immigration in the mid-nineteenth century. An Ackermann family with five children settled in the Salado Creek area in 1848. This road is thought to have divided the property of two of the brothers, Frederick and Johann Ackermann. As with the Rittimanns (p. 32), the name was originally spelled Ackermann but the second "n" was dropped when the roads were named.

Bellinger Street   This short street is named for a powerful African-American politician, Charles Bellinger (1875–1937). Born on a farm in Caldwell County, Bellinger moved to San Antonio in 1906 and made a substantial amount of money as a gambler. He parlayed that into extensive business and real estate holdings, as well as a "numbers" game and bootlegging operation during Prohibition. He organized African-American voters into a solid bloc comprising nearly one-fourth of all voters in the city. Because San Antonio was one of few Texas cities that allowed Blacks to vote in Democratic primaries, he was able to have a major influence on city politics for about 15 years, and was said to have been instrumental in electing John Tobin (p. 76) mayor in 1923. City government returned the favor with street paving and lighting, better plumbing, improved recreation facilities, a branch library and schools for the east side. In 1936 Bellinger was convicted of income tax evasion and sentenced to 18 months in Leavenworth, but illness led to his transfer to a government hospital and a pardon by President Franklin D. Roosevelt.

Binz-Engleman Road   This road just south of the new Brooke Army Medical Center on the fringe of Fort Sam Houston once connected properties of Ferdinand Binz and H. Engelmann. During World War I, about 200 acres was rented to the Army for training troops at Camp Travis. After the war the families sold the property to the War Department.

Can't Stop Street   One of the most frequently asked queries is about the origin of the name of this two block-long street. I regret that it remains a mystery. Express-News journalist Vincent T. Davis researched the name in October 2009, but was also unable to uncover the source. He did find that it has been on city maps dating back to 1889.

Dellcrest is a short street in the Dellcrest subdivision developed by George Delavan (p. 130), who apparently used part of his surname to name this development as the Winn family used theirs in naming Windcrest. Delavan also developed Dell View southeast of Loop 410 and IH-10.

Goliad Road   Established about 1720 by Spaniards as part of El Camino Real ("The King's Highway"), this road served for more than 150 years as a major thoroughfare for emigrant, commercial, and military traffic. Its importance diminished only after the railroads came to Texas in the late nineteenth century. Goliad, on the San Antonio River about 40 miles inland from the Gulf of Mexico, was the site of a Spanish mission and presidio moved inland from Matagorda Bay in 1749. In 1829 the name was apparently changed to Goliad to honor the revolutionary priest Father Hidalgo (Miguel Hidalgo y Costilla, 1853–1911). Goliad is thought by some to be an anagram of Hidalgo (the "h" is silent in Spanish). Born into a wealthy family, he became an iconoclastic priest who was frequently in trouble with the Catholic establishment. Living with and championing the cause of New Spain's poorer citizens as a parish priest in the small town of Dolores, Hidalgo is best remembered for his call for independence, el Grito de Dolores, proclaimed on September 16, 1910, the date celebrated as Mexico's Independence Day.

Holmgreen Road   Named for Julius H. Holmgreen (1854–1943), who came from Louisiana in 1883 to join his father, George, in running the company that became Alamo Iron Works. He is said to have created the Christmas tree tradition on Alamo Plaza by combining cedar branches to form a large tree.

Martin Luther King Drive   Formerly **Nebraska Street**, the name was changed in 1975 to honor the civil rights leader (p. 123).

Robinson Place   David Robinson and his wife Valerie were major founders and funders of the Carver Academy (p. 93), an elite preparatory school located on the north side of this street. Nicknamed "The Admiral" because he graduated from the U.S. Naval Academy before his two years on active duty, David Robinson is arguably the best-recognized face and name in the city. In addition to helping the Spurs win two NBA championships, he received virtually every NBA honor, including Rookie of the Year (1989–90), Most Valuable Player (1993–94), Sportsmanship Award (2001) and All-Star team (10 times). He is the only male basketball player to play for three U.S. Olympic basketball teams. Now a dedicated philanthropist and highly-sought after Christian motivational speaker, Robinson was further honored in 2003, when the NBA renamed its Community Assist Award the David Robinson Plaque. The award is given monthly to recognize players for charitable efforts. In his typically articulate fashion, Robinson gave a very moving acceptance speech when he was inducted into the Naismith Memorial Basketball Hall of Fame in 2009.

Former Spurs star David Robinson is now an inspirational speaker and philanthropist.

Toepperwein Road   Even if this thoroughfare turns out nor to have been named for Ad and Plinky Toepperwein, the name is so famous that it ought to be included. At one time, "The Famous Toepperweins" were once the world's greatest sharp-

Ad and "Plinky" Toepperwein were once the best sharpshooters in the world.

shooting team and perhaps San Antonio's best-known citizens. Adolph (Ad) Toepperwein (1869–1962) was born in Boerne and later moved to Leon Springs, where his father was a well-known gunsmith. Although his father died when Ad was thirteen, the boy had already become expert with a gun, and by the age of 21 all of San Antonio knew of his prowess. He toured with a circus for eight years, then represented the Winchester Repeating Arms Company for 50 years as an exhibition publicity agent and sales representative. On his first visit to the company factory in New Haven, Connecticut, he met an 18-year old woman that he would marry two years later. Although Elizabeth Servaty ("Plinky") Toepperwein (1882–1945) had never fired a rifle before she met Ad, she became his sharpshooting partner, and some said that she was the better marksman of the two. Plinky, whose nickname came from her exclamations when she hit a tin can—"I plinked it"—was the first woman to break 100 straight targets at trapshooting, a feat she repeated more than 200 times. Part of the act was for her to shoot chalk and crayons held in her husband's mouth. During a three-day exhibition at the St. Louis World's Fair in 1906, Ad made 19,999 hits out of 20,000, and the following year performed what the San Antonio Daily Express described as "the greatest shooting exhibition ever given." Using up all the ammunition for sale in San Antonio, he fired at 72,500 wood blocks and missed only nine during 68 1/2 hours of shooting. Despite such fame, I have never found any evidence that links this man from Leon Springs to the road that passes through Live Oak and Converse on the opposite side of town. A more plausible explanation is that one of the other many German families named Toepperwein in this area owned property nearby. Perhaps a reader will correct this. There is also a Toepperwein Road in Boerne, which is much more likely to have been named for them.

Walters Street   This prominent street that leads to the main south entrance of Fort Sam Houston has long been on the author's "mystery list." Then an alert reader, Ken Haase, pointed out that in 1890 the A. M. Walters Real Estate Investment Company of Nebraska set aside four acres in the center of their new East End subdivision and called the park by that name. The name was later changed to Lindbergh Park, and yet again to Dawson Park (p. 73). Since Walters Street runs along the eastern border of the park, one would assume that the developers named it for themselves.

W. W. White Road   William W. White was a farmer who bought large tracts of land in the Salado Creek Valley, settled by German and Belgian farmers. His land surrounded a school named for him, which is now part of the East Central Independent School District.

West

Biering Lane   This short street off Bandera Road just inside Loop 1604 is presumably named for the family that owned a ranch here. Friedrich August Biering was born in Saxony in 1837 and immigrated to Texas, where he and his three sons were all farmers and ranchers in this area.

Chennault Circle   Born in the east Texas town of Commerce but raised in Louisiana, Claire Chennault (1893–1958) was one of the most colorful and controversial generals of World War II. With the onset of World War I, he enlisted and eventually learned to fly, although he said that he was initially rejected by the Signal Corps for flight training three times. After the war, he was commissioned into the newly organized Air Service and became one of the military's first fighter pilots. Chennault was innovative and contentious, defending his "defensive pursuit" tactics that fighter planes could defeat unescorted bombers. Poor health and disputes with superior officers led him to resign in 1937 with the rank of captain. He immediately went to China as an advisor to Madame Chiang Kai-shek, who was Secretary General of the Chinese Air Force. As commander of the Chinese Air Force flight school, he was responsible for training a new generation of Chinese fighter pilots. Before the United States officially entered the war, Chennault recruited and led the American Volunteer Group, which gained fame as the "Flying Tigers" in their P-40C fighter planes. The group was incorporated into the U.S. Army Air Forces and Chennault rejoined the army, eventually becoming a major general in command of the 14th Air Force. After the war he returned to China, where he founded the Civil Air Transport, which supplied the Chinese Nationalists in their fight against the Communists. It later became Air America, a CIA-owned operation heavily involved in the Viet Nam war. His lifelong two-pack-a day cigarette habit finally caught up with him; he died of lung cancer and was buried in Arlington National Cemetery. He received an honorary promotion to lieutenant general one day before his death. A few months after his death, the Lake Charles Air Force Base was named Chennault in his honor. It is now Chennault International Airport.

Clarence Tinker Drive   Maj. Gen. Clarence Tinker (1887–1942) was the first Native American in the U.S. Army to attain that rank, and also the first American general officer killed in World War II. Tinker, one-eighth Osage, was born and grew up on the Oklahoma-Kansas border and entered the army as an infantry officer in 1912. Transferring to the Army Air Service, he served as an Air Services Advanced Flying School instructor at Kelly Field. Shortly after Pearl Harbor he was named commander of the Air Forces in Hawaii. In 1942, following the Battle of Midway, he led a force of early model B-24s in a bombing run of Japanese-held Wake Island. On June 6, four aircraft left Midway. Shortly after take-off Tinker's plane lost altitude, nosed into the overcast and went out of sight. He and his crew were declared missing. Neither wreckage nor bodies were ever located. Four months later, the newly created Oklahoma City Air Depot was named Tinker Field (now Tinker Air Force Base) in his honor.

Culebra Road   Culebra means "snake" in Spanish. There is some disagreement as to whether this road was named because of its circuitous, twisting course or because rattlesnakes inhabited the long, open stretches of the road as it led to ranches in Medina and northwest Bexar counties.

Cupples Road   One of the remarkable men in the history of San Antonio, Dr. George Cupples (1816–95), was a colorful Scottish-born and-educated physician who served as the first president of the Texas Medical Association, formed in 1852. He came to Castroville as director of transportation and a medical doctor. No stranger to armed conflict, he had been an assistant surgeon in the Spanish Civil War; in the Mexican War he was surgeon to the Texas Rangers Company and in the Civil War he was first surgeon of the Texas Mounted Volunteers. One of his era's most prominent medical men, he is credited with introducing the use of surgical anesthesia in Texas.

Donaldson Avenue   This name is probably related to the Babcock family (p. 34). Amos Babcock bought a 2,511 acre ranch in northwest Bexar County in 1877. When he died in 1899 he bequeathed 213 acres to his nephews, Arthur and David Donaldson, sons of the sister of Babcock's wife Carrie Lucas (1842–1923).

Duncan Drive   Angling off Billy Mitchell Blvd, this street is named for Lt. Col. Thomas Duncan. After his training at Kelly Field, Duncan was killed in 1923 in an airplane accident at Bolling Field in Washington, D.C. Two years later, Kelly Field Number 1 was renamed **Duncan Field**.

Foulois Street   Pronounced fooLOY, this street honors the U.S. Army's first aviator, Lt. Benjamin Foulois (1879–1967). He began his career as a cavalry officer but transferred to the Signal Corps, where he operated the U.S. military's first balloon. Seeking more favorable flying weather, the commanding general of the Signal Corps sent Foulois to Fort Sam Houston with orders to teach himself to fly and to establish a pilot training facility. The former he did in part through correspondence with the Wright brothers, after

Lt. Benjamin Foulois was the first military aviator in Texas.

only one hour of instruction by Wilbur. On March 2, 1910 Foulois made the first military flight in San Antonio—and Texas—which he described as "my first solo, landing, take-off and crash." His second order was carried out by building a small hangar near Fort Sam's Arthur MacArthur Field, then used for cavalry drill. Later he selected the site of what would become Kelly Field (p. 187). When America entered World War I in 1917, Foulois was promoted to brigadier general and assigned as Air Service Chief of the American Expeditionary Force, eventually—in 1931—becoming Chief of the Army Air Corps. An outspoken and aggressive promoter of the fledgling Air Service, Foulois clashed with many politicians and other military officers, including General Billy Mitchell (p. 59). Among his accomplishments was seminal work in the development of long-range bombers, so essential to winning World War II.

Frank Luke Road   Growing up in the sleepy town of Phoenix, Arizona (pop. 1,500 in 1880), Frank Luke (1897–1918) was a tough youngster who excelled in sports and participated in bare-knuckle boxing matches. He enlisted in the Aviation Section of the U.S. Army Signal Corps in September 1917, and was killed in action one year later. In the interim, he became an American fighter ace, ranking second only to Captain Eddie Rickenbacker in the number of aerial victories. His forte was attacking German observation balloons, which were heavily defended by anti-aircraft guns on the ground. On September 29, 1918 he was severely wounded by machine gun fire from a hilltop adjacent to a balloon site he had attacked. He immediately landed his plane, but collapsed and died while trying to run for safety. Described by Rickenbacker as "the most daring aviator and greatest fighter pilot of the entire war," Luke was posthumously awarded the Medal of Honor. Luke Air Force Base in his hometown Phoenix is named for him.

General Hudnell Drive   Maj. Gen. William T. Hudnell commanded the San Antonio Air Materiel Area at Kelly Air Force Base for almost five years and was instrumental in gaining support for construction of a nearly two-mile-long road to connect U.S. Hwy. 90 with Kelly. Its creation became a political football among state, federal and local funding sources. Originally named Kelly Access Road, it was renamed General Hudnell Drive in 1965, when the general retired from active duty.

General McMullen Drive   Maj. Gen. Clements McMullen (1892–1959) commanded the San Antonio Air Materiel Area at Kelly Air Force Base from 1948 to 1954. This Kelly access road opened in 1954. In 1918 McMullen was one of the first graduates of Kelly's flight training school. During a career that spanned three wars, he flew military aircraft from fighters to heavy bombers. Early on he was a flight commander in Billy Mitchell's Mexican Border Patrol. In 1930 he set a long-distance speed record of 52 hours and 30 minutes from New York to Buenos Aires.

John D. Ryan Boulevard   General John Dale Ryan (1915–83) is unique among high-ranking military officers because in 1962 he was named to the Sports Illustrated Silver Anniversary All-American football team. After graduating from West Point in 1938, this Iowa native received his pilot wings at Randolph and Kelly fields. In the early years of World War II he was a bomber instructor pilot, and was instrumental in establishing an advanced bombardier training school. In 1944 he commanded combat missions in Italy. In one of these he lost a finger to enemy antiaircraft fire, earning him the nickname "Three-Fingered Jack." After the war, he rose steadily through the ranks, becoming the seventh Air Force Chief of Staff in 1969. Twenty-eight years later, his son General Michael E. Ryan was named the Air Force's sixteenth chief of staff.

Josephine Tobin Drive   This road around Woodlawn Lake is named for the only woman who was both the daughter and mother of San Antonio mayors. Josephine Tobin was the daughter of John William Smith (p. 90), the first mayor after incorporation in 1837–38, and mother of John Wallace Tobin (p. 76), mayor in 1925–27 when much of the flood control work including Olmos Dam was done (p. 194). A landmark ornate rock and wrought-iron sign spanning the east en-

Josephine Augusta Smith Tobin, center front, was the only woman to be both the daughter and mother of San Antonio mayors. Her father was John William Smith and a son was John Wallace Tobin, standing at far right.

trance stood for more than 70 years, but was demolished when an 18-wheel truck ran into it in May 2000. Thanks to efforts of local businesses, the sign was restored in November 2001.

Kampmann Boulevard   This street around Jefferson High School was probably named for an early building contractor or a descendant. As a boy in Cologne, Germany, John Herman Kampmann (1819–85) trained in many facets of the builder's trade—carpentering, blacksmithing, stonemasonry and plastery. Fleeing to avoid conscription for military service, he arrived in San Antonio in 1848, penniless but well equipped to establish himself. His career as an architect and contractor was interrupted by the Civil War, during which he was stationed in Texas and saw no fighting. He resumed his profession and also built a sash and door company or lumber mill, where he is said to have installed the city's first steam engine. Among buildings he constructed were St. Mark's Church, the Menger Hotel (which he bought after Menger's death), the Steves mansion (p. 147) and the Lone Star Brewery, of which he was also president.

Leal Street   At age 54 the oldest of the Canary Island settlers, Juan Leal Goraz was also elected the first alcalde—mayor—of the new municipality of San Fernando, on August 1, 1731, though others can lay claim to that title; during Mexican rule in 1824–25 Juan Martin de

Veramendi was the first "alcalde of Bexar," and in 1837 John Smith was the first mayor after independence from Mexico. Juan Leal Goraz descendant John Ogden Leal was Bexar County archivist for 10 years.

Marbach Road   John Joseph Marbach and his wife, Agnes, emigrated from Wurtenheim, Germany in 1852 and established a large family in southern Comal County. Grandson Albert Marbach (1886–1941) moved to a farm west of San Antonio, where he was a street commissioner in the 1930s and became namesake of Marbach Road. Albert's uncle John was among the family staying in Comal County, where the town of Bracken named a Marbach Road for John Marbach. Once San Antonio spread west and that road became an important artery, Bracken sought to avoid confusion by changing its name to Marbach Lane.

Quentin Roosevelt Road   As the youngest (and said to be favorite) child of Theodore Roosevelt, Quentin (1897–1917) was three years old when his father became president, and he grew up in the White House. A mischievous and rambunctious youngster, he was also said to have his father's remarkable intellectual skills. He entered Harvard in 1916, but dropped out the following year to join the fledgling Army Air Service. At the time he was engaged to Flora Payne Whitney, great-granddaughter of Cornelius Vanderbilt. A courageous but reckless pilot, he was immensely popular with his fellow airmen. On July 14, 1918, he was shot down by two machine gun bullets that struck him in the head. Crashing near the front lines, his body was recovered by the Germans and buried with full battlefield honors. His body was later exhumed and buried in the World War II American cemetery above Omaha Beach in Normandy next to his brother, Brig. Gen. Theodore Roosevelt Jr., a Medal of Honor recipient in that war. Quentin's father was distraught over his son's death. Within six months the ex-president himself would be dead. An airfield on Long Island where he trained was later named Roosevelt Field in Quentin's honor.

Ray Ellison Boulevard   Few have dominated the home building of any American city as Ray Ellison (1917–2005) did in San Antonio. A local boy who attended Fox Tech High School, he started out as an auto and aircraft mechanic but soon turned his attention to building homes. Beginning with Valley Hi near Lackland and Kelly Air Force bases in 1955, Ray Ellison Homes and Rayco built more than 50,000 homes in more than 40 subdivisions during the next four decades, a number equaling between 45 and 60 percent of all new homes in San Antonio each year. In his later years Ellison limited his new construction to "only" 2,500 per year, for consistency and predictability of costs and profits. Along the way Ellison founded two banks and the largest private water/sewer utility in Texas, donated land for branch libraries and for Air Force Village, and received virtually every accolade given to builders on the state and local levels. In 1980 he was named National Builder of the Year by Professional Builder Magazine. He sold his company to a California corporation in 1998.

Robins Drive Augustine Warner Robins (1882–1940) has been called the Father of Logistics for the United States Air Force. Logistics is the complex science of implementing a system to have personnel, equipment, provisions and facilities in the right place at the right time, though anyone who has been in the military knows that this "science" doesn't

Ray Ellison, right, with company president Jack Willome, for several years were building half the new homes sold in San Antonio.

always work out as planned. His father had been a Confederate cavalry commander in the Civil War, and Robins himself was a graduate of West Point, class of 1907. One of his earliest deployments was with General John Pershing's (p. 30) 1916 expedition into Mexico against Pancho Villa. In 1919 Robins was assigned to Wright Field in Ohio, where he spent the next 20 years establishing the first official and workable supply maintenance and accountability system and creating guidelines for the training of logistics officers and civilians. The Warner Robins Air Logistics Center in Georgia was named in his honor.

Rogers Road The story behind this road started in Milwaukee in the late nineteenth century. D. G. Rogers was a millionaire lawyer and land speculator who in 1887 traded a resort hotel in Wisconsin for a 2800 acre ranch in Texas, and sent his son Henry to manage the property. Henry's interests lay in more pleasurable pursuits, and the ranch struggled until he married Mary Feldtmann, a woman 20 years younger, who took over its operation. Their daughter Blanche was born in 1903 and D. G. Rogers died shortly thereafter, leaving the entire ranch and its holdings to his 3-month-old granddaughter. When Blanche grew up, she married a man named Quintus Ellison, but he died of a brain tumor. The ranch fell on hard times during the Depression, forcing Blanche and her mother, Mary, to lease most of the property to a neighbor rancher. In 1933, Mary hired a young ranch hand named Ed Wiseman

"Papa Ed" Wiseman brought the Rogers Ranch back go profitability.

(p. 57) to help work the ranch, and he became Blanche's second husband. "Papa Ed," as he came to be known, soon brought the ranch operation back into the family and turned it into a prosperous venture, through good land management and animal husbandry. Because the family worked with the Woodbine Development Corporation to develop the Hyatt Hill Country Resort and Spa plus the surrounding area, several nearby streets are named for family members: **Feldtmann Trace** (for Mary); **Simpson Trace** (for Ed and Blanche's daughter Mary Ann "Tootie" Simpson); **Sugar Trace** (for Blanche's daughter "Sugar" by her first husband); **Polly Court** for Charles and Patricia's daughter, who died of cancer at age 31; and **Ed Wiseman Trace** (for "Papa Ed" himself). The only family member who didn't get a street is Ed and Blanche's son Charles Rogers Wiseman, a successful veterinarian, but Charlie's Long Bar in the Hyatt is named for him. The hotel's pool restaurant is called Papa Ed's and there is an Aunt Mary's Porch for Mary Feldtmann Rogers.

Ruiz Street   Although there is no clear evidence as to which Ruiz this street is named for, it is an important name in early San Antonio history. José Francisco Ruiz (1783–1840) was born in San Fernando de Béxar when it was part of Spanish-controlled Mexico. He was a young officer in the Mexican Republican army that fought to gain independence from Spain, and for several years was forced into exile in Louisiana to avoid arrest by Spanish authorities. After Mexico won independence in 1821, Ruiz returned to Texas and petitioned the President for a military command. In 1828, as a lieutenant colonel, he led the Alamo de Parras company (p. 3), and retired from the military in 1832. When Texans began their struggle for independence he joined the cause, and as a delegate to the Convention of 1836 was one of only three Hispanic signers of the Declaration of Independence, the others being his nephew José Antonio Navarro (p. 16) and Lorenzo de Zavala (p. 36). His son Francisco Antonio Ruiz was alcalde, or mayor, of the city during the battle of the Alamo. Prior to his military career, in 1803 Ruiz became the first schoolmaster of San Antonio, in a house on Military Plaza. The building was moved and reconstructed on the grounds of the Witte Museum in 1943.

Shearer Boulevard/Shearer Hills Street   Two streets in San Antonio bear the Shearer name, both probably named for auto dealer and civic leader H. J. Shearer, born in Pennsylvania in 1885. Shearer began his real estate career in San Antonio in 1917 remodeling homes into apartment buildings, then expanded to subdivision development. Shearer Boulevard runs just east of Jefferson High School in the Woodlawn Terrace area, which was platted and developed by Shearer and his partner C. M. Furr. Another of his developments was Shearer Hills, nestled in the triangle where McCullough Avenue and Jackson-Keller Road meet. Its major street, Shearer Hills Street, is named for him. Most of the subdivision's streets have women's names, such as **Susan Carrol**, **Audrey Alene**, **Veda Mac**, the names of secretaries who worked in his office building.

Wiseman Boulevard The Wiseman story begins with the Rogers family (p. 55). When Ed Wiseman married D. G. Rogers's granddaughter Blanche, he took over operation of the family property, which soon became known as "Papa Ed's" ranch." Conoco began drilling on the ranch during the 1950s. Although they did not strike oil, they hit something nearly as precious – water. At that time south central Texas was suffering from severe drought, and the water wells on the Rogers-Wiseman ranch allowed irrigation 24 hours a day. In 1990, with the city moving inexorably westward, the family sold 200 acres to Woodbine Development Corporation for the Hyatt Hill Country Resort and Spa. A stone marker on the hotel's driving range marks the site of the original homestead.

Zarzamora Street In Spanish, zarza means "bramble" and mora means "mulberry." It is postulated that Spaniards created a compound word when they encountered a new type of berry that reminded them of the familiar mulberry but grew on a prickly bush. Over time, their word zarzamora came to be the name for their new discovery, blackberries.

Wilson Boulevard John T. Wilson built the first of his many homes in Woodlawn Terrace in 1925. Arriving in Texas in 1878 from Georgia, he began as a telegraph operator for the new railroad. Eventually he became part owner in both a lumber company and a bank, thus becoming an important promoter of home ownership from both the financial and material directions. His was one of the first firms in San Antonio to sell products for monthly payments.

SOUTH

Billy Mitchell Boulevard Arguably the most controversial figure in American military aviation, William L. (Billy) Mitchell (1879–1936) is regarded by many as the father of the U.S. Air Force. In 1911, as the youngest member of the Army General Staff, he became inter-

Bob Billa was an influential civic leader on the south side.

Benjamin M. Hammond was a developer of Highland Park.

Anton Moursund was a legislator, judge and attorney.

ested in aviation and took private flying lessons. When the United States entered World War I in April 1917, Mitchell was immediately deployed to France, where he became a highly regarded and decorated combat leader commanding the Americans' fledgling flying service. After the war, his farsighted—and ultimately correct—views of the role airpower would play in the future kept him in constant conflict with Army and Navy brass, who considered airplanes of value only for reconnaissance. In 1924, after a tour in Hawaii and Asia, Mitchell filed a long report predicting a future war with Japan that would begin with an attack on Pearl Harbor. His outspoken public criticism of senior leaders in the military reached a peak when, after the Navy dirigible Shenandoah crashed in a storm killing 14 of the crew, Mitchell accused Army and Navy leaders of incompetence and "almost treasonable" disregard for aviation safety. In a court-martial trial made famous by a movie starring Gary Cooper, he was convicted of insubordination and resigned from the service in 1926. The B-25 bomber used by Jimmy Doolittle in the 1942 Tokyo raid was nicknamed the "Mitchell" for him. In 1946 Billy Mitchell was posthumously awarded the Medal of Honor.

Bob Billa Road Perhaps the most influential local civic leader to represent San Antonio's south side was Bob Billa (1921–95), affectionately known as the "Mayor of the Southside" (p. 141.

Hammond Avenue Benjamin Morton Hammond (1865–1955), a North Carolina Quaker, came to Texas with his parents in 1882 at the age of 17. After working at a variety of jobs, in 1896 he bought Bell Brothers jewelry store. He also traded actively in real estate, being a principal investor in the Highland Park development. In 1902 he married Nellie Rigsby, sister of his real estate partner, W. C. Rigsby (p. 61). They bought a house in Alamo Heights in 1919, where their grandson and his family now live.

Mauerman Street The names behind this short street near the intersection of IH-10 and IH-35 south of downtown were researched by Theresa Gold, one of the most knowledgeable persons in our city about German immigration. Although there are some discrepancies, it would appear that a man named Benjamin (or Bernard) Mauermann (1818–93) immigrated to San Antonio from either Germany or Bohemia around 1852. He was the first gunsmith in this area, and his family became prominent in city social circles. His son Gus A. became an alderman and later chief of police, and a grandson, Gus B., was mayor from 1943 to 1947. Current city maps show the spelling as Mauerman, which is typical of dropping the second 'n' in streets named for German families. The Mauermann family was tied to the Mitchell family (below) by intermarriage. There is also a **Mauerman Road** in south Bexar County near Mitchell Lake.

Mitchell Street In all likelihood, this street is named for Asa Mitchell (1795–1865), one of the Old Three Hundred, those settlers who received land grants in Stephen F. Austin's first colony. Mitchell moved his family to Texas in 1822 and settled at the mouth of the Brazos River. He took part in drafting the Declaration of November 7, 1835, a declaration of causes for taking up arms against Mexico that preceded the actual Declaration of Independence. He later fought as a sergeant in the Battle of San Jacinto.

Morrill Street An officer in the Confederate Army and later instrumental in forming groups of Civil War Veterans, Capt. David Morrill Poor (1838–1915) is better remembered for his middle name than for his last. His first wife Mary Mussey Poor, superintendent of the school at Mission San José, died giving birth to her sixth child in 1876. In

The court martial of Brig. Gen. Billy Mitchell, in uniform at table to right, was made widely known by a movie starring Gary Cooper.

her memory, Poor donated land for the Morrill Chapel School, built by his son Lawrence Frederick Poor in 1894. Twenty years later a new school was built and the name was changed to Morrill High School, though this served as a combined elementary and high school until the first Harlandale High School was built in 1926. From his mother, Eliza Dyer Poor, Captain Poor inherited land in the southeast part of town, where he developed several housing additions. Many streets were named for family members: **Mary Street**, for his first wife; **Mildred Street**, for granddaughter Mildred Neal Travers; **Neal Avenue**, for the Polk Neal family; **Hart Avenue**, for his mother-in-law, Susan Hart Mussey, who came to Texas from Kentucky; and **Morrill Avenue**, thought to be named for his bachelor son Morrill Hart Poor. Other neighborhood streets were named for friends: **Pyron Avenue** for Charles L. Pyron, Poor's commanding officer throughout the Civil War; **Octavia Place**, for Pyron's second wife; **Greenwood Street**, for the family into which Poor's oldest daughter Ellie married into; and **Merrick Street**, probably for his neighbor and friend Morgan Wolfe Merrick.

Moursund Boulevard   Judge Anton N. Moursund, (1877–1965) raised in Fredericksburg, attended the University of Texas at Austin, but finished his law studies at such an early age that he had to wait for his twenty-first birthday to take the bar exam.he began his law practice in Mason. When the governor seemed about to appoint to a vacancy on the Fourth Court of Civil Appeals in San Antonio a person whom a number of attorneys considered dishonest and disreputable, they delegated Moursund to go to Austin and convince the governor of his impending error in judgment. The governor was persuaded, and also impressed with the messenger. On the spot he appointed Moursund to fill the position. After completing his judicial term and a stint in the Texas legislature, Moursund joined his sons in private practice in San Antonio. Having written the state bar exam several times, he was asked by the St. Mary's University School of Law for guidance in improving their graduates' rate of passing. Some of his recommendations remain in effect, and Moursund's portrait hangs at the school. He maintained ownership of property in the area of Pleasanton Road. After his death, city council named part of Pleasanton Road in his honor.

Pop Gunn Drive   This street in a warehouse area on the south side is not named for a toy firearm but rather for a highly successful local businessman, Curtis E. "Pop" Gunn (1911–99). His mother wanted him to become a Methodist minister, but instead he obtained a bachelor's degree in philosophy at SMU in 1934, following which he was hired by Smith Motor Sales in San Antonio as an car salesman. After a decorated tour of duty as an officer with the 13th Armored Division in Europe, Gunn returned to Smith and became general manager and partner.

In 1955 he sold his interest in Smith and founded Gunn Oldsmobile, the first of some nine auto dealerships in his conglomerate. Perhaps as a result of his mother's aspirations, he was highly active in his sixty-five-year membership in Laurel Heights Methodist Church and was instrumental in the development of Methodist Hospital. Gunn Road on the northeast side off IH 35 is also named for him.

Curtis "Pop" Gunn was an auto dealer and churchman.

Rigsby Avenue The Highland Park development was on a pasture north of what is now Highland Boulevard. The original plan was for each of the six investors to set aside a square block on which to build a big house on a street named for himself, causing streets in the area to be named for W. C. Rigsby, Ben Hammond, Benno **Kayton**, L. P. **Peck**, and A. H. **Avant**. The sixth investor, Charles Peterson, did not want a street named for him, so **Highland Boulevard** is what would have been Peterson Boulevard. Although the first 20 years of his working life in San Antonio were spent with the railroads, Rigsby later bought into and ultimately headed Wolff and Marx Department Store. His wife, Emily, was the daughter of Capt. Charles Schreiner, Kerrville's leading citizen.

Retailer W. C. Rigsby helped develop Highland Park.

Samoth Drive There is a simple explanation for this weird-sounding name. One of the developers in this area, Alex Thomas, was running out of names and decided to spell his own surname backwards, with transposition of the last two letters, presumably, to make it more phonetic.

Southcross Boulevard Although not named for a person, part of this important artery was once the major thoroughfare of the city of **South San Antonio**, which grew with establishment of aviation training at nearby Kelly Field and had its own post office before being annexed as part of San Antonio in 1944. Originally called **Main Street**, then **Dwight Avenue**, it was finally given a name that describes its path.

Steves Avenue   In 1849, 20-year-old Eduard Steves arrived in Texas from Germany. He originally settled in New Braunfels, where he married another German immigrant, Johanna Kloepper, and started cutting cypress trees and shaping the wood into shingles. In 1866 the family moved to San Antonio, where he opened a lumber company behind the Menger Hotel. Before long he was shipping trainloads of building materials to the southwestern United States and northern Mexico. Five generations of Steveses have worked in the business (Steves Homestead Museum, p. 147).

EXPRESSWAYS

Charles Anderson Loop   Loop 1604 is named for former Bexar County Judge Charles W. Anderson (1892–1964), first elected in 1939 and never defeated in more than 25 years of public service. During World War II he took a leave of absence and served as an Army legal officer, rising to major. This is not the Charles Anderson who built the Argyle (p. 149).

Sgt. Cleto Rodriguez was San Antonio's most decorated World War II soldier.

Cleto Rodriguez Freeway   San Antonio's most decorated World War II veteran was Tech. Sgt. Cleto Rodriguez (1924–90). He was wounded in an assault upon a Japanese-controlled railway station during the Battle of Manila in the Philippines, in which he was credited with killing 82 Japanese soldiers and preventing the enemy from bringing up reinforcements. An 8.5-mile stretch of U.S. Highway 90 from Loop 410 West to IH-35 was named in his honor. His 20 medals—including a Silver Star, a Purple Heart, two Bronze Stars and the Medal of Honor—were donated to his former elementary school, named Ivanhoe when he attended but changed to Cleto Rodriguez Elementary after the war.

Connally Loop   Few San Antonians are aware that Loop 410 was named for former Gov. John B. Connally (p. 110), and fewer still actually refer to it as Connally Loop.

Frank Tejeda Memorial Highway   Highway 281 from Loop 410 South to the Atascosa County line is named for former Marine, attorney, state senator and congressman Frank M. Tejeda (p. 98).

José M. Lopez Freeway In the bitterly cold December days of 1944, José M. Lopez (1909–2005) won the Medal of Honor for his courage in the Battle of the Bulge. His actions were credited with saving his company from an attack by a much larger German force. Born in Mexico and orphaned at an early age, he hitchhiked for three days to Mission, Texas, where he lived with an uncle. Before the war he was a professional boxer, and won fifty-two of fifty-five bouts. U.S. Highway 90 (IH-10) from IH-37 to Loop 410 East was named for him in 1994. In 2000 Lopez, 89, and two other local Medal of Honor winners (including Lucian Adams, p. 63) were honored at a San Antonio Spurs game.

José M. Lopez was awarded the Medal of Honor for heroism during the Battle of the Bulge.

Lucian Adams Freeway IH-37 from IH-10 to Loop 410 South is named for Staff Sgt. Lucian Adams (1922–2003), decorated for valor on October 28, 1944 near St. Die, France. His company was surrounded by German troops and cut off from other friendly forces. Sgt. Adams was awarded the Medal of Honor for single-handedly clearing the forest of enemy soldiers, including three German machine guns, and reopening supply lines for his company. He was one of thirty-nine Hispanics to receive the Medal of Honor. Adams was discharged in 1945 and soon began a forty-year career with the Veterans Administration in San Antonio.

Sgt. Lucian Adams received the Medal of Honor for heroism in France.

McAllister Freeway A successful businessman who in 1921 founded San Antonio Savings Association, Walter W. McAllister (1889–1984) was co-founder of the San Antonio Union Junior College District (now the Alamo Community College District), mayor from 1960 to 1971 and honorary co-chairman of HemisFair '68. McAllister Freeway—the section of U.S. Highway 281 from downtown north to Loop 410—has been perhaps the only named local highway that people actually refer to by name. McAllister Freeway was to be in the federal interstate highway system as part of IH-37 from the Texas coast

Controversial freeway advocate Mayor Walter McAllister on the unfinished freeway that would be named for him.

though San Antonio and north, but construction was delayed for 10 years by conservationists who argued that the route would violate Brackenridge and Olmos Basin parkland. When federal funding was blocked for the section north of downtown, Mayor McAllister successfully obtained state funding instead and it was completed without federal aid, though it is otherwise indistinguishable from I-37. Controversy over construction occurred when San Antonio had two competing daily newspapers, the Express-News and the Light. The Light is said to have had a policy forbidding use in its pages of the word "express" in any form, thus rather than calling it an "expressway" always referred to the proposed project as a "freeway." A city government trying to remain neutral went with the safer designation, "freeway."

McDermott Freeway   IH-10 from downtown to Loop 1604 was named in 1991 for the man credited with the modern expansion of USAA,

Brig. Gen Robert McDermott was dean of the Air Force Academy, president of USAA and a trombone player.

a financial services institution established as United Services Automobile Association for active duty and retired military officers. Robert F. McDermott (1920–2006) graduated from West Point in 1943, flew as a combat pilot in World War II and was the first dean of the U.S. Air Force Academy. He retired as a brigadier general in 1968 to join USAA, and within a year was president. To consolidate scattered offices and prepare for growth, he acquired 286 acres that were, he said, "out in the boondocks." The expanse of USAA buildings on that property now dominates the west side of IH-10 from Huebner to Wurzbach roads. A plaque says that in his 25-year tenure as CEO McDermott and his wife "played an indispensable role in establishing San Antonio as a major business, medical, biosciences, educational, sports, and tourist center." Other facilities named for him include an elementary school and a Medical Center clinical science research building.

90th Infantry Division Highway   As part of the Texas Memorial Highway System, a four-mile segment of U.S. Hwy. 90/IH-10 between Loop 410 and FM 1518 honors a battle-hardened and highly decorated infantry division with Texas connections. The 90th was formed at Camp Travis, adjacent to Fort Sam Houston, in August 1917, and subsequently served in the American Expeditionary Force in World War I. Inactivated in 1919, the division was reactivated in March 1942, and first saw action on Utah Beach on June 6, 1944. From that day on, the 90th had at least one unit in contact with the enemy every day from D-Day to VE-Day, and had more days of combat than any other division in the European Theater of Operations. The division was first made up almost entirely of men from Texas and Oklahoma, and their shoulder patch reflected that, with a "T" superimposed on an "O." As the war progressed and replacements were drawn from every state in the union, the letters came to represent the unit's nickname, "Tough 'Ombres."

The 90th Infantry Division's T and O, shown in this patch, originally stood for Texas and Oklahoma, later for Tough 'Ombres.

Raymond E. Stotzer Jr. Freeway   Raymond Stotzer (1925–89) was director of the state highway department. Before that he was a district engineer in charge of San Antonio area projects. He died shortly after being instrumental in getting state approval for a west side freeway in San Antonio; he is credited with obtaining some $14 million in land and cash donations from private citizens. Begun in 1983 but not completed until 2004, this freeway—now known as Texas 151—connects US Highway 90 with Loop 1604.

SSgt. William J. Bordelon Freeway   The most recent addition to the city's list of named segments of local expressways is the section of IH-37 between IH-10 and IH-35. William J. Bordelon (1920–43) graduated from Central Catholic High School in 1938 and enlisted in the Marine Corps three days after Pearl Harbor. Rapidly promoted to sergeant, he was a member of an assault engineer platoon in the Battle of Tawara, where he was killed on November 20, 1943. On that day he single-handedly destroyed four Japanese pillboxes despite being seriously wounded. Killed instantly when a demolition charge exploded in his hand as he assaulted the final enemy pillbox, he was one of three Central Catholic graduates who died on Tarawa, and the first Marine from Texas to be awarded the Medal of Honor in World War II. He was initially buried on Tarawa a few yards from where he was killed, but his body was soon transferred to the "Punchbowl" Cemetery in Honolulu. At the request of his brother Robert, the body was again transferred in 1995, this time to his hometown, and he now rests in the Fort Sam Houston National Cemetery. Before that reburial, his remains lay in state in the Alamo, only the fifth person to be so honored. The destroyer USS Bordelon was named for him in 1945, and later San Antonio's Navy-Marines Corps Reserve Center as well as his high school alma mater's main foyer were renamed in his memory. Central Catholic High School's junior ROTC rifle team is called the Bordelon Rifles.

HONORARY STREETS

Several major streets in San Antonio bear dual names. In most instances, the name changes as proposed by City Council were either controversial, created confusion or met with substantial opposition from affected residents and business owners. The result was that the original name of the street was left intact but an honorary or memorial designation was appended. Thus such streets have dual names, though most residents use the original one.

Cesar Chavez Memorial Way Cesar Chavez founded the National Farm Workers Association in 1962 and fought for farm workers' rights until his death in 1993. He effectively used boycotts to demand better wages, housing and safer working environments for migrant workers. An intense battle over what site to name for him included suggestions that it be the airport or several major thoroughfares. The compromise was a 14-mile stretch of Commerce Street westward from IH 35. The memorial way is marked by signs along its entire course, but the street name is still Commerce.

Gaylard Fenley Way Although the official name of Fair Oaks Place in Alamo Heights has not changed, the segment of this street marking the northern boundary of the Alamo Heights High School campus is also named in honor of a revered football coach for nearly twenty years. Growing up in Houston where he was a multi-sport letterman, Gaylard Fenley (1943–2003) played football and baseball at the University of Houston and began his coaching career in that city, earning Greater Houston Coach of the Year Award in 1978. He became head coach at Alamo Heights in 1983, and in his second year took the team to the playoffs for the first time in 30 years. After two years as head coach at Baytown Sterling, he returned as head coach of Alamo Heights and led his team to its first undefeated season and district championship. As a mentor and role model to countless young men, Fenley lived his faith by being actively involved in the Fellowship of Christian Athletes. He earned the coveted Tom Landry award in 1994, and was inducted into the Athletic Director Association Hall of Honor in 2002 and, posthumously, to the Texas High School Coaches Association Hall of Honor in 2008.

Judge H. F. Garcia Memorial Boulevard   When a highly respected local judge died in 2002, the portion of Durango Boulevard from IH 35 to IH 37 was renamed in his honor. Opposition, mainly from residents and merchants in that area, objected on the grounds that the change was confusing and expensive. A compromise kept the original name and added the "memorial boulevard" designation. Hippolito F. ("Hippo") Garcia (1926–2002) was the son of Mexican immigrants, and spoke no English when he entered school in San Antonio. After his graduation from Brackenridge High School he joined the army and served with the Third Armored Division in Germany during World War II. After the war, he attended St. Mary's Law School on the GI Bill while working as a school janitor. After a stint in private practice he was elected to judicial posts in San Antonio before being appointed by President Jimmy Carter in 1980 as the first Mexican-American federal judge in the Western District of Texas, which includes 69 counties from San Antonio to El Paso. A lifelong bachelor, Garcia was also an avid history buff and Civil War scholar.

R. A. Callies Sr. Way   A 1.7 mile segment of Rice Road on the East Side was "renamed" for Rev. R. A. Callies, a long time civil activist. The pastor of First Gethsemane Baptist Church and for more than thirty years a shop teacher at Riley Middle School (a name he lobbied to have changed to Martin Luther King Middle School, p. 123), Callies organized the first MLK March, which has grown to become a well-attended annual event celebrating the birthday of that civil rights hero. As middle school teacher and pastor, he befriended many young people and worked tirelessly to champion and honor Dr. King and to upgrade living conditions in his eastside neighborhood. In 1997 City Council added his name to the MLK Boulevard Bridge over Salado Creek, but the following year the new council reversed the action. Two years later his supporters succeeded in appending the Callies name to Rice Road.

Rosa Parks Way   A three-block pedestrian walkway along Houston Street west of the Alamo is named for Rosa Parks (1913–2005), "Mother of the Civil Rights Movement." On December 1, 1955, she refused to relinquish her seat to a white man on a public bus in Montgomery, Alabama. Her arrest resulted in a 381-day boycott of the bus company and led the Supreme Court to rule Montgomery's segregated seating unconstitutional. This launched the career of the boycott's spokesman, the Rev. Martin Luther King Jr. (p. 121). Some forty years after the event, Parks received the Presidential Medal of Freedom and the

Congressional Gold Medal, the highest honor bestowed on a civilian by Congress. When she died she was the first woman to lie in state in the rotunda of the U.S. capitol.

MYSTERY STREETS

Despite persistent efforts, reliable documentation has not been located to explain the name origins of several of San Antonio's most well traveled streets, among them Foster, Gevers, Gibbs Sprawl, Potranco, Probandt, Roland and Vandiver. Identification of a few, such as Bitters and Toepperwein, is questionable. If a reader happens to have knowledge of the naming of these or any other streets included or not, he or she is encouraged to communicate this to the author via a Website created for this purpose: **www.sanantonionames.com**.

· 3 ·

PARKS AND PLAZAS

Aggie Park   Henry Weir's dairy farm was "way out in the country" where West Avenue now intersects Loop 410. A group of Texas A & M University alumni frequently rented part of his property for barbeques and get-togethers. When Weir left the dairy business, some of the men pooled their money and paid him $999 for 3.3 acres. Since then improvements have been added, including a large building where the traditional Aggie Muster is held each year.

A. J. Ploch Park   Anton Joseph Ploch (1905–85) served as precinct four's county commissioner for more than 30 years, the longest term of any commissioner since Bexar County was created in 1845. Part of what was originally Comanche Park on the southeast side was renamed for him. As a professional calf roper he had a keen interest in rodeos and stock shows, and was founder and trail boss of the Alamo Trail Ride. With Joe and Harry Freeman he was the major force in promoting and seeing to completion of a rodeo venue, the county coliseum, opened in 1949 (p. 154). San Antonio's Livestock Show and Rodeo was held here annually until the adjacent SBC (now AT&T) Center was built in 2002. Ploch was inducted into the Livestock Exposition Hall of Fame in 2003.

Alderete Park   This park honors former City Councilman Joe Alderete's daughter Clarissa Alderete, who died in her crib at the age of 16 months from strangling on a Venetian blind cord.

Bamberger Park   This 120-acre park was created in a flood plain where Leon, Maverick and Huesta creeks meet. Adjacent is the private Last Chance Forever Birds of Prey Wildlife Management Area. Land was donated by environmentalist J. David Bamberger, an early partner and former chairman of Church's Fried Chicken who transformed his overgrazed 5,500-acre ranch in Blanco County into an environmental showcase. It is the state's largest habitat restoration project on private land.

Bonnie Conner Park   Originally called Hausman Road Park, the name was changed in 2007 to honor a woman whose passion has been trees and the environment. Bonnie Conner taught school for 21 years before serving two terms as a San Antonio city councilwoman. Prior to her stint on the council, she co-authored an ordinance designed to preserve trees in the wake of population and building expansion. While on the council, she worked to ensure passage of the bond issue that provided funds for Voelcker Park—later renamed Phil Hardberger Park (p. 83)—and other improvements, and encouraged passage of two propositions establishing sales taxes to buy property to protect the Edwards Aquifer recharge zone. The 24-acre park is adjacent to the new Igo Library (p. 135).

Banker George W. Brackenridge was one of the city's major philanthropists.

Brackenridge Park Founder of San Antonio National Bank and the First National Bank of Austin, developer of the city's first water system, railroad investor and major philanthropist, George Washington Brackenridge (1832–1920) was one of San Antonio's most important figures. At the outbreak of the Civil War, his three brothers went off to serve in the Confederate Army, but George went into the lucrative cotton trade. One trading partner was Charles Stillman of Brownsville. Brackenridge's Union sympathies forced him to leave Texas for New Orleans, where he was a U.S. Treasury Department agent during the war. After the war he returned to Texas and came to San Antonio, where his friend Stillman invested $200,000 in Brackenridge's new National Bank of San Antonio. Brackenridge and his sister Eleanor, neither of whom married, lived with their mother at Fernridge, where Brackenridge kept an eye on the headwaters of the San Antonio River that supplied his water company. The estate included what is now the campus of the University of the Incarnate Word, the San Antonio Country Club and parts of the City of Alamo Heights, Olmos Basin and Brackenridge Park. In 1899 Brackenridge gave 320 acres adjoining the San Antonio River to the city. His close friend Ludwig Mahncke (p. 79), city parks commissioner, was largely responsible for designing the seven miles of roads that wind through the trees and along the river. Brackenridge's gift to the city came with several stipulations, including prohibition of alcohol on park premises. In the early twentieth century, Brackenridge Park gradually replaced San Pedro Park (p. 90) as the center for recreational activity in the city.

Japanese Tea Garden After the Alamo Portland and Roman Cement Company abandoned its quarry to move north to a new location at the site of the present-day Quarry Market, Parks Commissioner Ray Lambert used prison labor to convert it into a complex of walkways and ponds arched by stone bridges and a large stone pagoda. It became known as the Japanese Tea Garden until 1942, when anti-Japanese war sentiment caused the name to be changed to the **Chinese Sunken Garden**. The original name was restored in 1984. A $1.8 million renovation was completed in 2008.

Joske Pavilion   For more than a century the Joske name was well known to San Antonians. Julius Joske (1825–1909) brought his family to San Antonio from Prussia and opened a mercantile store in 1867. In 1903 his son Alexander Joske, born in 1857, purchased the business from his father and brothers. Their flagship store on Alamo Plaza was a downtown fixture until the company was purchased by Dillard's in 1987 and connected to Rivercenter Mall, the Dillard's location eventually closing. In 1921, Alexander's only son, Harold, drowned in the Guadalupe River. Five years later this pavilion was built as a memorial.

Koehler Park   Local brewers got revenge on Brackenridge's ban on alcohol in his park. In the early 1900s, the San Antonio Brewing Association—also known as Pearl Brewery—was the largest brewery in Texas. Its president was Otto Koehler. When he died in 1915, his widow, Emma, became president. Under her guidance, by producing near-beer, bottling soft drinks and operating other businesses, Pearl was the only Texas brewery to survive Prohibition. Emma acquired land adjacent to Brackenridge Park and donated it with the specific provision that malt liquors could be consumed there. To this day, the only place in greater Brackenridge Park where beer can legally be consumed is in Koehler Park.

Emma Koehler holds the first bottle of beer produced by Pearl Brewery after the repeal of Prohibition in 1933. Beside her is General Manager B. B. McGimsey.

Lambert Beach   When Ray Lambert was named parks commissioner in 1915, he inherited a parks system that was growing rapidly but was poorly financed. With additional funding, Lambert developed Brackenridge Park into the city's playground. He established a zoo and began construction of the city's first public golf course. He converted an abandoned limestone quarry into the Japanese gardens and developed a gravel-bottom swimming beach, later reconstructed as a concrete-lined pool and named in his honor after his death. The pool was closed for almost 50 years before being removed. The beach site is now indistinguishable in the area across from the Joske Pavilion.

Lion's Field   This is not named for nearby zoo animals but for the Lion's Club of San Antonio, which built playgrounds and clubhouse facilities here in 1925. The land was once a pasture for George Brackenridge's collection of animals, including buffalo and elk.

Sunken Garden Theater This portion of the abandoned rock quarry also utilized for the adjacent Japanese Tea Garden features a classic style open-air theater seating 2,700, designed by Harvey P. Smith in 1930, expanded in 1937 and renovated in 1984.

Tony "Skipper" Martinez Softball Field This is named for a 25-year employee of the San Antonio Department of Parks and Recreation. When he retired, Tony "Skipper" Martinez was superintendent of municipal athletics. He had also been a player, manager and umpire in city softball leagues, and for many years he was involved with Texas Amateur Athletic organizations.

Bryan McClain Park This 90-acre park was dedicated two years after the Aggie Bonfire in which 12 students died and 27 were injured. On November 18, 1999, the massive structure of logs being constructed for the pre-Texas game bonfire—a 90-year tradition—collapsed, trapping and crushing many students working on the project. Among those was a 19-year-old freshman from San Antonio— Bryan McClain, a 1998 graduate of Madison High School. A four-year member of the Madison swim team and captain in his senior year, he never hid his excitement about going to Texas A & M University and joining the Corps of Cadets. The park is just north of Madison High School, between O'Connor and Judson roads. Plans include outdoor classrooms and providing community recreation.

Casa Navarro State Historical Park This was the home of Texas independence hero José Antonio Navarro (1795–1871). The home, built about 1850, was restored by the San Antonio Conservation Society in 1964. At the entrance is this tribute: "Because of his determined efforts on behalf of Mexican American people, José Antonio Navarro is best known as The Strongest Champion of the Rights of the People." (Navarro Street, p. 16). It is easy to confuse this with the home of his son Celso Navarro, restored on the grounds of the Witte Museum (p. 147), and with the small city park named in honor of José Antonio (p. 80).

Cassiano Park Land for this park along Apache Creek was acquired by the city in 1898. More was added in 1936. Several Hispanic organizations petitioned city council in 1918 to name the park in honor of Frank Cassiano, a longtime civic and political leader who was a descendant of Giuseppe Cassini (1791–1862), a seaman born in Italy who settled in New Orleans and became a successful merchant. He changed his name to José Cassiano and in the 1820s moved to San Antonio, where he opened a store and acquired extensive property. During the Texas war for independence from Mexico he helped finance the revolution, in addition to allowing the revolutionary army full use of his home and store with all its supplies during the Siege of Bexar in 1835.

Chris Park This thoughtfully crafted and immaculately landscaped small oasis of green on Camp Street just south of downtown is unique in several respects. Although open to the public, the park was funded and maintained by ArtPace founder Linda Pace (p. 164) to honor her son Chris Goldsbury (1972–97), who studied art at Tulane University. Quarried limestone benches are inscribed with brief passages from his journal. Illuminated glass pavers on meandering paths alter a familiar nursery rhyme to highlight the day of his birth, Wednesday. Some plants were chosen to bloom annually in the spring month of his birth. Chris was the grandson of David Pace (p. 169).

Chris Goldsbury and his grandfather, picante sauce entrepreneur David Pace.

Crockett Park As part of a lawsuit settlement over ownership of property bordering an early irrigation ditch (acequia), the city agreed in 1875 to set aside this tract of land "forever . . . as one of its public squares." It was several years before people began to build homes this far north of downtown and several decades before the park began to be developed. In the mid-1920s the park was bisected by Main Avenue, causing it to be known as "Twin Parks" until conservationists pushed to have the original name restored, honoring Alamo hero David Crockett (p. 9).

Cuellar Park Uniformed officers from local, state and national law enforcement agencies gathered in 1968 for the funeral of Richard Cuellar, a highly decorated San Antonio police patrolman deeply involved in athletics for youth, who was killed in the line of duty by a bullet fired by a 14-year-old boy. The funeral procession, with some 513 vehicles stretched out over 10 miles, was said to have been the longest in San Antonio history. This 24-acre park and athletic area across the street from the old Edgewood High School was dedicated in his honor in 1975.

Dawson Park This small park on East Commerce Street has had three names. In 1890, a development firm set aside four acres for a park in the center of its new subdivision and called it simply East End Park. After Lindbergh's historic flight in 1927, the park was named in his honor. In 1986, area residents petitioned to rename the park for Robert A. Dawson, a 1935 Wheatley High School graduate who was San Antonio's first licensed African American pilot. Shortly before completing his training in the Army Air Corps in 1942, Dawson was killed in an air crash.

Dignowity Park This park east of downtown is named for Anthony Michael Dignowity (1810–75), who emigrated to the United States from Bohemia, studied medicine in Mississippi and came to San Antonio with a group of volunteers during the Mexican War. Recognizing a shortage of doctors in the city, he settled here and prospered as physician, businessman, and real estate developer. By 1850 **Dignowity Hill**, now designated a historic district, was a large residential area attracting affluent citizens. Its one-home-per-block mansions stood on an 80-foot elevation just east of the city, causing it to become the first exclusive neighborhood outside of downtown. Dignowity was a staunch abolitionist who opposed secession and fled North during the Civil War to avoid hanging. When he returned in 1869 he discovered his property had been confiscated. He was never able to rebuild his fortune.

Eisenhower Park Originally part of Camp Bullis (p. 183), these 323 acres were transferred to the city of San Antonio in 1988 and named for the World War II hero and 34th U.S. president (p. 102).

Emile and Albert Friedrich Wilderness Park Norma Friedrich Ward bequeathed 180 acres of Texas Hill Country property to the city in honor of her parents, Emile and Albert Friedrich. W. L. Matthews and associates contributed an additional 52 adjacent acres to create this hikers' paradise within the urban sprawl. In making the gift, Ward said, "I am particularly interested in seeing that, insofar as possible, the natural vegetation and native trees and shrubs be protected, and that the native birds and wildlife be protected and encouraged to use the park as a sanctuary."

Gilbert Garza Park An architect by profession and not a politician at heart, Gilbert Garza was drafted in 1971 by the Good Government League to run for city council. The son of immigrants from Monterrey, Garza was the third Hispanic to be elected mayor pro tem. He was serving in that capacity in the absence of Mayor John Gatti in 1972 when he suffered a heart attack and died two days later. The new **Mira Vista Park** was renamed for him later that year.

Gorrell Park Formerly called **Ridge Chase Park**, this park on De Zavala Road was renamed in April 2008 for a San Antonio police officer slain in the line of duty. Edwyn J. Gorrell was 34 when he was shot in February 1988 by a suspect he was attempting to arrest. An officer for less than two years, Gorrell lay in a coma for four months prior to his death. Sculptor Gilbert Barrera created a memorial for the park called

"The Widow's Letter," carved from a 3000-pound block of limestone. The poignant Madonna-like figure holds a dove close to her heart with her right hand and in her left a letter, to symbolize a tribute to all widows who have lost a uniformed husband.

Healy-Murphy Park This small park is adjacent to the Salvation Army Center on Nolan Street. Born in Ireland, where her physician father tended the needs of impoverished people, Margaret Mary Healy (1833–1907) emigrated to America and in 1849, at the age of 16, married John B. Murphy, later mayor of Corpus Christi. Healy-Murphy ministered to the poor and neglected of society. She tried without success to start schools for African Americans in Corpus Christi, Temple and Waco. Her husband died in 1884. Inspired by a sermon she heard in 1887, Healy-Murphy vowed to use the wealth left by him to further aid African Americans. She moved to San Antonio. Battling opposition and bigotry, she formed a church, school and convent, the first such school for blacks in Texas. The first church was on Nolan Street. Now the **Healy-Murphy Center**, its mission is education of young people at risk. The school was first named for St. Peter Claver (1580–1654), a Jesuit priest and Spaniard by birth, who spent 33 years ministering to slaves in Cartagena in what is now Colombia, the New World's primary Spanish slave market where 1,000 slaves landed monthly. Boarding slave ships as they entered the harbor, he cared for the sick and dying and followed slaves to plantations, encouraging them to live as Christians and entreating their masters to treat them humanely.

Highland Park In 1909, investors led by L. P. Peck bought a pasture owned by Albert Steves Sr. and developed the Highland Park subdivision. The city transportation company refused to run cars to this remote prairie, so the developers built their own streetcar line. Each of the six developers but one named a street for himself in the new subdivision (Rigsby Avenue, p. 61). A community center was completed in 1932 in spite of the Depression, and at one time it was the most active center in the city.

Hugo Lentz Park This plot of land facing Old Seguin Road in Kirby is hard to find unless you know exactly where to look. It is not part of the larger Kirby City Park, and the stone marker identifying the park is legible only when you are right upon it. The park is named for a man who served the city of Kirby as supervisor of public works, city secretary and tax assessor-collector.

Joe Ward Community Center An All-Southwest Conference tackle at the University of Texas in 1922, Joe H. "Papa Joe" Ward coached football at Edison High School from 1931 to 1943, when he went to work for the YMCA. He was instrumental in creating the association's northwest branch between Sunshine Drive and McNeel Road, where he mentored thousands of young people for more than 20 years. When the branch moved farther out to Wurzbach Road in 1978, the city bought the old property and created a public park and community center named in Ward's honor.

John James Park This park at the northeast corner of Fort Sam Houston is named for John James, one of San Antonio's pioneer builders, who is best remembered for restoring city property lines. When Mexican General Adrian Woll invaded San Antonio in 1842 and took 52 prominent citizens back to Mexico as prisoners, his army also destroyed or removed many public records. The loss of land records created

chaos, as citizens exercised squatter's rights to settle on vacant land. James was particularly well suited to help sort this out, as he was familiar with the field notes of some original land grants. With property lines restored by James, Judge Thomas J. Devine (p. 211) enforced the new lines and evicted squatters.

John W. Tobin was mayor during construction of Olmos Dam.

John Tobin Park and Community Center The name for this recreational center on Alazan Creek was one of several suggested by schoolchildren living in the vicinity and was selected by a committee of city officials. John W. Tobin (1867–1927), a descendant of Canary Island settlers and grandson of the city's first mayor, John Smith, was an engineer. After serving two terms as Bexar County sheriff, he was elected mayor shortly after the disastrous flood of 1921. He was influential in construction of Olmos Dam and other flood control projects, and he played a critical role in establishing the Witte Museum.

Western store owner Perry Kallison also bred registered polled Herefords.

Kallison Park Although clear documentation could not be found, this northeast park is probably named for Morris Kallison or perhaps for the entire Kallison family. Nathan and Anna Kallison were Jewish European immigrants who came to San Antonio via Chicago. A harness and saddle maker by trade, Nathan opened a store in 1899, which grew to sell a wide range of farm and ranch supplies and Western clothing. Morris Kallison (1897–1966), the oldest of four children, became a highly successful real estate developer, at one time said to be the largest landlord in the city. The youngest, Perry Kallison (1903–99), continued to run the store, from which emanated his daily "Kallison Trading Post" on KTSA radio from 1936 well into the 1960s. Broadcast over South Texas, the program was a combination of news pertinent to farmers and ranchers, weather, philosophy, swap shop, job searches and interviews. On the 3,400-acre ranch Nathan acquired off Culebra Road, Perry and his father started the breeding of registered polled (without horns) Hereford cattle.

La Villita   Meaning "little town" in Spanish, this area of downtown is originally thought to have been the site of a Coahuiltecan Indian village. In the early eighteenth century it was home to families of soldiers attached to the San Antonio de Béxar Presidio, separated by the river from the aristocratic Canary Islanders who lived around Main Plaza. After a flood in 1819 it was apparent that the higher ground of La Villita was a better place for a home. Many Canary Islanders moved across, and a fairly exclusive residential area grew beside the more humble dwellings of soldiers. By the middle of the century, German, Swiss and French immigrants had given a European flavor to the section. With at least two major renovation and restoration projects (in 1939–41 and in 1982–83), La Villita is maintained by San Antonio's parks department. For four nights each Fiesta it is the site of A Night in Old San Antonio, sponsored by the San Antonio Conservation Society to celebrate the city's multiethnic heritage and raise funds for historic preservation.

    Bolivar Hall   To the right of the Presa Street entrance to La Villita is a two-story stone building housing La Villita's offices. Built in 1940 and "Dedicated to Good Will in All the Americas," this structure was named for Simón Bolívar (1783–1830), nicknamed El Libertador ("the Liberator") for leading revolutions against the Spanish and a national hero in four South American countries—Bolivia, Peru, Ecuador and Venezuela. Son of a Venezuelan aristocrat of Spanish descent, Bólivar was sent to Europe for education and was inspired by writings of liberal French philosophers. Returning to the New World, he led the cause for independence in some 200 bloody battles, eventually becoming president (dictator) of both Colombia (1821–30) and Peru (1823–29).

    Cós House   In 1835, the dictator-president of Mexico, Santa Anna, sent his brother-in-law Gen. Martín Perfecto de Cós (1800–54) to quell the rising rebellion in Texas. Cós's troops occupied San Antonio but surrendered after a siege by the Texians. In a small white house in La Villita near the street level entrance to the Arneson River Theater, terms of the surrender were signed. Since neither army had sufficient provisions for a large group of prisoners, Cós was allowed to take his army back across the Rio Grande, with the promise that he would never again interfere in Texas affairs. Within a few months, however, he was back in San Antonio with Santa Anna's much larger force that took the Alamo. Rescued from destruction in the La Villita restoration projects, the Cós House serves as a frequent setting for parties and entertainment.

Dashiell House   Colonel Jeremiah Y. Dashiell (1804–88) was a physician with strong political connections. When the Mexican War broke out, President James K. Polk offered him the choice of surgeon or paymaster for the U.S. Army. He chose the latter. He bought this property in 1849 and built this house overlooking the river. A boat ferrying Army payroll sank while under his command, and Dashiell was forced to sell the house to settle his debt to the government. In 1942 the house was purchased by the San Antonio Conservation Society and now houses the headquarters of Fiesta's annual Night in Old San Antonio.

Juarez Plaza   Inside the Presa Street entrance to La Villita an open area honors a national hero of Mexico, Benito Juárez (1806–72). Born to poor Indian parents and orphaned at the age of three, he studied for the ministry but switched to law. After receiving his degree in 1831 he became involved in politics, eventually becoming governor of his home state of Oaxaca and then president of Mexico. Initially fighting against the strangleholds of the Catholic Church and the landed aristocracy, his ultimate battle was against the French-installed emperor, Archduke Maximilian of Austria, whom he helped to overthrow in 1867. Beneath his statue in the plaza is inscribed "El respeto al derecho ajeno es la paz," part of a well-known quote from Juarez loosely translated as "respect for other people's rights brings peace."

King Philip V Street   This short pedestrian walkway at right angles to La Villita Street, known before the restoration as Womble Alley, is named for the monarch who authorized importation of Canary Islanders to San Antonio in 1731. Founder of the Bourbon dynasty in Spain, Philip V, Duc D'anjou (1683–1746) ruled for 46 years.

Mayor Maury Maverick Plaza   In 1939, the city acquired the core neighborhood of La Villita from the city's utility company. Under the leadership of Maury Maverick (1895–1954), a third-generation San Antonio member of an influential family (p. 154), the first of two major restoration projects was carried out in 1939–41. His work is recognized by this large, open entertainment area, named Nueva Plaza when cleared at the time of HemisFair '68 and renamed in 1987. Maverick received the Silver Star in World War I and served two terms in Congress before being elected mayor; he is credited with bringing honest and efficient government to city hall.

O'Neil Ford Plaza   Behind the Little Church of La Villita and near Maury Maverick Plaza is this courtyard, named for San Antonio's nationally known architect O'Neil Ford (1905–82). Forced to drop out of college for financial reasons, Ford obtained his architectural training from a correspondence school, but in his later years he received honorary degrees from several prestigious colleges. A charismatic and colorful raconteur, he was a teacher and mentor for many young architects who worked in his firm. He was brought to San Antonio by Mayor Maverick to oversee the La Villita restoration. Some of his best-known local works are the Tower of the Americas and Trinity University's Parker Chapel and Laurie Auditorium (p. 129).

Lady Bird Johnson Park The park is east of Nacogdoches Road and north of Loop 410 is named in honor of the First Lady best remembered for her efforts to beautify America (p. 101).

Mayor Maury Maverick aided both the La Villita restoration and River Walk projects.

Lou Hamilton Recreational Center In 1974 this Lady Bird Johnson Park facility was named to honor Lou Hamilton (1908–75), for 34 years the superintendent of San Antonio's Parks and Recreation Department. She began as a playground leader at Roosevelt Park in 1930, taking over the department in 1941 when the city had only seven recreation centers and four public swimming pools. She was the first woman president of the Texas Amateur Athletic Federation.

Lindbergh Park When he made the first nonstop flight between New York and Paris, in 1927, Charles A. Lindbergh (1902–74) became an instant international celebrity. In a 48-state tour with his plane, the Spirit of St. Louis, he was seen by 30 million people, a quarter of the nation's populace. Many schools, buildings and other public facilities were named for him, including this park in the northwest corner of Kelly Air Force Base, where he received flying instruction after enlisting in the Air Service Corps. He reported for preliminary training at Brooks Field, graduated first in his class from the Air Service Advanced Flying School at Kelly Field in 1925, and was commissioned a second lieutenant.

Renowned architect O'Neil Ford came to San Antonio to oversee restoration of La Villita.

Mahncke Park Across Broadway from the Witte Museum is this long, rectangular strip of green that once connected the water works in

A bust of Parks Commissioner Ludwig Mahncke stands in Mahncke Park.

Brackenridge Park with a reservoir on the site of the present-day San Antonio Botanical Gardens. Ludwig Mahncke, alderman from 1897 to 1906 and also San Antonio's first parks commissioner, was largely responsible for laying out Brackenridge Park.

Main Plaza This onetime residential plaza was the site of the Villa de San Fernando de Béxar, established by Canary Island immigrants in 1731 and also called Plaza de las Islas. In 1868 a larger church designed by Francois Giraud (p. 11) was built around the walls of the original Spanish-era church, preserving the original apse. Six years later it was renamed San Fernando Cathedral, home of the new Archdiocese of San Antonio. City limits of San Antonio were determined by boundaries three miles in each direction from San Fernando (p. 5).

Mateo Camargo Park In 1927 the city acquired a gravel pit managed by Commissioner of Streets and Parks Paul Steffler, who preserved a stand of large live oak trees that came to be known as **Pablo's Grove**. In 1982 it was renamed for local Hispanic radio music and talk show Mateo Camargo. He had wished to be a doctor like his father, whose death when his son was 15 caused Mateo to pursue a less expensive education. In addition to becoming a radio technician and electrician, he learned to compose and play music, forming a group called Los Chihuahuas. Accompanied by his wife, Belia, on the bass guitar, he took his accordion and voice to hospitals, clinics and nursing homes.

Samuel Maverick Jr. donated the land for Maverick Park.

Maverick Park Land for this three-acre park on Broadway at Jones Avenue was donated to the city in 1881 by Samuel Maverick Jr. (1837–1936), son of Samuel A. Maverick (p. 154), whose home faced its southwest corner. Three blocks from the city's first railroad station, the park was originally surrounded by houses and businesses. Samuel Maverick Jr. fought in the Civil War with Terry's Texas Rangers. After the war he engaged in a variety of business and philanthropic ventures, including operation of an irrigated farm on family property that is now Brackenridge Park.

Mays Family Field of Dreams Although the name is in recognition of a generous contribution from the Lowry Mays family (p. 145), this multisport complex behind Wolff Stadium (p. 156) exists because of the dream and dedication of Michael Miller. When his wife Yvette was pregnant in 2004, the couple was told that the baby would be born with Down's syndrome. Even though their daughter, Sydney, turned out not to have the condition, Miller forged ahead with his idea of building a facility for children with special needs, inspired by a Georgia father who created the Miracle League. Miller set out to develop a Miracle League in San Antonio. Aided by former world champion boxer Jesse James Leija—for whom he once was co-manager—and other local philanthropists, Miller raised over $1 million to make the Field of Dreams a reality. Its rubberized playing surface and other amenities have been adapted to accommodate not only children with special physical and mental needs but also wounded soldiers and wheelchair athletes. Baseball rules have been changed in the Miracle League to allow each child to be a winner and a star.

McAllister Park This tract of land just north of the airport was named for former mayor W. W. McAllister (McAllister Freeway, p. 64). There are biking and hiking trails, campsites, picnic grounds, soccer fields and a Little League ballpark.

McGimsey Scout Park This 140-acre tract at Northwest Military Highway and Lockhill-Selma Road was the remote weekend retreat of B. B. and Mary Etta McGimsey (p. 71), who donated it to the Alamo Area Council, Boy Scouts of America in 1958. The wooded area was developed into an overnight camp where Boy Scouts learn basic camping skills.

Milam Park Benjamin Rush Milam is buried by his statue in this square-block park facing Santa Rosa Hospital. On the monument is inscribed a famous (but slightly altered) quote attributed to Milam as he gathered volunteers to retake San Antonio from the Mexicans: "Who will follow old Ben Milam into San Antonio?" (p. 16).

Military Plaza The Spanish established Military Plaza, or Plaza de Armas, in 1722 as a headquarters and parade ground, with barracks on the north side. Near the northwest corner of the plaza was the home of the presidio captain, restored in 1931 and known as the Spanish Governor's Palace. In the nineteenth century Military Plaza was the transportation hub for frontier wagon trains and associated market activity. This declined with arrival of the railroad in 1877. In 1892 the present city hall was built in the center of the plaza and market activity moved west to the area now called El Mercado (Market Square).

Monterrey Park Established in 1962 and originally named **Linda Vista Park**, this 51-acre parcel was renamed in 1963 for San Antonio's sister city in Mexico—Monterrey—which reciprocated by naming one of its parks Plaza de San Antonio. The **Sonny Melendrez Community Center** in the park was named for a local media personality who actively supported Parks Department youth programs.

Morgan's Wonderland Located adjacent to the North East Independent School District's Heroes Stadium (p. 106) in the old Longhorn Quarry, this bright and cheerful 25-acre facility is the world's first ultra-accessible family fun park designed for children and adults with special needs, their family members, caregivers and friends. Inspired by their daughter Morgan's boundless love and ability to transcend her own challenges, local philanthropist Gordon Hartman and his wife Maggie set out to raise funds for this unique concept, jumpstarting the campaign with a $1 million gift of their own.

Navarro Park This small park on the west side is named for Tejano patriot Jose Antonio Navarro. It is not the location of his restored home, which is designated the Casa Navarro State Historical Park (p. 72).

Normoyle Park This recreation area on the fringe of the former East Kelly Air Force Base was established in 1918 as a U.S. Army quartermaster depot called Camp Normoyle. At its peak it covered 590 acres with 12 miles of paved roads and 3.2 million square feet of storage space. In 1960, a 30-acre section of the original camp was deeded to the city for parks and recreation, opening in 1977 as Normoyle Community Park. Major James E. Normoyle (1866–1916) graduated from West Point in 1889. While stationed at Fort Sam Houston he directed Army transport operations during Mexican border mobilization in 1911. In 1912–13 he coordinated relief efforts for victims of major floods. At the 50th anniversary of the Battle of Gettysburg he organized support facilities for thousands of Union and Confederate veterans. Shortly after his death at the age of 49 this new facility was named in his honor.

O. P. Schnabel Park First called Bandera Road Park, the name was changed in 1977 to honor the cofounder of the Beautify San Antonio Association. Insurance executive O. P. ("Old Pushbroom") Schnabel kept in the media spotlight, exhorting citizens to keep the city clean and tidy with his own example and such catchy phrases as "Nice people don't litter."

Orsinger County Park Ward Orsinger was born in Des Moines, Iowa. After being a World War I army engineer lieutenant in France, he moved to San Antonio. In 1920 he and his brother Gunther founded the Orsinger Motor Company, selling such automobiles as the Haines, Star, Durant, and Hudson. The business closed in 1959, but the family name was kept in the business by his nephew Charles, who started Orsinger

Buick Company in 1955. In 1980, Ward and his wife, Genevieve, deeded more than 15 acres in northwestern San Antonio along Huebner Road to the county for a park in memory of his parents, the Charles G. Orsingers, so that the area's residents could enjoy pleasant times like the Orsingers experienced at MacArthur Park in northeastern San Antonio.

Oscar Perez Memorial Park Three new city skate parks were added to the existing five in the summer of 2006. Among these was this park in the Great Northwest area, named for a San Antonio police officer slain in the line of duty on March 24, 2000 at the age of 31 while serving a felony arrest warrant. A six-year police veteran, he was a resident of the neighborhood in which the park is located.

Phil Hardberger Park The land for this new park had been a dairy farm run by the Voelcker family, owners of the property for more than 100 years (Voelcker Lane, p. 30). In 2006 the city purchased 107 acres of this prime real estate surrounded by upscale residential neighborhoods, and the following year acquired an additional 151 acres. In 2009 the city named the park in honor of one of San Antonio's most successful mayors, who staked his political capital on passing a $550 million bond issue to provide funds for many city-wide park, health and infrastructure improvements. He was reelected to his second term in 2007 with 77 percent of the vote, and when he left office due to term limits two years later he had an 86 percent approval rating. Many were surprised when he ran for mayor in 2005 since he already had enjoyed several successful careers. Born in 1934, he is a 1955 graduate of Baylor University, piloted a B-47 bomber in the Air Force, was executive secretary of the Peace Corps during the Kennedy administration, worked as assistant director of the U.S. Office of Economic Opportunity, earned

O. P.—"Old Pushbroom"—Schnabel was tireless in his efforts to clean up San Antonio.

Mayor Phil Hardberger was instrumental in creating the park that bears his name.

a law degree from Georgetown University in 1965, served first as associate and then chief justice of the Fourth Court of Appeals, practiced law for nearly 25 years and only then became the first person in modern history to be elected mayor without a city council background. This is the first city park to have a master plan. Hardberger hopes that it will be the twenty-first century equivalent of Brackenridge Park (p. 70). Another of Hardberger's outstanding accomplishments as mayor was being instrumental, along with Bill Greehey (p. 175) in creating Haven for Hope, a national model for dealing with problems of the homeless.

Pittman-Sullivan Park   Dewey L. Pittman (1898–1918) and Edward B. Sullivan (also 1898–1918) were boyhood friends who played as children in the undeveloped area that would become their namesake park. Both died in France during World War I, aviation lieutenant Sullivan on July 7 and his friend Pittman with the Sixth U.S. Marines on July 19. Construction began in 1920 under supervision of city Park Commissioner Ray Lambert (p. 71), whose son Dick designed the park while taking a course in landscape architecture at Texas A & M. This park east of downtown was once a major city gathering place, with swimming pool, camping, places for picnics, a sunken garden and baseball diamond. In 1940, the baseball field was enhanced to attract major league teams for spring training, and a few games were played there by the St. Louis Browns and the Boston Braves. The park is now the site of the Davis-Scott YMCA (p. 143) and St. Gerard's High School.

Pletz County Park   In 1962, homebuilder Lee Roy Pletz donated this 15-acre tract near Joe Freeman Coliseum to the county. After 10 years with a pipeline company in Houston, Pletz established the Quali-Cut Company in his hometown of San Antonio, advertising "cut in the shop and built on the job" homes, garages and small commercial buildings.

Pytel Park   In 1993, nearly thirty-five acres on South New Braunfels Avenue was donated by Boyce H. Gaskin and NTL Land Holdings and developed as **South New Braunfels Park** with a grant from Texas Parks and Wildlife. On July 31, 1994, Bike Patrol officer Paul M. Pytel, 29, became the first San Antonio Park Ranger to die in the line of duty, while he was pursuing a fleeing suspect. The park was renamed in Pytel's honor in 1996. The city maintains the picnic facilities and exercise trail.

Raymond Rimkus Park   This neighborhood park in Leon Valley is named for the first mayor of that community, who was responsible for preventing annexation by the city of San Antonio. In 1940, Raymond Rimkus and his wife, Mary Louise, moved into this then rural area and established a meat market, grocery and variety store at the corner of what is now Bandera and Grissom roads. As the only such store for miles around, the Rimkus Store became a meeting place and information source for area residents. On March 12, 1952, a reporter drove out to the store to get Rimkus's reaction to news that the San Antonio city council had on its agenda for the following day a motion to annex substantial areas around the city, including Leon Valley. Rimkus alerted his land-owning neighbors, who gathered 133 signatures on a petition to incorporate. They submitted it to the council the next morning, blocking the annexation attempt. Rimkus was mayor for five years.

Raymond Russell County Park Raymond Russell (1892–1959) was an oilman who operated 22 refineries in Texas, Louisiana and Illinois. He was also developer of San Antonio's first horseracing track, Alamo Downs, in far western San Antonio. In 1951 he and his wife, Meta, donated 19.61 acres along what was to become IH-10, north of the future Loop 1604, to Bexar County for a park. Their son, Raymond Russell Jr., was a reform San Antonio city councilman in the 1950s.

River Walk From its beginning San Antonio has been intimately linked with the river. Today the city's most distinctive feature in the eyes of visitors is the linear park known as the River Walk, or Paseo del Rio. Its convoluted story is told in detail in Lewis F. Fisher's River Walk: The Epic Story of San Antonio's River. Much of this section was gleaned from that book.

Engineer Edwin Arneson helped plan the River Walk.

Arneson River Theater During the Depression, cities competed for funds from the Works Projects Administration (WPA), a federal relief program. WPA District Engineer was Edwin P. Arneson, who had done considerable research on waterways in Texas. He was persuaded by the San Antonio River Beautification Committee to make surveys and drawings to submit to the WPA for funding. Part of the project was an open-air theater to be called Broadcast Theater, where radio performances of plays were to originate. The name was changed to honor Arneson, who died at a relatively young age before the project began. The stage of this unique theater on a bend in the river is separated from the audience by the river.

Bowen's Island Not a true island and no longer in existence, this five-acre tract was a peninsula in the San Antonio River formed by a natural bend eliminated by a cutoff channel built in 1929. It resembled an island because across the base of the peninsula ran the Concepción Acequia's main channel and overflow channel. The irrigation ditch was constructed in the eighteenth century by Spanish missionaries. In 1845

The River Walk office sign of River Walk architect H. H. Hugman has been restored.

John Bowen, born in Philadelphia in 1867, paid $300 for the property, which first belonged to the Canary Island family of Juan Curbelo (p. 11). Bowen, the first postmaster of San Antonio, was an ardent Unionist and aided escaping slaves during the Civil War. With its gardens and amusement park, Bowen's Island became a popular spot for picnics, reunions, circuses and carnivals, and there were plans for a city coliseum on the island. In 1929 the river bed remaining around the "island" was filled in.

Hugman Bells   The five bells in the arches behind the Arneson River Theater stage were named in belated recognition of the man most responsible for the River Walk's design. As a 27-year-old architect recently returned to his hometown, Robert H. H. Hugman (1902–80) in 1929 presented a master plan for preservation, beautification and commercialization of the river, including use of gondolas like those in Venice. When the project was approved ten years later he was selected as the architect, though he had a falling out with Mayor Maury Maverick and the River Walk Board and was fired in 1940, halfway through the project. In 1978, two years before his death, he was at last recognized for his vision with the placement of five bells in the arches behind the stage of the theater, though no marker indicates that the bells honor his memory. His role is explained on a plaque near the entrance to his one-time river-level office in the Clifford Building at the Commerce Street Bridge, where a copy of his office sign is in its original place.

Jim Cullum's Landing   For nearly 50 years this has been not only a major tourist draw on the River Walk, but a magnet attracting world-class musicians to showcase their talents. The life of Jim Cullum Jr., born in 1941, has been about music, and his passion has been researching, preserving, and presenting jazz and popular songs from the first half of the twentieth century. With his father's interest in music, he grew up listening to Louis Armstrong and others, planning someday to play coronet or trombone. At around age 14, he bought a used coronet for $8 and an instruction book for $1, then taught himself to play. Because he couldn't read music, he was twice rejected for the Alamo Heights High School band before gaining acceptance. In 1962, while attending Trinity University, Cullum formed a seven-piece traditional jazz group, the Happy Jazz Band, with his late father, clarinetist Jim Cullum Sr. A year later, in the basement of the Nix Hospital a group businessmen established The Landing, a jazz club on the River Walk. For about a de-

Jim Cullum Sr. and Jr. in a River Walk session at The Landing.

cade the members hosted the World Series of Jazz, inviting such musicians as Benny Goodman and Pete Fountain to go head-to-head with their band. After Jim Sr. died in 1973, the group's name was changed to The Jim Cullum Jazz Band. The Landing's home has been at the Hyatt Regency since 1982. Sounds of the band are not confined to San Antonio; since 1989 River Walk Jazz has been broadcast nationwide weekly to over 200 Public Radio stations around the country. Venues have included Carnegie Hall and Lincoln Center, plus appearances in cities in Europe, Russia, Latin America and Australia.

Jones Bridge The Commerce Street bridge spanning the river is named for former mayor Augustus H. Jones, who inaugurated the first major beautification project of the San Antonio River shortly after taking office in 1912. This concrete and granite bridge replaced an 1880 iron structure, but before that there had been several bridges at this critical crossing spot, including one made famous by O. Henry in his short story "A Fog in Santone." Shortly before the battle for the Alamo an emissary from the besieged Texans met Santa Anna aide Juan Almonte on a wooden footbridge at this site.

Lila Cockrell Theater In 1968, San Antonio celebrated its 250th anniversary with a world's fair called HemisFair '68. Among the downtown improvements for this event was a new convention center, connected to the Great Bend section of the river by a man-made extension. In the lagoon at the end of the extension, buildings included a Theater of Performing Arts, renamed in 1981 to honor Lila Cockrell, born in 1922, San Antonio's first—and, as yet, only—woman mayor, who served in 1975–81 and 1989–91. At her 80th birthday celebration in 2002 she was recognized for her work in attract-

Mayor Lila Cockrell is honored in the naming of the Convention Center theater.

Rosita Fernandez, San Antonio's "First Lady of Song," entertained on the Arneson River Theater stage for 26 years.

Robert L. B. Tobin's Oakwell Farms estate includes a park named for him.

ing Rivercenter Mall, built on a nearby River Walk extension, and helping attract the adjacent Marriott Rivercenter Hotel, at 42 stories the tallest building in the city.

Rosita's Bridge Beginning in 1957 and continuing every summer for 26 years, singer Rosita Fernandez starred in the Alamo Kiwanis Club's Fiesta Noche del Rio in the Arneson River Theater. When she retired in 1983, the arching bridge over which she made her dramatic entrances to the stage was named in her honor. When making one of Rosita's many movie or live performances, before a roomful of ambassadors at the LBJ Ranch, Lady Bird Johnson introduced her as "San Antonio's first lady of song." After her retirement, she and her husband, Raul Almaguer, helped raise $600,000 for restoration of the Arneson Theater. Her life is celebrated in Mary M. Fisher's children's book, Rosita's Bridge.

Robert L. B. Tobin Park Shortly before his death, Robert Lynn Batts Tobin (1934–2000) gave 60 acres of his Oakwell Farms estate alongside Salado Creek in northeastern San Antonio for inclusion in a proposed city linear park system. The survey company founded by his father, Edgar Tobin, was the national oil industry's largest aerial mapmaking firm. Arts patron Robert Tobin joined the board of the Metropolitan Opera Company in 1976 and was later the board's vice president, and was a leading supporter of the Santa Fe Opera Company. He and his mother, Margaret Batts Tobin, donated much of their collection to the McNay Art Museum. His donation of the Tobin Collection of Theatre Arts made the McNay the nation's leading center for exhibition and study of scene and costume design.

Roosevelt Park Known also at various times as **Riverside Park** and **Lambert Park** (p. 71), Roosevelt Park was created from a gravel pit on the south side and named in 1920 for former President Theodore

Roosevelt (p. 1046), who trained his Rough Riders nearby. The Riverside name was later given to a park and municipal golf course half a mile south.

Rosedale Park   In 1892, an East Coast real estate company planned two residential neighborhoods in western San Antonio, Rosedale Park and Lake View. Apache Creek was dammed to form Elmendorf Lake and a streetcar extension was proposed. Largely because of the depression of the 1890s, the Rosedale subdivision never developed as planned. The 60-acre park includes almost the entire area intended for the subdivision.

    Fernando Arellano Sr. Little League Field   Within Rosedale Park is a baseball diamond named in honor of a man who organized, founded, and coached soccer, baseball, and softball for many decades. Fernando Arellano Sr. graduated from San Antonio Tech is 1933, was an amateur all-state soccer player in 1938, founded both the Colt and Little Leagues in San Antonio and coached three world-title Air Force softball teams. He did most of this while working at Kelly Air Force Base for 36 years, first as a maintenance man and later as recreational coach. There is also a soccer field named for him at Rodriguez County Park.

    Rudy Perez Sr. Field   Once a civilian worker at Kelly Air Force Base, Rudy Perez believed that young people who played sports were less likely to get into trouble. Beginning in 1979 with one baseball field in Cuellar Park and virtually no financing, Perez organized an eight-team league to participate in the citywide CYO (Catholic Youth Organization) program. To fund competition and purchase equipment for kids who could not afford it, he made deals with local businesses to donate soft drinks, chips and candy that he sold from the back of his pickup truck. By the time he retired as president of his league in 1994, there were nearly 30 teams and three baseball diamonds, one named for him and another for his grandson Reggie Perez, who died of leukemia at age 15. The third field is as yet unnamed. As a result of his efforts, scores of young boys and girls now play on teams in the nationwide PONY (Protect Our Nation's Youths) program.

Rusty Lyons Sports Complex   In 1995, the Olmos Sports Complex at Basse Road and McCullough Avenue was renamed in honor of Russell "Rusty" Lyons (1909–93), commissioner of amateur baseball in San Antonio for more than 35 years. His day job was being head cashier at the San Antonio Express-News, but his passion was amateur baseball. Thousands of local boys benefitted from his efforts. A three-sport athlete at Main Avenue High School, now Fox Tech, he played professionally for a brief time before spending 60 years organizing and working with baseball and softball. Also a longtime umpire of professional games in Texas and Mexico and in the Southwest Conference, he was a Southwest Baseball Umpires Association founder and served as its president for two years.

San Pedro Park   Also known as San Pedro Springs Park, this 46-acre tract is the oldest park in Texas and is said to be the second oldest designated public park in the United States; only Boston Common is older. San Pedro Springs was named to honor St. Peter by two Franciscan missionary priests, Isidro Felix de Espinosa and Antonio Olivares, who came across the springs on April 13, 1709. The reason for choosing St. Peter is not clear, as it does not adhere to the usual Spanish practice for naming places in honor of the saint on whose feast day the discovery was made. Espinosa's description of "the earth being terraced" suggests that Indians had long used this source of water.

Set aside as a public square in 1729 and formally established as a city park in 1858, San Pedro Park was for decades the most popular site in the city for recreational activities. It encompassed the city's first municipal zoo, first museum, a racetrack, pavilions for concerts and dances, an aviary, a theater, restaurants, a beer garden, ballpark and a Civil War prison camp, though it declined after Brackenridge Park grew in popularity in the early twentieth century.

McFarlin Tennis Center   John R. McFarlin (1913–90) gave much of his oil fortune to San Antonio charities, but he is best remembered for donations to the **San Pedro Tennis Center**, the largest public tennis facility in the city. It was renamed the McFarlin Tennis Center in 1974. He also funded a heart center at Santa Rosa Children's Hospital and made possible creation of the Children's Zoo at the San Antonio Zoo.

Koger Stokes Softball Center   Koger Stokes founded the Texas Amateur Athletic Association in 1925 and was its president until 1947. As the first chairman of the city Parks and Recreation Board he was superintendent of recreation until a professional could be hired. He also donated funds to help finance construction of this softball facility, which opened in 1966.

Seeling Park   Parkview Estates subdivision in the Jefferson High School area was owned and developed by the three daughters of real estate investor Edward Seeling. Adjacent **Pardo Circle** and **Lowery Drive** were the married names of two of the daughters. The third daughter's name (Jamieson) was a street in the original 1939 plat map, but this was later changed to **Comfort Street**.

Smith Park   This tiny park at Buena Vista and Smith streets was San Antonio's first municipal playground when developed by private citizens and given to the city in 1915. Which Smith the street and park were intended to honor has been forgotten, but the most likely candidate is John

William Smith (1792–1845), last messenger from the Alamo and first mayor of San Antonio. Born in Virginia, Smith moved to San Antonio in 1827 and married Maria de Jesus Delgado Curbelo, a Canary Islander descendant. He joined the Alamo defenders but was sent by commander William B. Travis as a final messenger to seek help, thus sparing his life. After the war, attorney Smith used his bilingual skills to broker deals between Spanish-speaking landowners and English-speaking buyers, becoming a successful land speculator himself. He held a number of city, county and Texas Republic positions, and was elected as the first mayor of San Antonio on September 18, 1837.

Travis Park   Named for the commander of the Alamo, William Barrett Travis (p. 19), the land for this tranquil downtown park was given to the city by Samuel Maverick (p. 153), who had an orchard here. The tract had been part of the upper farmlands of Mission San Antonio de Valero—the Alamo—and was purchased in 1851 by Maverick, who lived at the northwest corner of Alamo Plaza.

Vidaurri Park   Juan Vidaurri's parents fled Mexico in the 1910 Revolution. He worked for years as an auto mechanic. He lived in a tiny house across the street from the park named in his honor. He befriended high-profile politicians and indigent neighbors in his barrio and was a conduit between them. Juan "Don Juanito" Vidaurri combined the two preoccupations of his life¬—people and politics—and used them for the betterment of both. His political instincts helped elect many state and local candidates.

Walker Ranch Historic Landmark Park   Just west of the confluence of Panther Springs and Salado creeks, this area was a favorite camp-site of hunter-gatherers for several thousand years. University of Texas at San Antonio archeologists have concluded that the clay-based soil and the water source made this an ideal place for making ceramics. It is also believed that the area was occupied by soldiers and settlers in the Spanish Colonial period. It was then part of the 1.2 million-acre Monte Galvan, a supply ranch for Mission San Antonio de Valero—the Alamo. In 1858 Edward Higgins purchased a 2,556 acre tract, but when he defaulted on the note in 1874 Virginia Thompson Ganahl acquired the property. In 1899 her grandson, Charles Ganahl Walker, moved onto the land and established a ranch. He died in 1954, but his family continued to operate the ranch until 1972, when much of the land was sold to Dallas developers. The final parcel was sold in 1994. Listed in 1975 on the National Register of Historical Places, the ranch is now considered to be one of the most endangered historic places in the state. The park has been funded by the city and also by grants from several area foundations.

Wheeler Park   The land for this park was donated to the city in 2006 and two years later named to honor Patrolman John Randolph Wheeler, a San Antonio police officer killed in the line of duty in October 2005 when his patrol car was struck from behind by a car going 100 mph. Wheeler's wife, Kim, was a police department dispatcher on duty at the time of the accident.

Woodlawn Lake Park   In 1887, investors dammed Alazan Creek to create **West End Lake** and made it the centerpiece of the new West End development. In 1918, the city acquired the lake and surrounding property in lieu of back taxes and made these 62 acres a city park. The name of the lake was later changed to Woodlawn Lake Park.

Visit the Website of the San Antonio Parks and Recreation Department (www.ci.sat.tx.us/sapar) for brief histories of many city parks. The research was spearheaded by Maria Watson Pfeiffer, former special projects officer for the department, who provided much assistance in preparation of this chapter.

· 4 ·

SCHOOLS AND UNIVERSITIES

ALAMO HEIGHTS ISD

Alamo Heights High School and **Alamo Heights Middle School** in the Alamo Heights Independent School District (ISD) take their names from the city of Alamo Heights, incorporated in 1922 as Bexar County's first separate suburb. A one-room Alamo Heights school opened in 1909. A larger building was built in 1928 on the campus of what became Cambridge Elementary School after the separate high school building was built in 1950; the junior high was completed in 1958.

BOERNE ISD

Champion High School   Boerne's newest high school honors a man whose very name seems to have portrayed his character. Described as "a true champion," Samuel V. Champion (1953–2007) was associated with Boerne High School for most of his life. He played football there, then worked his way through San Antonio College and Southwest Texas State University. First a teacher/coach at Jay High School and then at Hobbs, New Mexico, he returned to Boerne in 1982 and never left. For 15 years he was the Boerne High School principal, which he once described as his dream job. He loved kids and inspired them to achieve, and it is said could call each of his 1,400 students by name. He elevated the school to recognition by Newsweek in 2001–02 as one of the top 150 high schools in the country. He next became the Boerne ISD director of student services, his main focus on at-risk students. Highly respected and loved, he received virtually every civic honor his community had to offer. Champion died of a brain tumor the year before his namesake school opened.

CARVER ACADEMY

In 2001 the privately run Carver Academy opened with 58 five- to seven-year olds in a black east side neighborhood adjacent to the Carver Community Cultural Center, its mission to challenge elementary-age children in "a nurturing family-like environment based upon the foundation of Judeo-Christian scripture" and prepare them for success in competitive high schools. Some $5 million of the $12.5 million initial funding was donated by San Antonio Spurs basketball player David Robinson and his wife, Valerie, for endowment and scholarships. One official said the school was named for George Washington Carver (p. 136) only because they couldn't persuade the major benefactor to call it David Robinson Academy. The closest they could get was to name a short adjacent street for the Robinsons (p. 47).

East Central ISD

East Central High School   The name of this school—and district—is a bit misleading, since it is actually located rather peripherally in the southeast part of San Antonio.

Heritage Middle School   This school is named for a group of people rather than for a single individual. When it opened in 1997, trustees selected the name as a memorial to local supporters of education. Although the intent is to add more names to the school's wall of honor, the board initially chose only five from those submitted:

The Campbell Family. In 1872 Neil Campbell, an Irish immigrant, donated one acre for a community school. For more than 100 years many of his descendants have been actively involved in education.

Ellen C. Cover, M.D. Among the first graduates of the Campbell School, Cover graduated from the University of Texas Medical Branch in 1913 and became the first woman "horse and buggy" doctor in the area. After her retirement, she donated 25 acres for establishment of the Cover Youth Center.

Robert E. "Bobby" Crow. A lifelong resident of the district, Crow established an auto mechanics program for the school that gained nationwide recognition.

Anthony B. Constanzo. Respected teacher, coach, athletic director and administrator, Constanzo ended his career with superintendency of the East Central district. A math/science center at the high school was named in his honor.

C. H. Griffin. A greatly admired middle school English teacher for 29 years, Griffin was active in organizing the Band Booster Club and Quarterback Club.

Oak Crest Middle School   When East Central High School moved to its current location in 1970, the old high school was renamed Oak Crest Junior High School.

Salado Middle School   Salado Creek meanders nearby before joining the San Antonio River to the south. Salado means "salty" in Spanish.

Edgewood ISD

In 1905 Carl and Friederike Frey sold a tract for one dollar to County Judge Robert B. Green (p. 148) to establish a school site. The name Edgewood was selected in 1942 from that of a new subdivision on a former farm on the edge of woods. Many families moved in, attracted by rich soil and the abundance of artesian water for irrigation.

Brentwood Middle School Brentwood Junior High School was named for the Brentwood Hills subdivision in which it is located.

Gus Garcia Middle School Graduating in 1932 as valedictorian of the first class at Jefferson High School, Gustavo Charles Garcia (1915–64) went on to obtain undergraduate and law degrees from the University of Texas, where he was captain of the law school debate team. After World War II he was the first Mexican American elected to the San Antonio ISD board. He was a legal adviser to the League of United Latin American Citizens and is best known for winning the Delgado case in 1948, making segregation of Mexican–Americans in public schools illegal. He is also known for participation in 1953 in Hernandez v. the State of Texas, in which the U.S. Supreme Court agreed with his argument that conviction of Pete Hernandez was illegal because he had been convicted by an all-Anglo jury. Arguing the case with him was fellow attorney Carlos Cadena (p. 150), who went on to a distinguished judicial career. Life was not as kind to Garcia. Alcoholism and mental illness caused his law license to be suspended for two years, and he died of liver failure at 48. In 2009 PBS released a documentary, "A Class Apart," about the Hernandez case.

President and Mrs. John F. Kennedy and Nellie Connally, wife of Texas Governor John Connally visited Brooks Air Force Base the day before he was assassinated.

Kennedy High School After the assassination of President John F. Kennedy, cities rushed to name schools, roads, streets and public buildings in honor of the martyred president. It would be natural to assume that the Edgewood ISD was part of that fever. In fact, the name was chosen more than a year earlier, in September 1962. Kennedy did visit San Antonio the day before he was shot but could not see his namesake school before he left for Dallas. He is said to have promised

Former President Harry Truman speaks at the dedication of Truman Middle School in 1960.

a local host, Congressman Henry B. Gonzalez, that he would return to dedicate the school. Instead, his brother Edward "Ted" Kennedy dedicated the school, belatedly, on October 22, 1980.

Memorial High School Memorial High School, opened in 1967, honors "all of those in the Edgewood family who gave their lives in defense of their country in all wars." In the Vietnam conflict alone, at least 50 Edgewood area residents were casualties.

Truman Middle School Selected by Franklin Roosevelt as his running mate in 1944, former Missouri senator and vice president Harry S. Truman (1884–1972) became president when Roosevelt died only 82 days into his fourth term. Truman, though ill prepared by his predecessor, turned out to be a strong leader who was willing to make tough decisions. This was the first secondary school in the nation (and the second school) named for Truman, who visited the campus for the formal dedication ceremony on October 11, 1960. Declining enrollment put the school on the district's closure list.

Wrenn Middle School In 1942, when schools were still segregated in Texas, Elizabeth Terrell Wrenn (1902–73), who had a bachelor's degree from Prairie View A&M, began teaching at George Washington Carver School, the school for blacks in the Edgewood Common District. She was the first black teacher in the district, and 17 years later was named the first principal of Lincoln Elementary School. She retired in 1966, and two years later the district's newest junior high school was named in her honor.

OTHER FACILITIES

José Angel Cardenas Early Childhood Center Starting as an elementary school teacher, Dr. José A. Cardenas, born in 1930, rose to high school science teacher, vice principal, principal and superintendent of the Edgewood district, a position in which he served from 1969 to 1973, all the while maintaining concern for early childhood education.

The José Angel Cardenas Early Childhood Center provides a focused learning environment for three- and four-year-olds preparing for kindergarten and elementary school.

Edgewood Communications and Fine Arts Academy This is in the Edgewood High School old building, opened in 1940 and closed in 1996.

HARLANDALE ISD

Though the Harlandale ISD was incorporated in 1924, schools in the district go back to 1888, when children first attended classes in the granary of historic San José Mission. Origin of the name Harlandale was difficult to uncover (p. 191).

Harlandale High School Built in 1926, Harlandale High School had a predecessor, Morrill High School, built on land originally donated in 1894 by David Morrill Poor; little wonder why they picked his middle name instead of his last for the school.

Kingsborough Middle School This school presumably was named for the subdivision in which it is located.

Leal Middle School Known as Southcross Middle School when built in 1954, this school was renamed to honor one of its own graduates. Armando Leal (1946–67) became a Navy corpsman after his graduation from Harlandale High School and was sent to Vietnam as a medic assigned to a Marine battalion. When his unit came under heavy enemy fire, despite sustaining three separate wounds Leal continued to aid wounded marines for two hours until he was killed by close range fire. He was posthumously awarded the Navy Cross along with his Purple Hearts.

McCollum High School Dillard McCollum graduated from Morrill High School in 1911 and spent his entire career as a teacher, principal and superintendent of the Harlandale ISD. One of his goals as superintendent was to establish a second high school. It opened in September 1962, three months after his death.

Terrell Wells Middle School **Terrell Wells** was an independent before being annexed by San Antonio in the late 1960s. It was a health spa named for sulfur and mineral wells on the property of Dr. Frederick Terrell (p. 193), who built a bathhouse and pools.

OTHER FACILITIES

Frank Tejeda Sports Complex and **Frank M. Tejeda Academy** At the age of 17, Frank M. Tejeda (1946–97) dropped out of Harlandale High School to join the Marines. After service in Vietnam, where he received a Bronze Star and Purple Heart, he earned a law degree at the University of California at Berkeley, a master's degree in public administration at Harvard and an advanced law degree at Yale. An enormously popular and effective politician, serving in the Texas House and Senate and in Congress, he died at age 51 from a brain tumor. He is remembered as being uncommonly generous with his time and money.

Attorney and legislator Frank Tejeda also served as a combat Marine.

Although the Harlandale School Board's policy prohibits naming district facilities after people, the rule was waived to honor Tejeda with both the new baseball complex and the alternative high school. They were completed in 1997.

JUDSON ISD

Judson High School and **Judson Middle School** Moses Campbell Judson (1861–1950) was born and raised on his parents' farm in northeast Bexar County. Financial restraints kept him from pursuing his dream to be a doctor, so when he graduated from high school in 1879 he and

Moses Judson was City Water Works superintendent and president of the County School Board.

his brother John William Judson formed a partnership with George W. Brackenridge (p. 70) that drilled the first artesian well in the San Antonio area. He was later superintendent of the San Antonio Water Works Company, predecessor of the City Water Board. Judson served 25 years on the rural Bexar County School Board, several of them as president. One goal was consolidating one-teacher rural schools into more versatile institutions. In 1958, the rural districts of Converse, Kirby and Selma combined to form a single district and named it in Judson's honor, later adding Live Oak and part of Universal City. The first member of the family in the area was George Henry Judson, who came from Connecticut, practiced law in New Braunfels, operated a general store on what is now Perrin-Beitel Road (p. 30) and married Martha Cornelia Perrin.

Kirby Middle School   Named for the town of Kirby (p. 190).

Kitty Hawk Middle School   Aviation began on the dunes of Kitty Hawk beach along the North Carolina coast on December 17, 1903, when Orville and Wilbur Wright's aircraft stayed aloft for 12 seconds and flew 120 feet, later that same day doing 59 seconds over 852 feet. This is an appropriate name for a school near Randolph Air Force Base (p. 188).

Metzger Middle School   Henry Metzger was born in 1885 in Fredericksburg but moved to Converse, where he began a teaching career that spanned fifty years. For 39 of those years he taught and was a principal in schools now part of the Judson ISD. He is also remembered as a community leader who helped form numerous civic organizations, but his greatest legacy appears to have been his encouragement of many students to pursue advanced study at a time when many in rural communities did not see the need for higher education.

Wagner High School   Promoted to Lt. Col. just a month before September 11, 2001, Karen Wagner (1961-2001) was killed in the terrorist attack on the Pentagon, where she worked as deputy chief of staff of medical personnel in the office of the Army surgeon general. A fourth generation soldier, Wagner was a 1979 graduate of Judson High School, where she excelled in academics and athletics, and where she had planned to return to teach at the completion of her army career. An All-City basketball player in her senior year, she also finished second in the 400-meter dash at the UIL state meet as a junior. The Wagner Sports Center at Walter Reed Army Medical Center in Washington and a building at Fort Sam Houston were also named in her honor.

Judson graduate Lt. Col. Karen Wagner was killed in the 9-11 attack on the Pentagon.

Arnold Athletic Facilities   Frank Arnold, born in 1941, has been described as the architect of Rocket Pride and the man who set in motion the football powerhouse that dominated San Antonio high school play for more than a decade. Head coach at five other area high schools before he went to Judson, Arnold's team won the school's first 5A state championship in 1983. The following year, he was elevated to athletic director, and his defensive co-coordinator D. W. Rutledge (see below) took over the football program and continued its remarkable success. Arnold was inducted into the Texas High School Coaches Association Hall of Honor in 2003 and into the San Antonio Sports Hall of Fame in 2010.

D. W. Rutledge Stadium   One of the most successful high school coaches in Texas history, D. W. Rutledge, born in 1952, took his Judson Rockets to the 5A state championship seven times, and won four state titles. As captain and All-American linebacker on Texas Lutheran's 1974 national championship team, he played under legendary motivator Jim Wacker. Much of Wacker's personality and coaching style appears to have worn off on Rutledge. Described by many former players as both inspirational motivator and mentor, Rutledge's passion was teaching young men how to become responsible adults. He stepped down from his Judson head coaching job in 2001 to take an administrative position with the Texas High School Coaches Association, and two years later he became the executive director. He has been named to the Texas High School Football Hall of Fame and the Texas High School Coaches Association Hall of Honor. Judson renamed its football stadium for him in 2006, and three years later he was inducted him into the San Antonio Sports Hall of Fame.

North East ISD

The North East ISD's board has held to its policy of naming high schools in honor of conservative American political and military heroes, with one possible exception.

Physician/astronaut Bernard Harris was the first African American to walk in space.

Bernard Harris Middle School   There are two Harris middle schools in San Antonio. This one honors physician/astronaut Dr. Bernard A. Harris, Jr. Born in Temple in 1956 and graduating from Sam Houston High School in San Antonio, he joined NASA as a clinical scientist and flight surgeon in 1987 and three years later was selected for the astronaut program. A veteran of two space flights, he became the first African-American to walk in space, logging some 438 hours in space. After leaving NASA in 1996, he has continued to do research. His Houston-based Harris Foundation supports programs encouraging disadvantaged individuals "to recognize their potential and pursue their dreams."

Gen. Omar Bradley wore five stars.

As First Lady, Barbara Bush promoted literacy.

Bradley Middle School   Graduating from West Point in the same class as Dwight Eisenhower, Omar Bradley (1893–1981) also achieved five- star rank when he was made the first chairman of the Joint Chiefs of Staff in 1950. Less flamboyant than some contemporaries, Bradley was an effective commander who won many battles and was highly regarded by the men who served under him.

Bush Middle School   This school is named for the wife and mother, respectively, of George and George W. Bush, the 41st and 43rd presidents. As First Lady, Barbara Bush, born in 1925, was noted for charm, family values and commitment to charitable and humanitarian efforts. In a speech at Wellesley College's commencement in 1990, Mrs. Bush said worldly success is no more important than being committed to family and friends. She dropped out of Smith College in her sophomore year to devote herself to her husband's career and to rearing their five children; a sixth child died at age four from leukemia. Literacy ranked highest among the projects she promoted as First Lady, and this has remained a lifelong passion. The Barbara Bush Foundation for Family Literacy has raised millions of dollars for this cause.

Churchill High School   This is an exception to North East's naming high schools for American heroes. The decision's defenders point out that the mother of Sir Winston Churchill (1874–1965) was the vivacious Jenny Jerome of New York, so he was American by blood, if not birth—though he was made an honorary citizen by President John F. Kennedy in 1963. One of history's most versatile, energetic and prolific characters, Winston Churchill is best known for leading the British people during World War II. North East departed from its school-naming policy at the urging of North East trustee Maxwell Higginbotham, an admirer of Churchill. Churchill never saw the

school, but his widow visited the campus in 1970.

Driscoll Middle School Born into a wealthy Irish Catholic family in Bayside, near Corpus Christi, Clara Driscoll (1881–1945) was sent by her parents to private schools in Texas, New York City and France. She was imbued with an appreciation for preserving historic sites in Texas for future genera-

Lady Clementine Spencer Churchill, right, widow of Sir Winston Churchill, receives a yearbook from Churchill High School Principal Nell Beukler in 1970.

tions. While in her 20s she worked with the Daughters of the Republic of Texas to acquire and preserve an enlarged Alamo site by advancing most of the purchase price for the Alamo's convento, or Long Barracks, earning the title "Savior of the Alamo."

Eisenhower Middle School Dwight David Eisenhower (1890–1969) was born in Denison, Texas, but his family moved back to Kansas when "Ike" was six months old. He loved sports but was an indifferent student, graduating from West Point in 1915 in the middle of a class of 125 students, of whom 59 became generals. Fort Sam Houston was his first assignment, and it was in San Antonio that he met his bride-to-be, Mamie Doud. In off- duty hours Eisenhower coached football at San Antonio's Peacock Military Academy and at St. Louis College, now St. Mary's University. Mamie was awarded a varsity letter for supporting the 1915 team; she was the only female to receive a football letter from the school. Eisenhower became commander of the D-Day invasion and 34th president.

Lt. Dwight Eisenhower appears in the center as an assistant football coach at what is now St. Mary's University in 1915.

Garner Middle School John Nance Garner (1868–1967) of Uvalde, west of San Antonio, served 30 years in the House of Representatives, including a term as speaker. Franklin Roosevelt named Garner his running mate in 1932 and made the vice president his liaison with Congress. As Roosevelt's New Deal became more liberal, Garner grew disenchanted and after two terms as vice president left Washington and spent his last 27 years in relative seclusion in Uvalde. Around the turn of the century, as a young Texas legislator he advocated (unsuccessfully) having the prickly pear be named the state flower, resulting in his nickname, "Cactus Jack."

Jackson Middle School Dr. Will W. Jackson (1890–1975) served for two decades as a member of the State Board of Education, half of that time as chairman. He was president of the University of San Antonio, a Methodist institution formed from the two-year Westmoorland College and open from 1935 to 1941. The school filed for bankruptcy—and later combined with Trinity University—after Jackson deposited the year's tuition receipts in a local bank that promptly failed. He was also first chairman of the board of the public KLRN-TV.

Will W. Jackson was chairman of the Texas Board of Education.

Johnson High School Claudia Alta "Lady Bird" Johnson (1912-2007) was one of America's great first ladies. A 1982 poll placed her third, behind Abigail Adams and Eleanor Roosevelt. Although named after her mother's brother Claud, during her infancy her nurse commented that she was as "purty as a ladybird," and the name stuck. Her father and siblings called her Lady, but her husband, Lyndon, called her Bird. Armed with three college degrees (St. Mary's College in Dallas in 1930, a University of Texas BA in 1934 and a UT bachelor's degree in journalism cum laude in 1934), her goal was to become a reporter. Those plans were derailed when she met a young congressional aide, Lyndon Baines Johnson, who proposed to her on their first date. They were married in St. Mark's Episcopal Church in San Antonio in 1934. In 1943 she spent $17,500 of her inheritance to purchase an Austin radio station, which she parlayed into a multi-million dollar communications enterprise under the name LBJ Holdings, of which she was president. Her greatest legacy was in preserving the environment. As First Lady, she started a capital beautification project and was instrumental in promoting the Highway Beautification Act. As a result of her efforts to clean up Austin's Town

As a child, Claudia Alta Taylor Johnson was thought to be "pretty as a lady bug," and the nickname stuck.

Lake and add trails to its shoreline, the lake was renamed Lady Bird Lake shortly after her death in 2007. She was the first president's wife to have a press secretary and chief of staff of her own, and hired employees to lobby congress and work specifically on her projects. Above all, she is remembered as a gracious lady, best described by Gerald Ford when, in awarding her the Presidential Medal of Freedom in 1977, he said "she made government human with her unique compassion and her grace, warmth, and wisdom. Her leadership transformed the American landscape and preserved its natural beauty as a national treasure."

Krueger Middle School Born in West Prussia, Walter Krueger (1881–1967) was brought to this country at the age of eight and at 17 became an Army private serving in the Spanish-American War.

Forty-eight years later he retired as a four-star general. Krueger was stationed at Fort Sam Houston from 1939 to 1943 in a series of positions, including commander of the Third Army. He organized the 200,000-member Sixth Army at Fort Sam and led it throughout the Pacific war theater, including recapture of the Philippines. After retiring in 1946 he returned to live in San Antonio.

Gen. Walter Kreuger organized the Sixth Army.

Robert E. Lee was stationed in San Antonio before he took command of the Confederate Army.

Lee High School Robert E. Lee (1807–70) was the son of a Revolutionary war hero and married a great-granddaughter of George Washington's wife, whose family owned a plantation named Arlington across the Potomac from Washington, D.C. He graduated second in his class at West Point in 1829, one of only two in West Point history to graduate having had no demerits; the other was Charles Mason, first in Lee's class. Lee forged a distinguished military career and was offered command of the U.S. Army on the eve of the Civil War. Although opposed to secession, Lee could not bring himself to take up arms against his beloved Virginia and resigned to fight for the Confederate cause. After the war he became president of Washington College, later Washington and Lee University. He was based in San Antonio in 1846 as a captain in the engineer corps and again as acting commander of the U.S. Army Department of Texas in 1860.

Lopez Middle School Opened in 2007, this school honors the same Medal of Honor recipient José M. Lopez for whom a section of IH-10 was named (p. 63).

MacArthur High School Like Lee, Douglas MacArthur (1880–1964) was the son of a military hero and an honor graduate of West Point, ranking first in the class of 1903. His own military career spanned half a century, including distinguished service in both World Wars and the Korean War. As military governor of Japan after World War II, he prevailed in drafting a radically new constitution that created a new way of life for the Japanese people. MacArthur had a strong attachment to San Antonio, having attended West Texas Military Academy (now Texas Military Institute) as a high school student when his father was stationed at Fort Sam Houston in the 1890s. He graduated as class valedictorian and was quarterback on the football team, shortstop in baseball and a tennis champion.

Gen. Douglas MacArthur was a student at what is now Texas Military Institute.

Madison High School The stature and legacy of James Madison (1751–1836) far surpass his physical attributes (five feet four inches tall and about 100 pounds). Called the father of the Constitution, he believed in a strong, well-balanced central government and was the driving force behind the first 10 amendments, the Bill of Rights. As fourth president, he was chief executive during the War of 1812, when the British burned the White House, the Capitol, and other public buildings. Henry Clay called him "after George Washington, our greatest statesman."

Nimitz Middle School The father of Chester William Nimitz (1885–1966) died before he was born in the Texas Hill Country town of Fredericksburg. His role model was his grandfather, Charles H. Nimitz, a German immigrant who bought a hotel on Fredericksburg's Main Street in 1855, remodeled the building to give it a steamboat appearance and named it the Nimitz Hotel. Nimitz dreamed of going to West Point, but when no appointment was available he took the exam for Annapolis and scored the top grade in his congressio-

Chester Nimitz with his grand-
father, German immigrant and
Fredericksburg hotelier Charles
Nimitz, who raised him.

Theodore Roosevelt in camp in San
Antonio, where he raised his First
Volunteer Cavalry, the "Rough
Riders."

nal district. He graduated in 1905. After the bombing of Pearl Harbor on December 7, 1941, he was named commander of U.S. Navy forces in the Pacific, achieving the rank of fleet admiral (five stars) and chief of naval operations after the war. To the Nimitz Hotel, restored as a museum, has been added the world-class National Museum of the Pacific War, ranked as one of the nation's ten best historical museums.

Reagan High School The early years of Ronald Reagan (1911–2004) as a sportscaster and movie actor propelled him into leadership as president of the actors' union, which, in turn, led him into politics. Originally a Democrat and an admirer of Roosevelt's New Deal, he became more conservative and shifted his support to the Republican party around 1950. He rose to the governorship of California and served two terms as President of the United States, receiving much credit for the collapse of the Soviet Union.

Roosevelt High School This school was named not for Franklin Delano Roosevelt but for his cousin Theodore (1858–1919). At the outbreak of the Spanish-American War, he organized the First Volunteer Cavalry ("Rough Riders"), many of whom he allegedly recruited in the bar of San Antonio's Menger Hotel (p. 155). Elected vice president in 1900, he ascended to the presidency when McKinley was assassinated, at 43 the youngest person to assume that office. He was reelected but failed in a bid for a third term against William Howard Taft (p. 113). He set aside some 125 million acres of western land as national forests and was instrumental in American acquisition of land for the Panama Canal.

White Middle School Born in San Antonio, Edward H. White II (1930–67) became a U.S. Air Force pilot upon graduation from West Point and a member of the second group of astronauts. On June 3, 1965, he was the first U.S. astronaut to walk in space. Two years later he died with Virgil Grissom and Roger Chaffee in a flight simulation fire on Apollo 1; they were the first casualties of the U.S. space program.

Ed White became the first American to walk in space.

Wood Middle School On a May morning in 1979, U.S. District Judge John H. Wood Jr. was shot in the driveway of his San Antonio town home. Known as "Maximum John" for his tough sentences to drug dealers, Wood was overseeing a drug case involving Jimmy Chagra, an El Paso attorney expected to be sentenced without parole. Chagra and his brother Joe were implicated in Wood's murder. Jimmy was acquitted of the charge but sentenced instead on a drug charge to 30 years in prison. His wife Elizabeth was sent to prison on related charges. In a deal to have his wife released, Jimmy admitted to his role in the murder. Hired hit man Charles Harrelson was also convicted and sent to prison, where he died in 2007. San Antonio's federal courthouse is also named for Wood (p. 154).

U.S. District Judge John H. Wood Jr. was shot in his driveway in 1979.

OTHER FACILITIES

Blossom Athletic Center Virgil T. Blossom, who died in 1965, was the first North East superintendent of national stature. Prior to becoming the revered pioneering superintendent of the newly formed North East district, Dr. Blossom was superintendent of schools in Little Rock, Arkansas. His intent to integrate Little Rock's all-white Central High School in 1957 prompted Gov. Orval Faubus to call out the Arkansas National Guard to block the entrance of nine black students. President Eisenhower

North East ISD Superintendent Virgil Blossom headed schools in Little Rock, Arkansas in 1957.

Jerry Comalander coached the Churchill Chargers to a state football title.

called out 1,200 Army paratroopers to escort the students into the school.

Comalander Stadium Jerry Comalander, the North East district's athletic director since 1988, was a star quarterback and basketball player at Dilley High School. After playing basketball at Rice, he coached at Devine and Uvalde with Marvin Gustafson (p. 118) before joining Gustafson's staff at Churchill in 1973. Two years later he succeeded his mentor, and as head coach took his team to the playoffs in eight seasons. In 1976 his undefeated team won the 4A state championship. Comalander was inducted into the San Antonio Sports Hall of Fame in 2008.

Josh Davis Natatorium A fifth-generation San Antonian, Josh Davis, born in 1972, became the only man in any sport to win three gold medals in the 1996 Atlanta Olympic Games. He went on to break the American record three times in his specialty event, the 200-meter freestyle. He added two silver medals at the 2000 games in Sydney as the USA Men's Swim Team captain. He continues to inspire younger athletes with swim clinics around the country, and is a popular faith-based motivational speaker.

Littleton Gymnasium Comalander's predecessor as North East athletic director was Jimmy Littleton (1922–2009), one of the most successful basketball coaches in San Antonio history. In 18 years as high school coach, Littleton won state championships at his alma mater—South San—in 1961 and at Lee in 1967. He coached for three years at Trinity University, but when Trinity ended athletic scholarships Littleton went back to school administration.

Josh Davis was the only athlete to win three gold medals in the 1996 Olympics.

Heroes Stadium Rapid growth in the North East district forced building of a second 10,000-seat football stadium, located in the former Longhorn Quarry adjacent to Wurzbach Parkway. It was originally to be named David Edwards Stadium in honor of a former Madison High School player who became quadriplegic in a 2003 playoff game and later died (p. 24), but, recognizing that similar accidents have befallen other players, the school board voted to name the new facility Heroes Stadium in honor of all such student athletes. The inaugural game in the stadium was played on September 4, 2009.

Northside ISD

With one exception, high schools in the Northside Independent School District are named for justices of the United States Supreme Court. Middle schools are named for Texans who have distinguished themselves primarily in the fields of government or education.

Anson Jones Middle School After his medical practices in New York and Pennsylvania proved unsuccessful, Anson Jones (1798–1858) drifted to Texas and developed a thriving practice in Brazoria. In the war for independence against Mexico he served as a surgeon but insisted on remaining a private. Afterward he devoted more effort to politics than to medicine, his positions including senator and secretary of state. He was the last president of Texas, earning the title "Architect of Annexation" for his role in negotiating union with the United States.

Brandeis High School Brandeis High School was named in honor of the first Jewish person appointed to the Supreme Court. Louis D. Brandeis (1856–1941) was born and raised in Louisville, Kentucky by immigrant parents from Prague, Czechoslovakia, and received his secondary education in Germany. Admitted to Harvard Law School at age eighteen without a college degree, he graduated in 1877 with what is said to have been the highest grade average in the school's history. He established a successful law practice in Boston and gained a reputation as an attorney for the people, often working without fees for such causes he believed in as minimum wage, trade unions and anti-trust legislation. His appointment to the court in 1916 by Woodrow Wilson was opposed by business interests and anti-Semites but was approved by the Senate, and Brandeis served until he retired in 1939. He became active in Zionist affairs during World War I, and worked for creation of an Israeli nation. Brandeis University in Waltham, Massachusetts, founded in 1948, is also named for him.

Brennan High School The son of Irish immigrants, William J. Brennan (1906–97) was only the tenth Catholic yet appointed to the U.S. Supreme Court when he was named in 1956. A graduate in economics of the Wharton School of the University of Pennsylvania and of Harvard University Law School, he was a New Jersey Supreme Court justice when President Eisenhower appointed him to the U.S. court in 1956. As an outspoken liberal who joined like-minded justices in the Warren Court (p. 116), Brennan subsequently found himself increasingly isolated in the more conservative Burger and Rehnquist courts. But due to his powers of persuasion in rallying support from conservative colleagues he was considered to be among the court's most influential members. A passionate supporter of individual rights, he wrote in one of his opinions: "Those whom we would banish from society or from the human community itself often speak in too faint a voice to be heard above society's demand for punishment. It is the particular role of the courts to hear these voices." His authorship of 1,360 opinions while on the Supreme Court bench was second only the number by William O. Douglas.

Clark High School   A Texan by birth and a University of Texas Law School graduate, Tom Campbell Clark (1899–1977) began his career in private practice in Dallas, where he became involved in Democratic party politics. He worked for the U.S. Department of Justice for several years before President Harry Truman named him attorney general in 1945. Four years later Truman appointed Clark to the Supreme Court. Clark resigned in 1967 when his son, Ramsey, was named Attorney General.

Connally Middle School   John B. Connally (1917–93) is probably best remembered as having been wounded while riding in the same car with John F. Kennedy during the assassination in 1963, but he accomplished much in his own right. Known as "Lyndon's boy," Connally started his career in 1939 at the age of 22 as legislative assistant to then Congressman Lyndon Johnson. He subsequently managed five of LBJ's major campaigns, including Johnson's election to the presidency in 1964. Connally served three terms as governor of Texas and was secretary of the Navy under Kennedy and secretary of the treasury under Nixon.

Hobby Middle School   Newspaperman William P. Hobby (1878–1964) began at the age of 17 as a circulation clerk for the Houston Post and eventually became owner of the Post and of other papers as well. As lieutenant governor of Texas when Gov. James E. Ferguson was impeached in 1917, Hobby became, at the age of 39, the youngest man to be governor. The next year he defeated Ferguson by the largest majority ever in a Texas Democratic primary and went on to serve as governor during World War I.

Dr. Hector P. Garcia Middle School   Although Hector Perez Garcia (1914–96) graduated from the University of Texas Medical Branch and practiced in Corpus Christi, one wonders how he found time to practice medicine. Born in Tamaulipas, Mexico, he was brought to Mercedes, Texas at age 3 by his schoolteacher parents to escape the

Mexican Revolution. He served in World War II as an infantry combat commander and later a doctor, and returned home to Corpus Christi with a Bronze Star and an Italian bride. As one of Texas's earliest and most ardent foes of discrimination and segregation, he fought tirelessly for the rights of veterans—he founded the American GI Forum—and for farm laborers and the voting rights of Hispanics. Appointed in 1967 by President Johnson as alternate ambassador to the UN, in 1984 he received the nation's highest civilian honor, the Presidential Medal of Freedom. from President Reagan. In 1988 the main Corpus Christi post office branch was renamed in his honor. After his death a nine-foot statue of him was dedicated at Texas A&M's Corpus Christi campus.

Holmes High School As a first child, Oliver Wendell Holmes, Jr. (1841–1935) got the same name as his famous physician/author father. His graduation from Harvard College in 1861 coincided with the start of the Civil War. He was wounded three times and rose to brevet (temporary) lieutenant colonel. His legal career began as a Harvard Law School professor and continued as chief justice of the Massachusetts Supreme Court and associate justice of the U.S. Supreme Court. Appointed to the Supreme Court by President Theodore Roosevelt in 1902, he retired in 1932 at the age of 91, having been the oldest sitting justice. Although known as "the Great Dissenter" for his sharp dissents, his most important role was as an advocate of judicial restraint.

John C. Holmgreen Junior and **Senior High School** This is the one exception to Northside's naming high schools for Supreme Court justices. The school itself has a different mission from other Northside high schools, as it enrolls only special education students. As a member and later chairman of the San Antonio Medical Foundation, John C. Holmgreen was instrumental in coordinating the efforts of the Foundation and the Northside district to establish Health Careers High School. It is fitting that these two schools are located side-by-side on the Medical Center's western edge.

Jay High School Appointed by George Washington to become the first chief justice of the Supreme Court, John Jay (1745–1829) had been president of the Continental Congress in 1778 and negotiated the Treaty of Paris with Great Britain to end the American Revolution. Convinced that the nation needed a strong centralized government, he profoundly influenced the Supreme Court in its formative years. In 1794 he was sent to Great Britain to negotiate lingering commercial differences between the two countries, and on his return discovered he had been elected governor of New York. After serving in that office for six years, he retired to his farm.

Jordan Middle School   Rather than being the sort of nationally known Texan for whom other Northside middle schools are named, Jack C. Jordan's career was dedicated to middle and high school education in San Antonio. Starting as a middle school teacher and coach, he became Northside superintendent in 1982, retiring in 1993. Twice he was named one of the state's top five educators.

Luna Middle School   More than 900 people, including the governor and half of Texas's state senators, crowded San Fernando Cathedral for the funeral mass of Gregory Luna (1932–99). Born in New Braunfels as the youngest of 17 children, his father died when he was 7 months old. His mother moved the family to San Antonio's West Side when he was three. A graduate of Lanier High School, he financed his education at Trinity University and St. Mary's University Law School through the GI Bill and by working full time as a patrolman and detective in the San Antonio Police Department. Luna was one of the founders of MALDEF—the Mexican–American Legal Defense and Educational Fund—in 1968, and was passionately dedicated to increasing educational opportunities and civil rights for low-income and minority persons. He served for 15 years in the Texas House of Representative and in the Texas Senate for 7 years. In his first senate term, he won authorization for $20 million in construction bonds for the downtown campus of the University of Texas at San Antonio.

Marshall High School   Although he had meager formal education, John Marshall (1755–1835) is credited as the nation's father of constitutional law. Before Marshall was named chief justice by John Adams in 1801, the Supreme Court was regarded as ineffective. His reorganization and the clarity, persuasiveness and force of his opinions established the power of judicial review of laws it considered unconstitutional. Northside's first high school was known as Northside Rural High School from its opening in 1950 until the name was changed to Marshall in 1960.

Neff Middle School   Pat Morris Neff (1871–1952) was twice governor of Texas, beginning in 1921. Considered a crusader and a moralist, he pushed reforms but did not develop a good relationship with the legislature, so many of his goals were not achieved. But he is given credit for establishing the state park system. For 17 years he served as president of Baylor University, which named its main administration building for him.

O'Connor High School   Sandra Day O'Connor was born in 1930 in El Paso but grew up on a ranch in Arizona. She married a Stanford Law School classmate who coincidentally had the same name as the first Chief Justice of the U.S. Supreme Court, John Jay O'Connor

III. After being state senator and a judge in Arizona, she was appointed in 1981 by President Reagan as the first woman associate justice of the Supreme Court.

Pease Middle School   Raised in Connecticut, Elisha Marshall Pease (1812–83) sought new opportunity, came to Texas at the age of 23 and became embroiled in the movement for independence from Mexico. After serving various roles in the fledgling government, he developed a successful law practice in Brazoria. Following an unsuccessful bid for the governorship he served

Justice Sandra Day O'Connor models the first letter jacket of her namesake high school at its dedication in 1998.

two terms, beginning in 1853. He eliminated the state's debt and lay the groundwork for financial support of public education. Using part of the $10 million settlement received from the United States in exchange for surrender of Texas land claims in the Southwest after annexation, he created the permanent school fund. By 1989 the fund had grown to more than $8 billion; interest is used for public education.

Rawlinson Middle School   While superintendent of the Northside ISD from 1995 to 2001, John "Ed" Rawlinson, born in 1943, took a risk most educational leaders would never take: he opened Holmes High School to a team of Express-News education reporters to undertake an in-depth study of the drop-out problem in a school that reflected the city's ethnic and racial diversity. Such openness was typical of the climate Rawlinson fostered throughout his district. Starting as an administrative assistant to the superintendent in 1971, he had worked his way up to the top job during his 30-year career with Northside. He was described by one colleague as being quiet, unassuming, and a brilliant problem solver, as well as a teacher's advocate. Originally a math teacher, when he was deputy superintendent he went back to the classroom for one year and taught a middle school math course to help him understand current problems from a teacher's perspective.

Rayburn Middle School   Samuel Taliaferro Rayburn (1882–1961) was a legendary politician. Elected to Congress in 1913, he served 48 continuous years in the House, 17 of them as speaker. A protégé and close ally of John Nance Garner (p. 102) and mentor of Lyndon B. Johnson, "Mr. Sam" developed mastery of congressional politics and was highly respected by members of both parties. He accepted no

Earl Rudder led his Second Ranger Battalion in a parade during the liberation of France.

money from lobbyists and in 48 years took no trip at taxpayers' expense.

Rudder Middle School After graduation from Texas A & M University, James Earl Rudder (1919–70) was a high school football coach and teacher, but his career was interrupted by World War II. On D-Day he commanded the Second Ranger Battalion, which scaled 100-foot cliffs at the Pointe du Hoc overlooking the beaches of Normandy to take out what were thought to be critical German gun batteries. His Rangers sustained nearly 50 percent casualties only to discover, when they reached the top, that the concrete bunkers were empty. The Germans had moved five 105 mm howitzers inland and had them lined up to fire on the landing beaches. Finding the guns camouflaged in an apple orchard, the Rangers rendered them inoperable with lignite grenades. Although wounded twice he continued to lead troops, including a regiment in the Battle of the Bulge, and became one of the most decorated soldiers of the war. He returned home and served as mayor of Brady for six years. In 1959 he became president of his alma mater.

Stevens High School When this school opened in the fall of 2005 on the site of the 1987 Papal Mass, its namesake was the most senior associate Supreme Court justice, second in time of service only to Chief Justice William Renquist. Appointed to the court in 1975 by President Gerald Ford, John Paul Stevens, born in 1920, avoided conservative or liberal labels, and was the least predictable justice in the Renquist court. Never involved in party politics and having no specific social agenda, his philosophy was to decide each case on its individual merits. He grew up in Chicago, where his father owned the Stevens Hotel—now the Chicago Hilton—and he excelled academically. His service on a naval code-breaking team in World War II gained him the Bronze Star. Stevens returned to Chicago and graduated from Northwestern University's Law School with the highest grades in the school's history. He retired from the bench in 2010.

Stevenson Middle School Born in a log cabin, Coke Robert Stevenson (1888–1975) was self-made and self-educated. He is the only person to have held the three top elected offices of state government: speaker of the House of Representatives, lieutenant governor and governor. As governor from 1941 to 1947 he established a policy to finance the state highway system. He is perhaps best known for the only election he ever lost. In 1948 he ran against Lyndon Johnson for U.S. senator, losing by 87 votes out of nearly one million cast. Stevenson appeared to have won until an uncounted ballot box from Duval County showed up. Many contend that the box was fraudulent. Johnson was nicknamed "Landslide Lyndon" and Stevenson went into permanent—and bitter—retirement.

Stinson Middle School   Aviation pioneer Katherine Stinson (1891–1977) originally intended to study music in Europe, but she became a stunt pilot to earn money for school. As she traveled the nation giving exhibitions, her success eclipsed any thoughts of music. She was the first woman to loop-the-loop, first woman mail pilot, first person of either sex to fly an airplane at night, first pilot to perform skywriting at night and first woman to fly in the Orient. Her family operated the Stinson School of Flying on the parade grounds at Fort Sam Houston until the Army started its own aviator's school (Kelly Air Force Base, p. 187), at which point the Stinson school moved to 750 acres southeast of town on what is now known as Stinson Field. All three of Stinson's siblings were renowned pilots. Brother Eddie founded the Stinson Aircraft Company.

Sul Ross Middle School   Originally called Northside Junior High School, it was renamed Sul Ross Middle School in 1960. The early ambition of Lawrence Sullivan ("Sul") Ross (1838–98) was to be an Indian fighter like his father. He was seriously injured in a battle with the Comanches during a summer vacation from college. After graduation he joined the Texas Rangers. He resigned to enlist in the Confederate Army, rising to brigadier general and commanding the Texas Cavalry Brigade. He was elected sheriff of McLennan County and state senator before serving two terms as governor of Texas, beginning in 1886. Leaving Austin, he stepped into the presidency of Texas A & M University, then Agricultural and Mechanical College of Texas. He is credited with putting that institution on a firm foundation during his seven years as president.

Taft High School   William Howard Taft (1857–1930) is the only person to have been both U.S. president and chief justice of the Supreme Court. He hated politics and loved the law, so it is not surprising that many regard him as an

President William Howard Taft lays the chapel cornerstone at Fort Sam Houston in 1909.

ineffectual president yet one of the great chief justices. A trusted cabinet member and close friend of President Theodore Roosevelt (p. 106), he twice turned down a seat on the Supreme Court. As Roosevelt's handpicked successor he became president in 1908, but the two men had a serious falling out and Roosevelt ran against Taft in 1912. They split the Republican vote, giving the election to Democrat Woodrow Wilson. Taft returned to Yale as a professor of constitutional law. In 1921, President Warren G. Harding appointed him chief justice.

Vale Middle School After graduating as valedictorian from St. Mary's University Law School in 1954, Robert L. Vale (1931–92) served in the U.S. Army in Korea and returned to San Antonio, where he became immediately involved in community activities and political campaigns. Beginning in 1965 he served for 20 years in the Texas legislature, seven terms as a representative and two as a senator. He is credited with being instrumental in securing funding for the University of Texas at San Antonio and the Health Science Center. Having a passion for education, he championed better opportunities and facilities for students, increased salaries and benefits for teachers and higher standards for public education. In fighting for legislative reform he is remembered as one of the 1971 "Killer Bees," the dozen state senators who fled the state to prevent a vote and thereby successfully blocked a bill they opposed. In 1979, he and other liberal legislators joined the "Dirty Thirty" to implement legislative reforms.

Wallace Jefferson Middle School A 1981 graduate of John Jay High School, Wallace Jefferson, born in 1963, is the youngest Northside school namesake and the first Northside alumnus for whom a school was named. After graduating from Michigan State University and the University of Texas Law School, in 1991 he and two colleagues founded one of the first appellate firms in Texas. He successfully argued two cases before the U.S. Supreme Court in his mid-thirties. In 2001, at 37, he was appointed as the first African American to serve on the Texas Supreme Court, and three years later was appointed chief justice. In 1990 he received the Northside district's first Pillar of Fairness, an honor now bestowed annually on distinguished Northside alumni. He has also been named Outstanding Alumnus of both Michigan State and the University of Texas Law School.

Warren High School Earl Warren (1891–1974) wanted to be President of the United States. When he lost the 1952 Republican nomination to Dwight Eisenhower, he may have been promised a Supreme Court appointment in return for delivering the California vote to Eisenhower. In 1953, the sitting chief justice died and Eisenhower did appoint Warren to be the new chief justice. As a district attorney and attorney general of

California who was tough on criminals and racketeers and as the governor of California who supported the internment of Japanese-Americans during World War II, Warren was thought to be much more conservative than he turned out to be. The famous 1954 Brown v. Board of Education case that ruled segregated schools to be unconstitutional was only the first of many rulings by his court that defended and expanded individual rights of citizens. The Warren Court was not only more liberal than anticipated, but also became much more proactive than the Supreme Court had been previously. Warren himself was reviled and vilified by right wing conservatives. In 1963, he chaired the Warren Commission that investigated the assassination of President Kennedy, and their "lone gunman" conclusion has been challenged since by many others who have offered up a variety of conspiracy theories. An interesting footnote to Warren's life is that the only election he ever lost was as the vice-presidential running mate of Thomas Dewey, who was upset by incumbent Harry S. Truman in the 1948 election.

Zachry Middle School   Graduating from Texas A & M University in 1922 with a degree in civil engineering, Henry Bartell "Pat" Zachry (1901–84) formed his own construction company, which became one of the largest in the country. One of his best-known jobs was his innovative modular completion of the 500-room Hilton Palacio del Rio Hotel in a record 202 working days just in time for the start of HemisFair '68. Much of his fortune was used to create college scholarship funds; he directed school officials not to disclose the amount of his contributions.

Construction magnate H. B. Zachry used much of his fortune to create scholarship funds.

OTHER FACILITIES

Dub Farris Athletic Complex   As the second major sports complex for the Northside ISD, this area is still under development, but the football stadium is named for a former athletic director of the district: James Walter "Dub" Farris, born in 1944, who stepped down in 2003 after a 13-year tenure. Farris became an athletic administrator after serving as head football coach at Odessa, Marshall–San Antonio and Dickinson high schools. One of the most significant changes he helped bring about was addition of a third playoff team from each 5A district to compete in playoffs, as well as creation of two divisions in 5A. He was named to the Texas High School Coaches Association Hall of Honor in 1997.

Don Hardin Athletic Complex   When he retired from the NISD in 2004, Don Hardin, born in 1937, had been assistant athletic director of facilities for 24 years. In fact, he never worked for any employer other than the Northside school district. A 1957 graduate of Harlandale, he went to work as a teacher and coach at Neff Middle School upon his graduation from Southwest Texas in 1962. Moving in 1964 to Marshall High School, where he taught and coached football and track until 1979, he then spent the remainder of his career working tirelessly to improve the athletic facilities of the NISD. He is remembered by colleagues at the NISD as working harder and putting in more hours than anyone else on the staff.

Annemarie Tennis Center   As director of the NISD tennis program for eight years, Annemarie Walson Murillo (1967-2004) helped develop this part of the Hardin Athletic Complex into a first class facility. Shortly before she died of breast cancer at age 37, parents and players petitioned the school board to name the new tennis center in her honor. A dedication ceremony that she could attend was planned, but it was to have been held one day before she died, and the ceremony was cancelled. A native of the Netherlands, she graduated from Texas Tech and played professional tennis before becoming director of the NISD tennis program in 1996.

George Block Aquatics Center   In January 2010, Northside ISD named the aquatics center in the Hardin Complex in honor of the man responsible for developing a strong district swimming program. George Block opened the center in 1978, and was not only the driving force behind the development of the swimming, diving and water polo teams, but also started the Learn to Swim program for elementary school children and was instrumental in the creation in 2006 of the district's second natatorium, in the Dub Farris complex. In 1997 he was named Top Aquatics Director by the United States Water Fitness Association. Upon his retirement in 2009, he became the chief operating officer of Haven for Hope (p. 12).

Gustafson Stadium   Before becoming athletic director of Northside, Marvin Gustafson was a high school football coach. He led his Uvalde team to a 3-A state title in 1973 and later the Churchill Chargers to state quarterfinals in both years he coached there. Northside's football stadium was named for him in 1994, three years before he died of a rare neurological disease. He was the older brother of Cliff Gustafson, legendary baseball coach at the University of Texas.

Northside ISD Athletic Director Marvin Gustafson also coached winning football teams at Uvalde and Churchill high schools.

Jake Inselmann Baseball Stadium   J. H. (Jake) Inselmann was city clerk of San Antonio from 1962 until his death in 1975. He supported many projects and programs benefiting the youth of the city and he had a great interest in athletics. At a eulogy by city council shortly after his death Councilman Henry Cisneros made the suggestion that some sports facility be named for him.

Paul Taylor Field House   A graduate of Edison High School and Trinity University, Paul Taylor was the first basketball coach at Holmes High School when it opened in 1964. He taught and coached with passion and enthusiasm, but he died of leukemia in 1970 at age 34. When the new Northside sports complex was built a few years later, the basketball facility was named in his memory.

Reddix Center   The Northside Vocation Transition Program was named for Nellie M. Reddix, Northside's first black trustee and the first woman on the board in several decades. Coming from a background as a PTA president, Reddix is credited with urging that a reading specialist, music teacher and art teacher be put in each school and that athletic opportunities for girls be increased.

OUR LADY OF THE LAKE UNIVERSITY

In 1895, Mayor Henry Elmendorf donated 18 acres of land for a school south of Elmendorf Lake to the Sisters of Divine Providence on the condition that they spend $75,000 on improvements in 10 years. They eventually acquired 71 acres for their college and convent. The name of this school in English is the same as the full name in French of its better-known counterpart in South Bend, Indiana—Notre Dame du Lac.

ST. ANTHONY CATHOLIC HIGH SCHOOL

San Antonio is, of course, Spanish for Saint Anthony (p. 1). In 1890 the Catholic Church purchased a tract on McCullough Avenue in what is now the Monte Vista Historic District for a "great Catholic college" to train Mexican priests. Such training, however, became prohibited by Mexican law. Instead, Rt. Rev. Dionede Falconio came from Rome in 1903 to lay the cornerstone for **St. Anthony Seminary,** later renamed St. Anthony Catholic High School. The present building includes the chapel wing of the 1903 structure.

ST. MARY'S HALL

Founded by the Episcopal Church as a girls' school in 1865, the school was forced to close in 1866 because of a cholera epidemic. It is named for the Virgin Mary, as stated by the organizers of the school in 1876: "What we want is an institution, even though with small beginnings, which shall take the daughters of the church and train them upon in gentleness and grace and true loveliness of character, to be like her that was 'blessed among women,' true handmaids of the Lord." In 1879 the school was reorganized as West Texas College for Girls, primarily through efforts of St. Mark's Episcopal Church. St. Mary's Hall is now an independent coeducational college preparatory school in the Marymont subdivision off Loop 410 NE.

St. Mary's University

The Society of Mary (Marianist brothers and priests) was founded in France in 1817. Four priests of the order arrived in San Antonio in 1852 and opened their first school above a livery stable on the southwest corner of Military Plaza. Moved to College Street on the river, behind St. Mary's Catholic Church, the school eventually outgrew this site as well. In 1892 the order purchased a 75-acre tract in Woodlawn Hills, far beyond city limits. The new campus for boarders on this site was called **St. Louis College.** In 1923 remaining downtown collegiate work was transferred to this campus and the name was changed to St. Mary's. The College Street campus became St. Mary's School of Law until it was sold in 1966 to a group of St. Mary's graduates, who renovated the old buildings into La Mansion del Rio Hotel in time for HemisFair '68 (p. 8).

V. J. Keefe Field   This was the home of minor league baseball in San Antonio in the 1970s and 1980s. It was named for a man in the concrete business whose widow, Margaret Keefe, cosigned a loan to refurbish the field sufficiently to support a team.

Bill Greehey Arena   St. Mary's basketball facility, which opened in November 2000, was named for the man who raised the money to build it—Valero Energy Corporation CEO William E. "Bill" Greehey, not only chairman of the fund-raising committee but also the largest single contributor. Born in Iowa, Greehey came to San Antonio to serve a tour of duty at Lackland Air Force Base and later studied accounting at St. Mary's. First an internal auditor for Coastal States Gas Corporation in Houston, at age 37 he was named president of a subsidiary that evolved into Valero (p. 172). Greehey was named Distinguished Alumnus of St. Mary's in 1986 (p. 177).

St. Philip's College

In 1898 the Episcopal Church began a sewing class for six black girls in an old adobe house across from the Cos House in La Villita. It evolved into an industrial school for girls, then a high school and is now part of the Alamo Community College District, with an enrollment of more than 8,000. St. Philip was one of the 12 apostles of Jesus.

San Antonio ISD

Since its first school opened 120 years ago, this district's schools have undergone a dizzying number of name changes. About 1920 the board began naming most middle schools for American writers.

Brackenridge High School This was established in 1917 and named for businessman and philanthropist George Washington Brackenridge (1832–1920) (p. 70). Most of his fortune went to support public education in San Antonio, Austin, Galveston and Seguin and to the University of Texas at Austin. On his statue at a Broadway entrance to Brackenridge Park is inscribed "a great friend of lower and higher and eternal education." In 1974 a new building was built and the name changed to Wheatley High School (p. 125). The Brackenridge name was restored in 1988.

Burbank High School Luther Burbank (1849–1926) was a horticulturist, botanist and pioneer plant breeder who developed more than 800 new strains and varieties. Born and reared on a farm in Massachusetts, he used the profits from his first successful creation, the Burbank potato, for travel fare to California. For the next 50 years he worked on his experimental farms in Santa Rosa, and at the time of his death was growing more than 5,000 botanical distinct species native to many parts of the world.

Connell Middle School In the 1890s, hot sulfur springs were discovered on open land just north of San Antonio State Hospital. The Hot Wells Hotel and other spas were built, and the local population increased to the point where schools were needed. On this site was the original campus of Hot Wells School, which eventually housed all grades through high school. By 1952 only Hot Wells Junior High School remained. It was renamed in honor of former principal Wilbur B. Connell, after his death in 1964.

Cooper Middle School James Fenimore Cooper (1789–1851) is considered to be the first major U.S. novelist. His most popular works were of frontier adventure, including The Last of the Mohicans.

The name of educator Stonewall Jackson Davis replaced that of Jefferson Davis at a San Antonio ISD middle school.

Davis Middle School This school was first named for Confederate President Jefferson Davis (1808–89). After the neighborhood's predominant makeup changed from Anglo to African American, the name was changed in 1991 to honor the late local civil rights leader, real estate broker and St. Philip's College professor S. J. Davis. Those initials also stand for Stonewall Jackson, another Confederate hero. Davis's widow was quick to point out that most people called him "S. J." or "Stoney," few of his friends even knew what his initials stood for and, after all, he was black and the first African American to serve on the district's board.

Edison High School Although he had only a few months of schooling, Thomas Alva Edison (1847–1931) was America's most prolific inventor. He held 1,093 patents, including for the electric light bulb, phonograph and critical elements for telephone, microphone and motion pictures.

Fox Tech High School First called **High School and Central Grammar** when it shared space with the grammar school in the Vance Barracks (p. 19), this school got its first permanent home on Main Avenue in 1882 and was named San Antonio High School in 1908. When a second high school, Brackenridge, was built on the south side in 1917, **San Antonio High School** was renamed **Main Avenue High School** after its location. In 1932 it became San Antonio Vocational and Technical High School. Louis William Fox (1889–1978) spent 47 years with the district, primarily as a teacher of vocational and industrial arts but then as principal of the school, working to develop a curriculum combining classroom instruction with on-the-job training. Fox retired in 1949, and the school was subsequently renamed in his honor.

Fox Tech bears the name of vocational educator Louis J. Fox.

Harris Middle School As recorder of the Uncle Remus tales, Joel Chandler Harris (1848–1908) was one of the first American writers to use dialect. A southern newspaperman, Harris attempted to authentically reproduce local black folktales, until then passed on only by word of mouth.

Highlands High School This is on the crest of a hill above the surrounding area and adjacent to Highland Park and Highland Hills subdivisions.

Houston High School Houston High School was named for Texas patriot Sam Houston (Fort Sam Houston, p. 186).

Irving Middle School   "America's first man of letters," Washington Irving (1783–1859) is best known for his short stories "The Legend of Sleepy Hollow" and "Rip Van Winkle."

Jefferson High School   Thomas Jefferson (1743–1826) was primary draftsman of the Declaration of Independence, third president of the United States, the person responsible for the Louisiana Purchase, sponsor of the Lewis and Clark Expedition, founder and architect of the University of Virginia, and perhaps the most versatile and well-read man to occupy the White House. Built in 1930 in the Spanish Colonial Revival style, Jefferson High School was named a National Historical Landmark in 1983. Life Magazine once termed it "the most beautiful high school in America."

King Middle School   Originally opened as **James Whitcomb Riley Elementary-Junior High School** in 1957, this school was renamed in 1982 for Martin Luther King (1929–68), one of the most important leaders of the American civil rights movement. In 1964 he was awarded the Nobel Peace Prize; he is its youngest recipient.

Lanier High School   This school is named for poet and musician Sidney Lanier (1842–81), who spent time in San Antonio in 1872–73 hoping the sunshine and mild climate would heal his chronic lung condition. While here he wrote eloquently about San Antonio and its river. The school opened in 1915 as McKinley Elementary School and in 1923 became **McKinley Junior High School** when Superintendent Jeremiah Rhodes began grouping grades seven through nine as a preparation for high school. About this time the policy began of naming middle schools for American writers, and Lanier was chosen. In 1929 it became a six-year school when high school grades were added. When Tafolla Junior High School opened across the street in 1969, Lanier became a high school only.

    Nemo Herrera Alumni Center Basketball Court   It's hard to recall a time in which everything was not so specialized. One non-specialist was coach Nemo Herrera (1898–1984), who coached all major sports at Lanier High School for 17 years (1928-45). His basketball teams won two state championships, in 1943 and 1945) When he moved to El Paso a year later, his Bowie High School Bears won the state baseball championship in 1949. A tough, no-nonsense strict disciplinarian, he was idolized by his former players as a great man and inspirational role model. Four of the players on his championship Lanier teams established a scholarship in his name in 2000. A 1918 graduate of Brackenridge High School, he went on to graduate from Southwestern University in Georgetown, which honored him with a citation of merit in 1974. He was named to the Texas High School Coaches Hall of Honor in 1967. At least two other facilities bear his name: the Youth Center at Kelly AFB, where he served for 11 years as civilian sports coordinator after "retiring" from coaching at age 70, and an elementary school in El Paso.

Longfellow Middle School   The most popular American poet of the nineteenth century, Henry Wadsworth Longfellow (1807–82) was fluent in French, Spanish, and Italian. Many of his poems immortalized events in North American history, such as "Paul Revere's Ride" and "Evangeline."

Lowell Middle School   Born into a distinguished New England family, James Russell Lowell (1819–91) succeeded Longfellow as Smith Professor of Modern Languages at Harvard University. His best writing was done before the age of 30. Lowell also served as U.S. minister to Spain and later as ambassador to Great Britain.

Mann Middle School   Horace Mann (1796–1859) was the first great American advocate of public education, championing the then relatively novel concept that education should be free, universal and nonsectarian, and taught by well-trained professionals. A decade before the Civil War he served briefly in Congress, and was a fierce enemy of slavery.

Page Middle School   A Virginian whose writings fostered romantic legends of southern plantation life, Thomas Nelson Page (1853–1922) seems an ironic choice for the name of a school in a predominantly black neighborhood, although the neighborhood was predominantly white when the school was named.

Pickett Academy   The building that houses this middle school for students with special needs was built in 1894 on Starr Street, later made part of Houston Street, as Starr Street School. In 1902 it was renamed Fannin School in honor of Colonel James W. Fannin, commander of 300 Texan troops killed by order of General Santa Anna in the so-called Goliad Massacre of 1835. Fannin School closed in 1971 because of declining enrollment, and the building lay vacant for 25 years. In 1998, $2.2 million was spent to renovate the building. The name was again changed, this time to honor Dorothy Mae Carter Pickett (1918–95), longtime district teacher, librarian, counselor, dean and principal. She was the 1935 graduating class salutatorian at Wheatley High School and went on to earn a bachelor's degree from Prairie View A & M University and a master's in education from Our Lady of the Lake College. She was active in numerous civic, social, church and civil rights organizations.

Poe Middle School   Plagued by alcohol abuse and possibly drug addiction, Edgar Allan Poe (1809–49) lived a tortured existence. His depression and melancholy were frequently evident in such works as The Raven. He is considered the first master of the short-story form, and his novels of detection are regarded as predecessors of the modern mystery.

Rhodes Middle School   Jeremiah M. Rhodes, superintendent of the San Antonio district from 1920 to 1925, is best remembered for implementing the junior school system in San Antonio in 1923 so that grades seven through nine could prepare students for high school.

Rogers Middle School   This school is named for Harry H. Rogers (1877–1957), president of the district's board from 1948 to 1953. An attorney, Rogers spent 10 years as a schoolteacher and county school superintendent in Missouri before attending law school. Active in civic and church affairs, he served as president of Rotary International at the time of its 1926 world convention in Belgium.

Tafolla Middle School   Fidel Leon Tafolla (1899–1971) served for 50 years in public schools, 46 with the San Antonio district as teacher, vice-principal and principal of Lanier Junior-Senior High School.

Twain Middle School   Writer and humorist Samuel Langhorne Clemens (1835–1910) used the pen name of Mark Twain, a Mississippi River man's term for water two fathoms deep, barely safe for navigation. He became a licensed steamboat pilot on the Mississippi River in 1859 after a four-year apprenticeship, but the outbreak of the Civil War two years later disrupted river traffic and caused him to find another line of work—writing.

Wheatley Middle School   Phillis Wheatley (1753–84), the first noted black woman poet in the United States, was taken to Boston on a slave ship in 1761 and purchased by a tailor named John Wheatley as his wife's servant. The Wheatleys recognized her considerable talents and gave her privileges unusual for a slave. Learning to read and write, she mastered not only English but Greek and Latin as well. Opened in 1933 as a segregated school for black students, Wheatley High School was closed in 1970. The name was given to a new high school building that opened in 1974 on the site of the old Brackenridge High School, but in 1988 Brackenridge replaced Wheatley as the name of this high school and **Emerson Middle School** was renamed Wheatley Middle School.

Whittier Middle School   John Greenleaf Whittier (1807–92) was a nineteenth-century poet and probably the most influential writer in the Abolitionist movement for several decades prior to the Civil War.

SPECIAL FACILITIES

Estrada Achievement Center   Previously known as the **Alamo Achievement Center**, this alternative school serving the district's eight high schools was renamed in 2006 for Ramiro Estrada, a pioneer Hispanic physician. Despite having to drop out of school during the Depression to help support his family, Estrada was his Lanier High School class valedictorian and went on to earn degrees in pharmacy, medicine and law, all with honors. Although his pediatric residency was also interrupted to take care of his family, he returned to San Antonio after completing his training and practiced for more than 35 years. He was the first Hispanic pediatrician on the staff of Robert B. Green Hospital. A staunch believer in the power of education, he was also honored by having Barkley Elementary School in the San Antonio district renamed for him. In addition, a Santa Rosa Hospital wing is the Dr. Ramiro Estrada Respite Center.

Gonzales Achievement Center   Created in 1986, this school is designed to meet the needs of the district's severely emotionally disturbed and behaviorally disordered students, and to serve as an alternate setting for students violating the student code of conduct. It is on the site of the original **Don Rafael Gonzales Elementary School**, long known as the "rock quarry school" because of its proximity to the rock quarry that became Brackenridge Park's Sunken Gardens. A new structure with the same name was built in 1948. Rafael Gonzales (1789–1857) was a San Antonio native active in the Mexican independence movement and, from 1824 to 1826, the governor of the Mexican state of Coahuila and Texas. The town of Gonzales is also named for him.

Navarro High School   This non-traditional high school in the SAISD honors the same famous Texas patriot José Antonio Navarro for whom a street, county, and state park are also named (p. 16).

SCHERTZ-CIBOLO-UNIVERSAL CITY ISD

J. Frank Dobie Junior High School   Born on a ranch in Live Oak County and raised in Alice, Texas, J. Frank Dobie (1888–1964) called upon early life experiences to write about Texas ranch life and southwestern folklore. As a student at Southwestern University in Georgetown, Dobie was encouraged by an English professor to become a writer. After earning a master's degree at Columbia University in New York in 1914, he joined the faculty of the University of Texas at Austin, with whom he seems to have had a love-hate relationship. After serving in World War I, Dobie returned to the university as an English instructor, but became disillusioned and left teaching to work on his uncle's ranch. Not having a Ph.D. blocked him from promotion at UT, and he served as chairman of the English department at Oklahoma A & M University for two years (1923–25) before returning to Austin. Although dismissed from the UT faculty in 1944, his funeral was held in Hogg Auditorium on the UT campus. His Marble Falls ranch was deeded to UT as a place for scholars to study and write, and the largest student housing property in Austin is the Dobie Center. An outspoken liberal who poked fun at Texas state politics, he was nonetheless awarded the Medal of Freedom by President Lyndon Johnson four days before his death. His most famous book, The Longhorns, is credited with being instrumental in saving this noble breed from extinction. As secretary of the Texas Folklore Society for 21 years he worked to generate interest in folklore, in part by promoting publications by that organization.

Ray D. Corbett Junior High School Lifelong educator Ray D. Corbett (1924–86), who had a bachelor's degree from Austin College and a master's in Education from Southwest Texas State, was a teacher and coach in various Texas school districts for 10 years before, in 1961, joining Schertz-Cibolo-Universal City ISD, where he spent the remainder of his career. When ill health forced his retirement in 1984, the school board voted unanimously to rename O'Henry Junior High School, where he had served as principal for 20 years, in his honor.

Wilder Intermediate School Although she has become one of the best-known authors of pioneer life in the late nineteenth and early twentieth centuries, Laura Ingalls Wilder (1867-1957) did not publish her first book until she was 65. Famous now mainly because of her "Little House" series, adapted to television, she apparently did not try writing until after her daughter Rose Wilder Lane had developed her own literary career. Some have concluded that they were collaborators, Laura's vivid storytelling strengthened by her daughter's editing skills. Most of Wilder's subject matter was autobiographical, stemming from a hardscrabble life as a child and from the medical, physical, financial and emotional struggles she and her husband endured. She was inducted into the Hall of Famous Missourians in 1993, and a bronze bust of Wilder is in the rotunda of the Missouri state capitol. Her longtime home, Rocky Ridge Farm in Mansfield, Missouri, where she wrote the Little House stories, is now the Laura Ingalls Wilder Home and Museum.

Steele High School A native of San Antonio, Byron P. Steele II, born in 1935, worked his way through San Antonio Junior College and St. Mary's University as a professional boxer, winning 20 of his 22 fights. He began his 45-year career in education as a teacher, but he left the classroom in 1965 to serve as the first director of the Bexar County Head Start Program. After leaving that post in 1968, he spent the remainder of his career as an administrator in several school districts in and around San Antonio, the last 18 years as Schertz-Cibolo-Universal City ISD superintendent.

SOUTH SAN ANTONIO ISD

Dwight Middle School   Several longtime residents of the area say this school honors a famous American by his first name. Main Street was the thoroughfare in incorporated South San Antonio, which was annexed by San Antonio in 1944. Since San Antonio already had a Main Street, the name had to be changed. Local citizens apparently wanted to honor then war hero Dwight David Eisenhower, but San Antonio already had an "Eisenhauer" Road, albeit spelled differently and honoring a different man (p. 24), so they used his first name. The middle school took its name from **Dwight Street**—which was again changed, so as to be consistent with its ongoing route, the already named Southcross Boulevard.

Abraham Kazen Middle School   Abraham "Chick" Kazen (1919–87), a lifelong resident of Laredo of Lebanese descent, spent his life in public service. After nearly 20 years in the Texas house and senate, he was elected to Congress in 1996 to represent the newly created 23rd district, which stretches 800 miles from El Paso to San Antonio. He was reelected eight times with virtually no opposition until 1984, when he was defeated in the Democratic primary by Albert Bustamante. He is credited in being a major force in creation of the San Antonio Missions National Historical Park.

Alan B. Shepard Middle School   A graduate of the U.S. Naval Academy, Alan Bartlett Shepard Jr. (1923–98) was one of the original seven astronauts. On May 5, 1961, he became the first American in space, going up 115 miles in a 15-minute suborbital flight. He later commanded the Apollo 14 moon mission, during which he spent a record 33 1/2 hours on the surface of the moon.

Alan Shepard, first American in space, is honored by President John F. Kennedy.

South San Antonio High School is the name of obvious origin of one of the district's high school. A second, **West Campus High School**, opened in 1975, was closed in 2008.

SOUTHSIDE ISD

This district has Southside High School and Southside Middle School, and one other middle school, **Losoya Intermediate School**. This school honors a Tejano defender of the Alamo, Jose Toribio Losoya (p. 15).

Southwest ISD

Christa McAuliffe Junior High School   On January 28, 1986, the space shuttle Challenger exploded just 73 seconds after lift-off, killing all seven astronauts aboard. Among those was the first civilian in space, schoolteacher Sharon Christa McAuliffe (1948–86), of Concord, New Hampshire. In 1984, NASA sought to rekindle the excitement that once surrounded the space program partly by sending an "ordinary citizen" along with professional astronauts. More than 11,000 people applied. McAuliffe was chosen and was to present lessons about those on board to be beamed to the viewing public on earth. Her motto was, "I touch the future, I teach."

Christa McAuliffe enjoys zero-gravity training prior to her ill-fated flight on the space shuttle Challenger.

Francis Scobee Middle School   In keeping with its precedent of naming middle schools for astronauts killed in the Space Shuttle Challenger disaster, Southwest ISD named its next two middle schools for other members of that seven-member crew. Francis Richard "Dick" Scobee (1939–68) grew up in Washington state and enlisted in the Air Force. While working as a mechanic at Kelly AFB he attended San Antonio College and then earned a degree in aerospace engineering from the University of Arizona, following which he was awarded a commission. After flying combat missions in Vietnam, he became a test pilot and was selected for the astronaut program in 1978. In April 1984 he piloted a Challenger mission that successfully deployed one satellite and repaired another. He was then elevated to spacecraft commander of the ill-fated 1986 Challenger flight. Delayed several times because of bad weather and technical glitches, the launch finally took place on January 28, but exploded only 73 seconds after liftoff. Subsequent investigations revealed the "O' rings designed to seal the rocket against fuel leakage failed because of near-freezing temperatures.

Ronald McNair Middle School   Another member of the Challenger crew was Ronald Ervin McNair (1950–86), an African-American physicist/astronaut. A native of South Carolina, he received a bachelor's degree in physics at North Carolina A&T State University and a Ph.D. in physics from MIT. Nationally recognized for his work in lasers, he received three honorary doctorates and worked at the Hughes Research Lab in Malibu, California. In 1978, McNair was selected from a pool of 10,000 applicants to the astronaut program, and in 1984 became the second African American to fly in space. He held a black belt in karate and was an accomplished saxophonist and had planned to record a saxophone solo on the flight.

SUNSHINE COTTAGE SCHOOL FOR DEAF CHILDREN

Sunshine Cottage School for the Deaf founder Dela White, left, and her daughter Tuleta, right, with Heather Whitestone, the first deaf person to become Miss America.

Sunshine Cottage was established in 1947 under the leadership of Mrs. Dela White, whose daughter, Tuleta, was born profoundly deaf (p. 33). It began in a former Landa Library caretaker's building that needed painting. A paint store donated surplus paint that happened to be bright yellow, leading to the school being named Sunshine Cottage. Five years later the school moved to a site north of Alamo Stadium, where it gained a national reputation for educating students in listening and spoken language rather than in sign language. The student body has grown to more than 200, with children from early childhood through fifth grade taught in Sunshine Cottage classrooms and students in sixth through twelfth grades mainstreamed on the campuses of partner schools. In 2010 Sunshine Cottage moved to a 20-acre campus designed by Lake/Flato Architects on Hildebrand Avenue across from Trinity University.

TRINITY UNIVERSITY

Trinity University was formed in Tehuacana in 1869 by the Presbyterian Church from resources of three Presbyterian colleges that did not survive the Civil War. The name refers to the Holy Trinity of Christianity—Father, Son and Holy Spirit. Trinity's campus later moved to Waxahachie, and in 1942 to the buildings of the former University of San Antonio/Westmoorland College on San Antonio's near west side. Its present campus on a bluff overlooking San Antonio, near what became the Monte Vista Historic District, was begun in 1950. Formal ties with the Presbyterian Church were dissolved in 1969 at the time of its centennial celebration.

Delavan Tennis Stadium Trinity's tennis stadium with 8 Laykold courts and 1,000 seats was completed in time to host the 84th NCAA Championships in 1968. The donor, George W. Delavan, was a local

Legendary coach Clarence Mabry with some of his players, including, far left, Trinity University Tennis Director Butch Newman.

developer whose other major contribution to the city was as one of four San Antonians who gave the original 200 acres to establish the South Texas Medical Center (Von Scheele Drive, p. 183). Delavan pioneered the first air-conditioned shopping mall (North Towne Plaza) in San Antonio in 1955, and developed several subdivisions including Dell View and Dell Crest.

Mabry Pavilion Dedicated in 2008, the Mabry Pavilion at Delavan Tennis Stadium honors the man who put San Antonio (and Trinity University) tennis on the map. As Tigers tennis coach from 1956 to 1974, Clarence Mabry, born in 1926, led his men's team to a Division I NCAA national championship in 1972. His induction into the San Antonio Sports Hall of Fame, the Trinity Hall of Fame and the U.S. Professional Tennis Association Hall of Fame acknowledge his stature in local and national tennis circles. Director of Trinity Tennis Butch Newman, a two-time All-American under Mabry, quotes his former coach as teaching him the principles of "S-A-T:" first be a person with spiritual values, then focus on academics and then tennis. Although Trinity downgraded its tennis program from Division I to Division III in 1990, the sport has continued to be pursued with excellence at the school. In 2000, both men's and women's teams captured Division III national championships.

E. M. Stevens Stadium When the campus was first moved to its present site in San Antonio, part of the master plan was an athletic complex. A track and football practice field was constructed in 1965, and seven years later, a 6,272-seat football stadium was built on the site. Both were given by E. M. Stevens, founder and chairman of Great Western Finance Company. A native of Kerrville, Stevens moved to San Antonio in 1919, graduated from Main Avenue High School and shortly there-

President James W. Laurie directed major growth at Trinity University.

after bought a loan company that was operating out of a single room. Over the next 43 years, he expanded the firm into 34 branch offices in 26 Texas cities.

Laurie Auditorium This is named for the president credited with the initial growth of the endowment and physical facilities of the skyline campus. James W. Laurie (1903–70), an ordained Presbyterian minister, became president in 1952 when there were two administrative/classroom buildings, one dormitory and an endowment of less than $1 million. When he retired in 1970, 42 new buildings had been erected and the endowment had reached nearly $50 million.

Margarite B. Parker Chapel This was designed, like the rest of the new campus, by architect O'Neil Ford. It was a gift in honor of Margarite Bright Parker by her husband, George Parker (1886–1965), a pioneer in the oil business in the southwest. Mrs. Parker served for more than 30 years on Trinity's board of trustees.

UNIVERSITY OF TEXAS AT SAN ANTONIO

Most streets on the UTSA campus are named for former members of the University of Texas board of regents.

Bartlett Cocke Drive Bartlett Cocke (1901–92) was one of San Antonio's eminent architects and engineers. His projects with O'Neil Ford (p. 79) created not only the UTSA campus but also master plans and buildings for Trinity University and the UT Health Science Center. He was the first University of Texas alumnus honored with a professorship in architecture in his name at the University of Texas at Austin.

Edward Ximenes Avenue A physician who practiced internal medicine in San Antonio for 45 years, Edward T. Ximenes (1915–92) was the first Latino on the board of regents. He was appointed in 1967 by Gov. John Connally, a former classmate in their hometown of Floresville and later at the University of Texas. Ximenes was instrumental in establishing the San Antonio campus and in creating scholarships at the school to help young Mexican Americans enter the field of medicine.

George Brackenridge Avenue George Brackenridge's commitment to education is outlined on page 70.

James Bauerle Boulevard An oral and maxillofacial surgeon in San Antonio since 1952, James E. Bauerle (1927–2007) graduated from the University of Texas in pharmacy and earned a dental degree before entering the Army during World War II. He served a term as president of the Texas Dental Association and was recognized by the Health Science Center for his role in the establishment of the Dental School in San Antonio in 1969. He was a regent of the University of Texas system from 1973 to 1979.

John Peace Boulevard   As a San Antonio attorney, John Peace (1917–74) was active in state Democratic politics and influential in John Connally's three races for governor. He was named a regent in 1967 and served as chairman from 1971 to 1973. Peace was a driving force behind creation of the University of Texas at San Antonio.

Margaret Tobin Avenue   The daughter of a former chairman of the board of regents, Margaret Lynn Batts Tobin (1900–89) was appointed a regent in 1947 and served until 1955. One of San Antonio's cultural leaders, she was instrumental in organizing a symphony orchestra in 1939 and establishing an opera series a few years later. In addition to other activities, she served as president of the McNay Art Museum trustees. Her husband, Edgar Tobin, founded a pioneer aerial survey company.

Marshall Hicks Drive   Marshall Hicks, born in 1865, had already accomplished much when he served briefly on the board of regents in 1923. Elected mayor of San Antonio in 1899 at 34, he served two terms before resigning to run for the state senate. During his tenure George Brackenridge deeded his large plot of land to the city for a park (p. 70). The other major achievement of his administration was bringing together the four independent streetcar lines into a single company.

O'Neil Ford Road   This street was named for the noted architect who designed much of the campus (p. 79).

Ransom Road   Harry Huntt Ransom (1908–76) joined the faculty of the University of Texas as an instructor in the English Department in 1935, and 26 years later he was named chancellor of the entire university system. A noted accomplishment of his administration was expanding library special collections to among the best in the world.

Thomas Devine Avenue   San Antonio city attorney, district judge, Confederate diplomat and Texas Supreme Court justice Thomas Jefferson Devine (p. 209) is unique among this group of names because he served on the board of regents before there was a state university, in 1881–82, when the university was in the planning stages. It formally opened in Austin on September 15, 1883.

Walter Brenan Avenue   A San Antonio attorney and longtime personal friend of Gov. Price Daniel, Walter "Spike" Brenan, who died in 1971, managed most of Daniel's statewide campaigns. Daniel appointed Brenan interim Bexar County judge and later to the board of regents, on which he served from 1961 to 1967. Most city maps misspell his name as "Brennan," but UTSA street signs spell it correctly.

University of the Incarnate Word

The Roman Catholic Sisters of Charity of the Incarnate Word originated in Lyons, France and first came in San Antonio in 1869, when the city was recovering from a cholera epidemic. That December 1 they opened the first hospital in the city, known then as Santa Rosa Infirmary (p. 158). In 1881 they chartered a college that enrolled its first students in 1910 on the present campus, purchased in 1897 from George Brackenridge (p. 70). Its **Academy of the Incarnate Word** evolved into **Incarnate Word High School** across U.S. 281 above the university campus. The name is from the opening verse of both the Gospel of John and the First Letter of John in the New Testament: Jesus is the Incarnate Word, or, in other words, the Word made flesh, God given a human form.

Dreeben School of Education Armed with a University of Texas degree and, later, with an executive MBA from Harvard, Alan Dreeben from Dallas married a San Antonio woman named Barbara Block, whose family started Block Distributing in 1939. Joining the business in the mid-1960s, Dreeben and his associates partnered with similar corporations throughout the United States to form Republic National Distributing, now the nation's second-largest wine and spirits distributor. Having a passion for education and wanting to give back to the community, the Dreebens endowed the University of the Incarnate Word's School of Education.

Feik School of Pharmacy In May 2010, UIW graduated the first class from its new school of pharmacy. Made possible through a gift from John Feik, born in 1946, his wife Rita and other donors, the school is located just west of the main campus. The son of a World War II fighter pilot, Feik earned degrees in both chemistry and finance at UT

Tom and Gayle Benson's New Orleans Saints finally won the Super Bowl in 2010.

Arlington through a work/scholarship program of the LTV Company. After a tour of military duty, Feik went to work for Alcon Laboratories, a pharmaceutical firm in Fort Worth, and by 29 had become president and general manager. In 1990 he created a pharmaceutical manufacturing company, DPT, whose major plant and research facilities are in San Antonio. DPT became a component of a larger holding company, DFB, an acronym for owners, Dorman, Feik and Burnett.

Gayle and Tom Benson Stadium When the University of the Incarnate Word decided to field a football team, an important factor was the contribution of Tom Benson, born in 1927, to build a stadium and field house. Although a resident of San Antonio, where he owns several car dealerships, Benson was born in New Orleans and is a passionate supporter of that city. He purchased the New Orleans Saints in 1985. Both owner and team went through tumultuous times before finally winning the 2010 Super Bowl, their first trip to the game in 43 years of the franchise. Benson became widely known for his "Benson Boogie" as he line-danced down the field carrying a black and gold umbrella , Mardi Gras style, in the closing minutes of a team victory.

Ursuline Academy

Founded in Italy in 1535, the Order of Saint Ursula is a Roman Catholic teaching order named for a 4th-century British princess reputed to have gone to Rome accompanied by 11,000 virgins but to have been killed with them by Huns at Cologne on their return. In 1851 seven sisters of the order arrived in San Antonio and established a school for girls on Augusta Street along the banks of the San Antonio River. The earliest building was designed by Francois P. Giraud (p. 11). The campus moved to Vance Jackson Road north of Loop 410 in 1965, but enrollment continued to decline. The school closed in 1992 and was sold, becoming Cornerstone School. The saga of the old campus is told in Maria Watson Pfeiffer's *School by the River: Ursuline Academy to Southwest School of Art and Craft, 1851–2001*.

The Winston School of San Antonio

The Winston School was established in 1985 as part of the Winston School in Dallas, became independent in 1989 and in 1998 opened its new campus in the South Texas Medical Center. Its mission is "to educate children with learning disabilities in an atmosphere that addresses their personal learning styles and promotes self-esteem." It is named for Winston Churchill (p. 101), who, apparently due to dyslexia, had difficulty in normal school environments.

· 5 ·
LIBRARIES, LEARNING CENTERS
AND MUSEUMS

LIBRARIES

Bannwolf Library at Reagan High School   Former councilman Tim Bannwolf came up with the idea of housing a public library branch in a high school library, saving taxpayers more than $3 million. Bannwolf, a commercial lending, real estate, and employment attorney, was District 9 councilman from 1997 to 2001, and has served on numerous boards. He holds a bachelor's degree in foreign service from Georgetown University, a law degree from the University of Texas, a master's from the LBJ School of Public Affairs at the University of Texas and a master's degree with honors from England's University of Lancaster. The branch library was named for him in 2006.

Bazan Branch Library   Isabel G. Bazan went to work for the city library soon after graduating from Our Lady of the Lake University in 1942. She soon became main library supervisor, staying in the position until her death in 1977. This branch is near her home in the Prospect Hill area.

Carver Branch Library   The first Carver library was in a small wooden building established by black army officers at Fort Sam Houston during World War I. The present building, dating from 1973, was built on donated land on East Commerce Street next to the Second Baptist Church. The name honors African American scientist George Washington Carver (1861?–1943). Born of slave parents in the early years of the Civil War, he was freed when he was 10 or 12 years old. Overcoming adversity to obtain a high school and college education, he became director of the Department of Agricultural Research at Tuskegee Normal and Industrial Institute (now Tuskegee University), where he developed hundreds of industrial uses for peanuts, sweet potatoes and soybeans. He also developed a new hybrid of cotton, taught soil improvement and during World War II produced textile dyes formerly imported from Europe. In 1940, he donated his life savings to establish Tuskegee's Carver Research Foundation.

Cody Branch Library   Land for this branch was donated by the Northside Independent School District, of which Edmund Cody, born in 1926, was superintendent for 17 years. A graduate of Jefferson High School who earned a master's degree from Trinity University, Cody was instrumental in promoting the community library system.

Collins Gardens Branch Library   Finis Foster Collins was a Confederate Army captain who settled in San Antonio where this branch stands. He traveled to cities and ranches throughout Texas and Mexico selling the windmills, pumps and tanks manufactured at his plant on Houston Street at the river. His Collins Gardens home and adjoining property south of downtown were donated to the city in 1917, and a branch library bearing his family name was built there.

Finis Collins and his wife on their golden wedding anniversary in 1916.

Cortez Branch Library   This was named for Raul Cortez, founder of the nation's first full-time Spanish-language radio and television station.

Guerra Branch Library   Not long after Henry A. Guerra Jr. (1918–2001) graduated from Central Catholic High School, he took a job with WOAI radio on two conditions: having a work schedule that allowed him to finish his degree at St. Mary's University and also the right to use his surname. He thus became the first Hispanic announcer to use his own name at a major English language radio station in Texas, his deep resonant voice being instantly recognizable. He later was the city's first Hispanic television

Henry Guerra's stirring "Thirteen Days of the Alamo" stories aired on WOAI Radio each spring.

announcer. Guerra became a beloved local historian. The most popular of his stories was "Thirteen Days of the Alamo," broadcast each spring. He considered himself neither Hispanic nor American, but a Tejano. In 1957 he help found the Mexican American Friendship Committee to strengthen business ties between the United States and Mexico.

Igo Branch Library   It would be hard to imagine a more appropriate person for whom to name a library in the northwest part of San Antonio. John Igo, born in 1927, has lived his entire life in this area. The library

is nestled on a 24-acre site once part of the Woller Ranch, home of his Bavarian stonemason ancestors who settled there more than 140 years ago. Location aside, his name is appropriate because he is a man of language and letters. With bachelor's and master's degrees from Trinity University, he taught at San Antonio College for 45 years, where he was known as a stickler for correct use of the English language. He had a radio talk show to answer questions about grammar. He is a poet—with 12 books to his credit—and playwright, having written 15 plays and also having been a producer, director and critic. In 1985 he received a special Emmy in 1985 for Linguistics, probably the only Emmy given in that category, to recognize his work on a documentary about effects of gang warfare on young children. He credits his parents with instilling in him a love of learning. As a San Antonio historian he generously shared with this author many fascinating stories about places and personalities for the first edition of this book, one of the stories being the origin of Tioga Drive (p. 44).

Longtime San Antonio College professor John Igo remains a stickler for correct grammar.

Johnston Branch Library   Leah Carter Johnston was the city's first children's librarian, establishing the library's children's department in 1922 and organizing the nation's first children's poetry competition in 1927. When she retired in 1955 she helped organize the Friends of the San Antonio Public Library.

Julia Yates Semmes Branch Library   This branch, opened in November 2005, ushered in a new concept in library design. The library is set within a park and is intended to blend in with its surroundings, including an outdoor classroom and hiking trails. It is named for Julia Yates Semmes (1904–2002), who grew up on a ranch in West Texas and had a lifelong love of reading. In the 1930s she served as president of the Women's Club of Santa Fe, which established and operated that city's public library. As she lost her sight late in life to macular degeneration, she made frequent use of large-print books and books on tape. She served as a director of Semmes Foundation, which donated funds for the construction of the

Library namesake Julia Yates Semmes as a young lady.

main library and for creation of an endowment to purchase materials for the visually impaired, as well as for site enhancements for this new branch library at Comanche Lookout Park on Judson Road. She was the widow of independent oil producer and businessman D. R. Semmes (p. 143).

Landa Branch Library   Within what is now the Monte Vista Historic District, this Mediterranean-style building was designed by Robert B. Kelly in 1928 as the home of New Braunfels textile magnate Harry Landa and his wife, Hannah Mansfeld Landa. They furnished it with treasures from their travels in Europe. After his wife's death, Landa gave the home as a library and children's playground in her memory. It opened in 1947.

Maverick Branch Library   Few felt neutral about Maury Maverick Jr. (1921–2003). Scion of one of San Antonio's oldest and most renowned families, Maverick was a study in contradictions. He was a proud marine veteran of World War II, but defended many mainly poor conscientious objectors during the Viet Nam war. As a congressman during the McCarthy era, he fought rampant Red-baiting, and as a lawyer later won several important civil rights victories. As a man of ideals and principles, champion of the underdog and iconoclast, he cared passionately for what he believed was right. Perhaps best known in San Antonio for the highly opinionated and polarizing newspaper column that he wrote in the Express-News for more than 20 years, his direct, in-your-face writing style evoked both praise and abuse. Maverick did indeed epitomize the family name as one who was a nonconformist (p. 154). An annual lecture series in his honor was inaugurated at Trinity University in 2008.

Library namesake Maury Maverick Jr., far left, watches as his father, Maury Sr., is sworn in as mayor in 1939 by his father, Albert Maverick Jr., who stands beside a portrait of his father, onetime mayor Samuel A. Maverick.

McCreless Branch Library   The land for this branch was donated by twin brothers G. S. and S. E. McCreless. They weighed three pounds each at birth, and their mother kept them warm in two shoeboxes on top of a wood-burning stove. They thrived, growing up to be highly successful businessmen (p. 154).

Parman Library at Stone Oak   As master developer of the entire Stone Oak area, Dan Parman, born in 1935, had a vision of what the north side of the city would one day look like, and eventually transformed a huge area of brush, stones and oaks into his dream. His path to becoming a developer took a circuitous route. Armed with a degree in math and physics from Texas A & I, he returned to his hometown of Uvalde and began to buy and fix up ranches and farms. When he discovered his cattle being shot and butchered on his property, he decided that a better use of the land might be to develop it, thus his first project was in Uvalde. He next began to build Gibson and Food City stores before focusing on northern San Antonio. In the 1970s, when Loop 1604 was a two lane farm-to-market road, he studied the northern spread of the city with serial aerial photographs and saw where it was heading. When the city lifted moratoriums on development over the Edwards Aquifer recharge zone, he entered into partnership with other investors to acquire some 9,000 acres. The first stage of development, in conjunction with Tom Turner (p. 171), was Sonterra. It is fitting that his role in this major expansion be remembered with the library named in his honor, to open in 2011.

Tobin Library at Oakwell   Oakwell Farms was the estate of Robert L. B. Tobin (p. 88). Property for the **Oakwell Branch Library** was donated in memory of his grandfather, Judge Robert Lynn Batts. Additional funding was provided by the estate of Elizabeth Evelyn Beike. In 2007 the Tobin Foundation augmented additional city funding for expansion, and the library reopened under its present name.

Westfall Branch Library   Once the city's busiest branch library, this first major branch was built on the north side in 1963 with funds created by a gift of 1,000 acres of farmland to the library in 1891. Edward Dixon Westfall (1820–97) came to San Antonio in 1845 and served in the war against Mexico. Later a Texas Ranger, he was known as a trail guide and Indian fighter. Westfall had little formal education but a passion for books, and he wanted to pass on to future generations his love of reading.

LEARNING AND COMMUNITY CENTERS

The city has several Learning and Leadership Development Centers, funded by a 1989 bond issue and managed under its Literacy Services Division. Under its Department of Community Initiatives, central facilities for private, federal, state and city agencies deliver a comprehensive program of recreational activities and social services.

Albert J. Benavides Learning and Leadership Development Center
A native of western San Antonio, the Rev. Albert Benavides rose to citywide prominence in the 1970s as a leader of Communities Organized for Public Service (COPS). The Catholic priest helped unite

and represent citizens of poor neighborhoods, demanding equal distribution of water and flood control. In 1984 he drowned in the Gulf of Mexico during a religious retreat, when, while swimming alone, a strong undertow pulled him from shore. Twelve years later this center was named in his honor.

Barbara Jordan Community Center   Barbara Jordan (1936–96) was born in a poor African American neighborhood in Houston. She began to develop her talent as an orator in high school, later leading her Texas Southern University debate team to a draw in competition against the Harvard University team. She was one of two black women among 600 graduates of Boston University's law school in 1959. After two unsuccessful campaigns for state office, in 1965 she won a landslide vote to become the first black woman elected to the Texas Senate, and in 1972 became the first black woman in Congress from the South. In 1976 she was the first African American woman to be keynote speaker at a Democratic national convention. Reelected to Congress twice, she retired to become a professor at the LBJ School of Public Affairs at the University of Texas at Austin.

Barbara Jordan was the first black woman elected to the Texas Senate.

Bob and Jeanne Billa Learning and Leadership Development Center   Affectionately known as "Mayor of the Southside," Bob Billa (1921–95) was an influential San Antonio city councilman and strong supporter of single-member districts. A graduate of Brackenridge High School, he was a fighter pilot in the Pacific during World War II and later one of the first to fly jets in Korea. His wife, Jeanne, was an Army Air Corps nurse. They met while both were in military service. She was active in the San Antonio Conservation Society and St. Margaret Mary Catholic Church. Their daughter, Lynda Billa Burke, later served as a city council member.

Carver Community Cultural Center   At the beginning of the twentieth century, the city public library system was segregated, and the governing board did not provide adequate library services for the African American community. The problem was addressed by the private sector, and in 1918 a new Colored Library Association built a community house and assembly building. A new facility built in 1929 was originally called the Colored Library Auditorium, but was renamed in honor of George Washington Carver (Carver Branch Library, p. 136) in 1938. For the next two decades many nationally acclaimed black musical artists performed at the Center. In 1973 library functions were moved to the new Carver Branch Library. Periodic additions and renovations kept the building in operation until 2000, when it closed for extensive remodeling. Re-opened four years later, it has resumed its role as an African American cultural, educational and social center. The building is listed in the National Register of Historic Places.

Claude Black Community Center   For 49 years, the Rev. Claude W. Black (1916–2009) used the pulpit of Mount Zion First Baptist Church to speak against racism and injustice. Returning to a still segregated San Antonio in 1943 after graduating from Morehouse College in Atlanta and Andover Newton Theological Seminary in Massachusetts, he began to speak out against civil rights abuses. Recognizing his power on the east side, the Good Government League tapped him as a candidate for city council. Black sought to work within the system, but split with the Good Government League and supported Charles Becker for mayor. Becker, in turn, appointed Black the city's first African American mayor pro tem. This center was named for him in 1993. He officially retired from his church in 1998, but continued to preach and champion civil rights until his death at the age of 92.

Sportswriter Dan Cook was also an early TV sportscaster.

Dan Cook Youth Center   Started in the basement of St. Mary's Catholic Church in 1984 and first called the Downtown Youth Center, this is one of six San Antonio youth centers providing a safety net for young people at risk. It was renamed in 2004 for the man who helped keep it alive financially for 20 years by hosting an annual golf tournament and by otherwise cajoling his many friends to contribute. Dan Cook (1926–2008) was for several decades the city's most recognized and best loved TV sportscaster and journalist. In 51 years with the San Antonio Express-News Cook racked up numerous awards and honors. He served twice as president of both the San Antonio Press Club and the Texas Sports Writer's Association, and in 1996 was among the second round of inductees into the San Antonio Sports Hall of Fame. With innumerable personal contacts in the sports world, Cook always seemed to have the inside "scoop" on all pending changes in the world of athletics. If he predicted something was going to happen, it usually did. He wrote with great humor but also with honesty and humility. If ever mistaken in the facts, which was rare, his apology and a correction were printed as soon as he knew the true story.

Davis-Scott YMCA As a founder and the only paid staff member of what was then called the Alamo Branch YMCA, Odie E. Davis, Jr. (1912–75) served as the executive director of the branch for 28 years. Dedicating his life to helping youth and families on the east side of San Antonio, Davis created the "36 Men's Club" to help finance the facility. Among board members was Dr. S. T. Scott (1914?–94), who raised more money than any other YMCA volunteer city-wide. Before becoming assistant superintendent of the San Antonio ISD, Scott was principal of Douglass Junior High School and Wheatley High School (p. 125). The current executive director of this branch is Odie's son Nathaniel, who came on staff shortly after his graduation from college to carry on the work started by his father.

Dorie Miller Community Center On December 7, 1941, Dorie Miller, a Waco native and high school football star, was a cook on the battleship USS West Virginia, lying at anchor in Pearl Harbor. For heroism during the Japanese attack, Miller was presented the Navy Cross by Admiral Chester Nimitz. Miller died later when his ship was sunk by a Japanese submarine. He is played by Cuba Gooding Jr. in the movie Pearl Harbor. Family members say that his given name was Doris, but apparently he went by Dorie because Doris was considered too feminine for a sailor.

Adm. Chester Nimitz pins the Navy Cross on Dorie Miller for heroism during the attack on Pearl Harbor.

D. R. Semmes YMCA The YMCA's downtown branch is named for Douglas Ramsay Semmes (1892–1976), born in Virginia and the son of an Episcopal clergyman. Earning a Ph.D. in Geology from Columbia University, he became a professor, author, Sarnosa Oil Corporation president and international consulting geologist. In 1952 he established the Semmes Foundation, which supports charitable organizations including the YMCA.

D. R. Semmes was a geologist, oilman and philanthropist.

Dr. Frank Bryant Health Center Elected as the first African American president of the Bexar County Medical Society in 1986, Frank Bryant (1930–99) served as a role model and inspiration for many younger physicians. Among others, he urged a young woman physician, Dianna Burns, to become involved in organized medicine, and in 2005 she became the first black woman to be elected to that same office. Bryant was co-founder and first medical director of the Ella Austin Health Clinic, and devoted his career to helping economically struggling families get medical care. As a trustee and chairman of the City Public Service Board, his priority was to insure that CPS workers had suitable training and health-care benefits. Opened in 2005 as part of CommuniCare Health Centers, the Bryant facility's major goal is to serve uninsured patients on the city's east side.

Ella Austin Community Center   Although this facility has been in existence for more than 100 years, the woman whose name it bears remains for the most part a mystery. Ella Austin (1856–1902?) was an African American who apparently enlisted the help of the Women's Progressive Club to found a home for orphans in 1897, but virtually nothing is known of the person herself. Her photo does appear on the center's Website, but the accompanying biography is a single sentence. Said variously to be the wife of a barber or a physician, Austin's personal story was perhaps lost when office files were burglarized in 1979. The children's home was converted into a multi-purpose community center in 1968, and despite a somewhat turbulent political history continues to provide a variety of social services on the city's near east side.

Enrique M. Barrera Community Center   The large building that houses this center was once the Levi Strauss sewing plant, where some 800 employees produced four million pair of jeans annually for 27 years. When the plant closed in 2004, the city bought the buildings and 58.9 acres to accommodate this community center and the Operations Headquarters of the City Parks and Recreation Department, named in honor of longtime director Ronald R. Darner. Enrique M. Barrera (1937–2006) was a city councilman from 2000 to 2005, an ordained deacon at San Fernando Cathedral and a board member of the Edgewood Independent School District, Bexar County Mental Health and San Antonio Development Agency.

Frank Garrett Center   Frank Garrett, born in 1917, was a multiposition player for the San Antonio Black Sox, an all-black semiprofessional baseball team, in the 1950s and 60s. As a Parks and Recreation Department employee for 47 years, Garrett directed the West End Multi-Service Center from 1940 to 1987. There, he said, "my job was to teach the kids. Those kids needed a friend, a father, everything."

George Gervin Youth Center   The "Iceman" was the San Antonio Spurs' first true superstar. Given that nickname because of his unflappable demeanor under pressure and the matchless grace of his movements on the floor, George Gervin, born in (1952, started his professional basketball career in the old ABA, but his glory years were during the decade that he played for the Spurs, 1974–85. Known primarily for his offensive shooting skills and his trademark "finger roll," he spent countless nights practicing shots in his high school gymnasium in Detroit after barely making the JV team as a sophomore. Both his college (Eastern Michigan University, where he was an All-American) and the Spurs (where he was a 12-time consecutive All-Star) retired his number. He founded the George Gervin Youth Center in 1989 as a non-profit organization focusing on the development of disadvantaged at-risk youth. The center provides vocational training, remedial education, mentoring, tutoring, job placement and supportive services.

"Iceman" George Gervin was known for his soft touch with a basketball.

Margarita R. Huantes Learning and Leadership Development Center Born in Mexico, raised on San Antonio's west side and an honor graduate of the University of Texas at Austin, Margarita R. Huantes (1914–1994), founder of the San Antonio Literacy Council, devoted her life to literacy before it was popular after learning a neighborhood baby had died because the mother could not read the label on the medicine bottle.

Mays Family YMCA Unlike most YMCA facilities with indoor gymnasiums, this complex in far north San Antonio focuses on such outdoor activities as soccer, baseball and softball. Made possible through a donation from Lowry and Peggy Mays, the athletic fields on this 46-acre site are carved into the rolling hills. Lowry Mays, born in 1935, was an investment banker in 1972 when he founded the San Antonio Broadcasting Company with the purchase of a single radio station. Later changing the name to Clear Channel Communications, the company grew to become the largest radio station owner in the country, with more than 1,200 radio stations, television stations, outdoor advertising displays and a live entertainment company, operating in 63 countries and having more than 50,000 employees. Mays has served as chairman of the Board of Regents of Texas A & M University, where he obtained a degree in Petroleum Engineering, and as a board member of the Harvard Business School, where he received his MBA.

Virginia Gill Community Center Originally called Lackland Terrace, the name was changed in 2003 by a vote of the Lackland

Terrace Neighborhood Association to honor Virginia Gill, who had been president of the organization. A Michigan native, she was a former teacher and member of the state PTA Board. She served in the military and was at one time stationed at Lackland Air Force Base.

Virginia Marie Granados Community Center and Park The property for this adult and senior citizen center was donated by the Granados family in 2003 and named in memory of Virginia Marie Granados, who died in 1990 and lived one mile north of the park. The five-acre estate was originally owned by the Gillespie family, but was purchased by Virginia Marie's youngest son Mark in 2000 and donated to the city. Mrs. Granados, a San Antonio native, was a city police officer until she started raising her three sons, at which time she became secretary for Whittier Middle School, Lee High School and the San Antonio Independent School District.

William C. Velasquez Learning and Leadership Development Center In 1995, Jane Velasquez stood in the East Room of the White House to accept the Presidential Medal of Freedom on behalf of her late husband, civil rights advocate C. "Willie" Velasquez, who died in 1988, the first San Antonian and one of few Hispanics to receive the award. During the ceremony, President Clinton said, "Willie is now a name synonymous with democracy in America," quoting Velasquez's appeal to the Hispanic community: "Su voto es su voz"—"your vote is your voice." A graduate of Central Catholic High School and St. Mary's University, Velasquez founded the Southwest Voter Registration Education Project in 1974 and founded the Southwest Voter Research Institute in 1986.

MUSEUMS

McNay Art Museum Marion Koogler McNay (1883–1950) was the only child of Dr. and Mrs. Marion Koogler. Dr. Koogler, an Ohio physician, lived frugally, using income from his medical practice to acquire land on which to grow bluestem, the best native grazing grass for cattle. She went to the Art Institute of Chicago in 1902 and in 1917 married Don McNay. Her father's wedding present was 160 acres of land he had purchased in Kansas, by then producing oil. Ten months later Don McNay died at an Army camp in Florida during the flu epidemic. Their final days together had been spent at the Menger Hotel. She last saw him as his company assembled at the Alamo for the march to the railroad station. Each time after her four later marriages ended in divorce she reverted to the name of her first husband. In 1927, while married to her third husband, San Antonio ophthalmologist Donald Taylor Atkinson, McNay began her dream house, Sunset Hills. An artist in her own right, she was involved with architect Atlee B. Ayres in the design and building of the home as she continued to collect art. In 1942 her friend Ellen Quillin (Witte Museum, below) convinced her that Sunset Hills would be an ideal location for a fine arts museum. Mrs. McNay provided for that in her will, and it became the McNay Art Institute—later the McNay Art Museum—after her death in 1950. It was the first museum of modern art in Texas.

Marion Koogler McNay at her home, which became the state's first museum of modern art.

Steves Homestead Museum This elegant King William Street mansion was built by Eduard (Edward) Steves (1829–90) in 1876 and was the family home until 1952, when it was donated to the San Antonio Conservation Society to become a house museum. Steves came to Texas from Germany in 1849 and worked with his father establishing a farm in New Braunfels. He settled in Comfort in 1854, cleared 160 acres and developed a business threshing neighbors' crops and hauling the wheat to Eagle Pass. After the Civil war, Eduard and his wife, Johanna, sold their possessions and eventually built their home near the end of the fashionable King William Street in San Antonio. Having been trained as a carpenter, with his savings Steves started a lumberyard that became known as Steves and Sons. The bulk of his fortune came from local land investment and development. After retiring in 1880 he was active in civic improvements, including paving Commerce Street with mesquite blocks and burying power and telegraph lines to eliminate poles.

Witte Memorial Museum Ellen Dorothy Schulz Quillin (1892–1970), head of the science department at Main Avenue High School, saw the need for a city museum. She convinced Mayor John Tobin to donate city land and $75,000. Originally intended for San Pedro Park, the site was changed in 1926 when Alfred G. Witte left a $65,000 bequest for a museum with stipulations that it be built in Brackenridge Park and named in honor of his father and mother. "Ellen D" served as director for 34 years at the salary of one dollar per year, and wrote books and articles on botany. The museum focuses on natural history, anthropology and Texas and regional his-

Alfred G. Witte left a bequest for a museum named in honor of his parents.

tory, much of it interpreted in buildings moved and reconstructed on the grounds.

Celso Navarro House   Celso Navarro, born in 1830, was the son of José Antonio Navarro (p. 16). In 1947 his home on Camaron Street was to be torn down for expansion of Fox Tech's athletic fields. It was saved from a bulldozer literally at the last minute.

Ruiz House   This building originally stood on the south side of Military Plaza in downtown San Antonio. Early in the nineteenth century it housed the city's first public school, with José Francisco Ruiz (c.1804–76) the first schoolmaster. It was moved and reconstructed in 1943 at the Witte.

Twohig House   In 1941, the century-old home of Irish merchant and banker John Twohig on the banks of the San Antonio River was rescued before it was to be torn down. Irishman John Twohig (1806–91) established a mercantile business in San Antonio in 1830. When the city was invaded by Mexican troops in 1842, he blew up his store to deny ammunition to the enemy—after opening the doors to the poor to help themselves. He returned from imprisonment in Mexico, became a wealthy banker and built one of the first two-story houses in the city. Although he and his wife entertained lavishly, he also created what was thought to be the first bread line in America. It was his custom for many years to have women of poor families come to his home to receive large loaves of bread, which he gave in abundance.

Yturri-Edmunds Museum   Adjacent to Mission Concepción, the name of this museum honors a venerable old San Antonio family. Manuel Yturri Castillo, who died in 1843, was born into an aristocratic Spanish family but as a young man immigrated to Mexico, where he worked for prominent merchants. He was sent to San Antonio to represent the business and was awarded a land grant from the Mexican government in 1824. His daughter Vicenta married Ernest B. Edmunds in 1861, and they built a house adjacent to a grist mill owned by her father. This homestead, which now houses the museum, was willed to the San Antonio Conservation Society by their daughter, longtime teacher Ernestine E. Edmunds. The first Manuel and his wife died when their eldest son Manuel II was quite young, and much of the son's early training was under the supervision of William and James Vance (p. 19).

· 6 ·
LANDMARK BUILDINGS

The Argyle In about 1859 Kentuckian Charles Anderson erected a house on a bluff above Olmos Basin as headquarters for his 1,400-acre horse ranch. Anderson, whose brother commanded Fort Sumter at the outbreak of the Civil War, remained loyal to the Union and in 1861 was forced to sell his ranch and leave Texas. In 1890 it was purchased by the Denver-based Alamo Heights Land and Improvement

The Argyle in 1909, shortly after its front portico was added.

Company (p. 190) and became a hotel, named the Argyle by company principal J. W. Ballantyne Patterson; the surrounding bluffs reminded him of Argyleshire in his native Scotland. In 1893 the hotel was purchased by Robert O'Grady, who added the two-story front columns in 1907. O'Grady was elected the first mayor of Alamo Heights in 1922 after citizens meeting on the Argyle's front lawn organized the city. His sister, Alice O'Grady, later managed the hotel. It was purchased in 1955 by the Southwest Foundation for Research and Education, which operates it as a private club benefiting the foundation.

Brady Building On Houston Street near the corner of St. Mary's Street, the four-story "Little Brady" Building is sandwiched between the Majestic and Empire theaters. Expansion of the Majestic's stage into a 25-foot section of the Brady Building was made possible when the Brady Building was purchased in 1995 by a joint venture of the City of San Antonio, the nonprofit Las Casas Foundation and Arts Center Enterprises, which manages the properties. Following renovation of the 2,300-seat Majestic and 900-seat Empire, it became the traffic center and central storage facility for both. It is referred to as the "Little Brady" Building because beside it on the corner is the eight-story Brady Tower, both among the properties owned by Dublin-born Thomas F. Brady (1836–1923), who came to New York at the age of nine and in 1866 ended up in San Antonio. Here he established the first agency of the

Aetna Life Insurance Company and was among the first to drill artesian wells. His daughter helped fund the Brady-Green Clinic.

Brady-Green Clinic   West of the intersection of interstates 10 and 35 just north of downtown is a beige five-story building, for many years the city-county hospital. Opened in 1917 and named in honor of Robert Berrien Green (1865–1907), it was the primary hospital for the care of indigent patients until Bexar County Hospital was built in the Medical Center in 1968. Elected a district judge at the age of 28 and later county judge, he was chosen state senator in 1906 but died the following year at the age of 42. He was called the "incorruptible judge" for his uncompromising honesty and integrity. He urged creation of a charity hospital for the city, though this was not built until ten years after his death. His wife was Rena Maverick Green (1874–1962), granddaughter of Samuel A. and Mary Maverick (p. 154), an artist, women's rights leader and a founder of the San Antonio Conservation Society. Now an outpatient facility for the University of Texas at San Antonio health care system, it has been the Brady-Green Clinic since the early 1970s, when a clinic was built adjacent to the renovated hospital with a bequest from Lady Patricia Brady. She got her unusual first name when her father (p. 149), believing she would never hold a title of her own, gave her one at birth. Never married, she loved theater and contributed to local productions. As she sat daily by the bedside of an employee at the Robert B. Green Hospital in 1965, she is said to have been so impressed with the care that she gave a substantial portion of her estate to the hospital.

Cadena-Reeves Justice Center   In June 2002, a new justice center for Bexar County was dedicated in honor of two former chief justices of the 4th Court of Appeals. Carlos C. Cadena (1917–2001) is remembered as a brilliant attorney and judge with a tenacity for truth and honesty

and also as a caring, gentle, and self-effacing man. Following his graduation summa cum laude from the University of Texas Law School, he served as San Antonio's city attorney, maintained a private practice, taught as a professor of law at St. Mary's University and served for 25 years on the Fourth Court of Appeals. His strong principles are spelled out in the guiding philosophy he formulated for the school of law, which is reprinted on the front pages of the Law School Bulletin. His greatest legacy was as a champion of the civil rights movement that helped end segregation in Texas. In 1954 he won a case before the U.S. Supreme Court that struck down re-

Carlos Cadena was a champion of civil rights.

strictions barring Hispanics from serving on juries (see Gus Garcia p. 93). Other cases he won helped lessen discrimination against Mexican-American children in Texas public schools and to eliminate restrictive covenants prohibiting the sale of property to Mexican-Americans. Blair "Bruzzie" Reeves (1925–97) spent more than 50 years in a wheelchair, the result of a World War II injury that left him paraplegic. After the war he earned a law degree and eventually became chief justice of the Fourth Court of Appeals, where he earned the reputation of integrity, unfailing cheerfulness, a passion for clean, efficient government and a deep desire to help the underprivileged (see page 178).

Charline McCombs Empire Theater

Acquisition of the Brady Building made possible the restoration of the Empire Theater, but financing came from the nonprofit Las Casas Foundation led by Jocelyn Straus. The foundation raised nearly $5 million, $1 million coming as a gift of B. J. "Red" and Charline McCombs, listed by Texas Monthly as among "The Most Generous Texans." Auto magnate McCombs, at one time majority owner of the San Antonio Spurs (p.170), the Minnesota Vikings football team and other ventures. He is the namesake of the University of Texas at Austin's McCombs School of Business.

Charline and Red McCombs were major donors for restoration of the Empire Theater.

Dullnig Building George Dullnig was listed by the San Antonio Light in 1886 as one of the city's leading capitalists. An immigrant from Austria, he started a grocery store in 1863 that developed into a large wholesale and retail business. He also founded the Alamo National Bank and helped establish the San Antonio and Gulf Railroad. The three-story brick building that still bears Dullnig's name was constructed in 1883 where Losoya and Alamo streets meet at Commerce Street. One of its picturesque cupolas was removed when the building was cut back for the widening of Alamo Street, and the other was removed years later as the building declined. Restored, its upper floors are now the Riverwalk Vistas bed-and-breakfast, while street level tenants include McDonald's.

Emily Morgan Hotel Originally the Medical Arts office building when built in the 1920s, the Emily Morgan Hotel is just north of the Alamo. Its name represents an entertaining Texas myth. Emily Morgan, the "Yellow Rose of Texas," is said to have kept Gen. Santa Anna occupied in his quarters as Sam Houston's troops surprised and routed the Mexican Army at the Battle of San Jacinto. The legend of Emily Morgan, however, appears to have been based on Emily D. West, a free black born in New Haven, Connecticut, who signed on as a hotel housekeeper with Col. James Morgan on Galveston Bay. When seized along with others by Mexican troops, it was apparently assumed that because of her mulatto skin she was a slave. She was taken to Santa Anna's encampment at Buffalo Bayou about 10 miles away. Santa Anna is said to have had a penchant for expensive surroundings and beautiful women, so historians say it is possible that he added Emily to his entourage but unlikely that she kept the general in his tent as part of a planned military operation. The legend appears to have grown out of an overheard conversation recorded in the diary of a traveling Englishman. The folksong "Yellow Rose of Texas" was first published about 1838.

Frost Bank   The founder of this financial dynasty took a circuitous route to the banking business. Thomas Claiborne Frost's (1833–1903) first job in Texas was an assistant professor of Latin at Austin College in Huntsville, Texas in 1854. He studied law and passed the bar. At the outbreak of the Civil War he was a member of the Secession Committee and later served as a lieutenant colonel in the Confederate army. After the war, because he had been a Confederate officer he was not allowed to resume his law practice. Joining his brother and another partner, he went into the freight, mercantile and auction business, and later added a wool commission enterprise. He established the practice of storing local wool producers' goods until market conditions were favorable, and made loans as a convenience to his customers. This led him to abandon his wool commission business and concentrate solely on banking, and the Frost National Bank received its national charter in 1899.

T. C. Frost expanded his mercantile business into a banking enterprise.

G. J. Sutton State Office Building   In 1972, Garlington Jerome Sutton (1909–76) became the first black elected to state government from San Antonio. When he died, his wife, Lou Nelle Callahan Sutton, succeeded him, the first woman to represent Bexar County in the legislature. It was his idea for the state to buy the abandoned east side buildings of the San Antonio Machine and Supply Company to revitalize the neighborhood. His father, Samuel J. Sutton, was one of the first black teachers in San Antonio, serving as principal of three high schools during his 53-year career. His wife, Lillian Viola Sutton, was also a teacher. All 12 of their 15 children who survived to adulthood earned college degrees. Four daughters were prominent teachers and a fifth was the first woman graduate of Howard University Medical School. One son was an inventor. Son A. C. worked for many years with disadvantaged youth from the eastside, Oliver Carter was a judge on the New York Supreme Court and Percy was president of New York's Borough of Manhattan.

Gunter Hotel   When it opened at the main downtown corner of St. Mary's and Houston streets on November 20, 1909, the Gunter was said to have been the most modern hotel between New Orleans and Los Angeles. On the site stood the first U.S. military headquarters in Texas, from 1861 to 1865 headquarters for the Confederate Army in Texas. After the Civil War, it was converted into a hotel known as the Vance House (p. 19). In 1886 Ludwig A. Mahncke (p. 79) and Lesher A. Trexler took over and renamed it the Mahncke Hotel. Jot Gunter, a Texas political power broker who came to San Antonio in 1902 after a career in cattle and real estate in North Texas, was the major financial backer of the new hotel, though he died two years before its completion.

Henry B. Gonzalez Convention Center   San Antonio's ever-expanding downtown convention center is named for one of its most enduring public servants. After starting in city politics as a councilman in 1953, Henry B. Gonzalez became the first Hispanic elected to the Texas Senate and in 1961 the first Hispanic congressman from Texas. He was a champion of minorities and a staunch defender of federal employees in San Antonio. Considered quixotic because of his passion for lone wolf crusades, "Henry B" lived by his values and principles. Lyndon Johnson once said, "Henry's for the people." He was chairman of the House Banking Committee during the savings and loan crisis of the 1970s. He retired from the House in 1998, and his congressional seat was won by his son Charles. He died in 2000.

In 1961 Henry B. Gonzalez became the first Hispanic congressman from Texas.

Jesse James Leija Gym   Located just east of Christus Santa Rosa downtown, this gymnasium was built before World War II and dedicated by the Catholic Church on December 3, 1950. In the mid-1970s the Archdiocese of San Antonio donated it to the city, and the gym is managed by the Parks and Recreation Department. Although there is a full-sized basketball court on the second floor, it is the first floor boxing training facility for which the gym is best known, and where many local boxers trained. James Leija was born in 1966 into a boxing family—his father Jesse was the first San Antonian to reach the national Golden Gloves finals—but his parents would not let him start boxing until he graduated from Harlandale High School. His middle name was added later, partly in honor of his father and grandfather and partly as a marketing ploy. He won world championships in three weight divisions during his 16 -year career, long for a boxer. San Fernando Gym was renamed in his honor by city council in 2006.

Brothers Joe Freeman, left, and Harry with rodeo entertainer Judy Lynn.

Joe and Harry Freeman Coliseum Joseph Freeman (1885–1971) had a dream—to build a huge coliseum for rodeos and also provide space for exhibitions of livestock by young people. Although small in stature, he was highly respected, and his efforts were a major force in bringing the Bexar County Coliseum to reality in 1949. The name was changed to Joe Freeman Coliseum in 1958 and, when Joe's younger brother Harry (1889–1985) died, to Joe and Harry Freeman Coliseum. The brothers' partnerships involved an automobile dealership, oil drilling, ranching, cotton exporting, pecan-shelling, show horse exhibitions, even promoting Siamese twins who toured the world as a singing act. Harry once said, "We were in everything except undertaking." In addition to quietly giving scholarship aid to college students, they supported numerous local charities.

John H. Wood Federal Courthouse Built as the United States Pavilion for HemisFair '68, it was later converted to the federal courthouse and named for the federal judge who was gunned down by an assassin in his own driveway (p. 107).

Maverick Building This plain-looking building at North Presa and Houston streets was intended to be 21 stories, so planned top-story architectural embellishments were not in place when construction stopped at nine stories in 1922. Builder was the estate of George Madison Maverick (1845–1913), who on the site had constructed a two-story headquarters for the U.S. Army that he later remodeled as the French Second-Empire-style Maverick Hotel. The Maverick Building occupies the eastern part of the site of the hotel, razed when North Presa Street was extended to meet Houston Street. At the southwest corner of Houston and St. Mary's streets, one of George Maverick's commercial buildings, built in 1898 and designed by Alfred Giles, has been restored as the George Maverick Building, part of the Valencia

Hotel complex. These are not to be confused with the Victorian two-story Albert Maverick Building, built on Houston Street to the north and east by George's brother Albert (1854–1947) and restored in 1983. Their father was Samuel A. Maverick (1803–70), Texas Declaration of Independence signer and lawyer/landholder whose name came into the English language when his unbranded cattle kept on an island in Matagorda Bay wandered ashore during low tide and were identified as "Maverick's." Their mother was diarist Mary Adams Maverick (1818–98). Albert's youngest son was San Antonio's reform mayor and congressman Maury Maverick (p. 78).

Maverick-Carter House   Tucked behind mesquite trees near Municipal Auditorium, this three-story limestone house was designed by Alfred Giles and built in 1893 by William H. Maverick (1847–1923), one of Samuel Maverick's sons (above). A real estate developer who traveled extensively, he filled the home with fine art and lavish furnishings from Europe. The house was sold in 1914 to attorney Henry C. Carter, whose wife, Aline, was poet laureate of Texas from 1947 to 1949. In the 1930s Mrs. Carter, a devout Episcopalian, remodeled its library into a chapel with stained-glass windows and added a landmark domed observatory above the ballroom. Their son David restored the house and moved his law practice there.

McCreless Shopping City   Although it never reached the magnitude imagined by its developer, Gordon Sealie McCreless, "Big M City" was state of the art when it was completed in 1962. G. S. McCreless was also one of four owners of the original 200-acre Oak Hills site donated to start the South Texas Medical Center (p. 173). Co-developer on the project was his twin brother, Sollie Emmett McCreless, who founded the American Security Life Insurance Company. As a divinity student at Perkins School of Theology in Dallas, S. E. McCreless sold life insurance part-time, and learned of a new concept called prepaid hospitalization insurance used at Baylor Hospital. When he returned home in the early 1930s, McCreless used this forerunner of Blue Cross as his model to create a similar type of insurance in San Antonio. His wife Lilla was the first actuary for the company. She later served as secretary of the board of Southwest Texas Methodist Hospital. Among their many civic contributions, the McCreless brothers donated land for a branch library (p. 139). It is now known as **McCreless Mall**.

Menger Hotel   Arriving from Germany at the age of 20, William A. Menger (1827–71) built the first brewery in San Antonio—and Texas—in 1855. Hops and malts came from Germany to New York, by boat to Indianola and by wagon to San Antonio. To house customers from New Braunfels, Seguin and Fredericksburg, Menger in 1859

William A. Menger built the Menger Hotel.

built a hotel on the brewery's site. It soon began to attract the rich and famous. Capt. Richard King, founder of the King Ranch, lived and died in the suite that now bears his name. Theodore Roosevelt recruited his Rough Riders in the hotel bar.

Menger Soap Works   In 1847, Johann Nicholaus Simon Menger, a teacher, came to Castroville from Germany as one of Henri Castro's colonists (p. 211). Shortly afterward he moved to San Antonio, where he is said to have become the city's first music teacher. Until his death at 85 he played a major role not only in teaching music but also in organizing singing clubs. In 1850 Menger established a soap and candle factory near the present-day Santa Rosa Hospital on the banks of San Pedro Creek, called the Menger Soap Works, believed to be the first industry in San Antonio. The surviving limestone building, with its tall windows to aid ventilation, was restored in the 1980s as offices for the adjacent **Soap Works Apartments**.

County Judge Nelson Wolff donned a Yankees cap to visit with Yankees star Darryl Strawberry.

Nelson Wolff Municipal Stadium Built in 1994 as Municipal Stadium for the San Antonio Missions baseball team, this was renamed the following year for Mayor Nelson W. Wolff, an avid ballplayer whose family built and sold the Alamo Enterprises building materials chain and Sun Harvest Natural Food Stores. Wolff was active in the upgrading of St. Mary's University's V. J. Keefe Field in 1968, but minor league baseball in San Antonio finally outgrew it. When elected mayor in 1991 he started looking for a new ballpark site. The Levi Strauss Company sold adjacent land on U.S. 90 near Kelly Air Force Base and the city built the stadium. Its twin towers resemble the old Mission Stadium, built by the St. Louis Browns in 1947, used by the San Antonio team until 1968 and torn down in 1974. City council named the facility in honor of Wolff the week before he left office in 1995. He became Bexar County Judge in 2001.

Nix Medical Center   Built downtown beside the San Antonio River in 1930 as a combination medical office building, hospital and parking garage, the Nix was named by and for its builder, J. M. Nix (1866–1932), a local businessman and real estate developer. Nix died a year and a half after the building was completed, and its management was assumed by his brother, Joe J. Nix.

Norton-Polk-Mathis House This home at 401 King William Street was built in 1876 by hardware merchant Russel C. Norton, enlarged by stockman Edwin Polk in 1881 and then sold to a succession of owners. Walter Nold Mathis (1919–2005) restored the mansion to its original elegance. Shortly after his graduation from the University of Texas, on the morning after Pearl Harbor, Mathis enlisted in the Army Air Corps and became a highly decorated B-26 pilot, with 65 combat missions. After the war he returned to San Antonio and started his successful career as an investment banker. When he purchased this house in 1967, the King William area was in a state of severe decline. He not only spent 18 months renovating the house, but also purchased 14 more homes and sold them to people who would do similar restorations. A descendant of San Antonio's first mayor, John W. Smith (Smith Park, p. 88), he served as the first chairman of the San Antonio River Walk Commission. Asserting he would take on no more preservation projects personally, Mathis named his home Villa Finale and willed it to the National Trust for Historic Preservation. After further restoration, it opened to the public in September 2010, the first National Trust property in Texas.

Walter Mathis flew 65 combat missions in World War II.

Peacock Center The Salvation Army's San Antonio headquarters on the near west side includes the Peacock Center, Peacock Boys and Girls Club and Peacock Village, a girls' home. It incorporates the former **Peacock Military Academy**, one of the first private preparatory boarding and day schools for boys in Texas. Known as the **Peacock School for Boys** when founded in 1894 by Wesley Peacock (1865–1941), the name was changed in 1900 when military training was added. It became known as the West Point of Texas because of its rigid military and academic standards. The football coach in 1915 was a second lieutenant at Fort Sam Houston, Dwight David Eisenhower (p. 102). In 1926 Col. Wesley Peacock Jr. became superintendent and Col. Donald W. Peacock became commandant of cadets. When the school closed in 1973 the 20 acres and 15 buildings were deeded to the Salvation Army. Wesley Peacock Sr.'s two-story home, built in 1890, has been restored and designated a state historic landmark.

Pearl Brewery   In 1883 San Antonio was introduced to a new beer called City Pearl, first brewed in Bremen, Germany and given that name by a brew master who thought the foamy bubbles in a freshly-poured glass resembled sparkling pearls. The most important person in the company's history, Otto Koehler (p. 99) became president and manager in 1902. During Prohibition, Pearl changed its operations and name to Alamo Industries, and under the leadership of Otto's wife Emma not only survived the dry years but also was well positioned to revert to beer brewing when Prohibition ended in 1933. That, of course, was during the Depression, and Emma also skillfully guided the company through those difficult times. In 1985 Pearl's parent company purchased the Pabst Brewing Company. In a twist of irony, Pabst shut down the San Antonio brewery in 2001. A year later, the 14-acre property was bought by Christopher "Kit" Goldsbury (p. 159). Since then there has been a meticulous renovation, restoration and renewal of the old brewery. One of the first major tenants (in 2007) was the Culinary Institute of America, which at Pearl opened its third campus, this one to concentrate on Latin American cuisine. In addition to entertainment venues, an abundance of office and retail space is in the Full Goods Building. With addition of a weekly Farmers' Market and other activities, plus becoming the northern terminus for the extension of the River Walk, the Pearl Brewery promises to become increasingly active in San Antonio business and entertainment life.

Quarry Market   The tall smokestacks towering over this shopping center are a lasting reminder of the Alamo Cement Company's longtime presence. Alamo Cement's home since 1880 became part of Brackenridge Park in 1908, when the company gained a new source of rock and a rail link by moving north to a 450-acre site three miles beyond the end of the streetcar line. But in 1985 civilization caught up with the company again, and it moved to an even larger facility beyond Loop 1604. The large hole left was developed by the Lincoln Heights Development Company as the **Quarry Golf Course**, the rim of the crater lined with luxury homes. Razed for the larger **Lincoln Heights** development was the rest of Cementville, San Antonio Portland Cement's company town of 91 three-room cottages rented to its workers. The close-knit community of predominantly Mexican-American families had its own swimming pool, clinic, assembly hall and recreation facilities. They and streets named for early employees—**Robles, Pena, Ortiz, Ponce**—have disappeared beneath the redevelopment of upscale homes, shops, restaurants, Alamo Heights Methodist Church and commercial properties in the area.

Retama Park   After a 50-year absence, pari-mutuel betting was legalized in Texas in 1987. It didn't take long for horseracing to re-emerge. In 1989, the Retama Park Association was formed and purchased an option to buy the 488-acre **Retama Polo Center.** With private financing and additional funding from the sale of tax-exempt municipal bonds, the site later moved from the polo property to its now familiar location adjacent to IH-35 in Selma. Racetrack construction began in 1994, and the inaugural racing season was held in August 1995. After emerging from bankruptcy in 1997, the track has gradually increased its profits, aided by simulcasting such other horse races as the Kentucky Derby and dog racing in Corpus Christi. The name comes from the original 1880 Retama Ranch, in turn named for the deciduous shrub native to Mexico and the Rio Grande Valley, well adapted to drought and intense sun and adorned with fragrant, bright yellow flowers and needle-sharp thorns.

Robert Thompson Transit Station Visitors to the Alamodome will notice this name on the main hub of activity for VIA buses there. After finishing his military service at Lackland AFB in 1963, Robert Thompson (1939–93) went to work as a bus driver for the city and became active in the Amalgamated Transit Union. As its president and business agent for 16 years, his major efforts were to secure improved wages, benefits and working conditions. His most important victory was obtaining time-and-a-half overtime pay. Although it took nine years, the Supreme Court finally ruled in the union's favor, giving public employees a benefit already enjoyed by workers in the private sector. Thompson died of cancer in 1993, the year that the transit station opened.

Santa Rosa Hospital In the years following the Civil War, Texas was in dire need of medical and nursing facilities. The Roman Catholic Bishop of Galveston recruited three nursing sisters from Lyon, France to form the nucleus of the Sisters of Charity of the Incarnate Word (p. 122). Led by Sister Louise (Mother Madeleine) Chollet, 23, they arrived in San Antonio in 1869 and established the first hospital in the city, Santa Rosa Infirmary. The name is believed to honor Saint Rose of Lima, (1586–1617), born of Spanish parents in Lima, Peru. She chose to serve God by self-denial, suffering and humility and in 1671 became the first canonized saint in the New World. St. Rose is the patroness of Latin America and the Philippines. Another naming theory suggests that a wealthy benefactor offered to donate a substantial sum for the hospital's construction if it were named for his sister, an Ursuline Nun who was named Sister Mary Rose. Santa Rosa's David Christopher Goldsbury Center for Children and Infancy was funded by David's father, Kit Goldsbury, and named for the same person for whom ChrisPark (p. 73) was created.

Stinson Field The nation's second oldest airport in continuous operation, Stinson Field is named for a family rather than for an individual. Although the most famous member was Katherine (Stinson Middle

Stinson family aviators include, from left, Marjorie, Eddie and Katherine.

School, p. 115), other family members were also aviators. The **Stinson School of Flying** was first located on the parade grounds at Fort Sam Houston, but when the Army started its own aviators' school in 1915 (Kelly Air Force Base, p. 187), the Stinson School moved to 750 acres southeast of town where they trained Canadian Air Force pilots. All three Stinson siblings were renowned pilots. While Katherine toured the world to raise money and set flight records, sister Marjorie was the school's chief instructor. Brothers Jack and Eddie also held aviation records, and Eddie founded the Stinson Aircraft Company. Serving as the city's main airport when commercial air traffic first came to San Antonio in the 1920s, it was briefly named **Winburn Field** in honor of William D. Winburn, a young San Antonio Light city hall reporter who died in an ill conceived publicity flight in 1927. That name seems not to have been widely used, and the name was officially changed to **Stinson Municipal Airport** in 1936.

Sunset Station The building that houses this nightspot was once a real train station. Railroad service was brought to San Antonio in 1877 by the Galveston, Harrisburg & San Antonio Railway, shortly thereafter purchased by the Southern Pacific Railroad. The Sunset Limited, begun in 1894, was the line's premier train, running from New Orleans to Los Angeles and at one time continuing on to San Francisco. Sunset Depot was built in San Antonio in 1904, and for more than half a century was a hub of transportation activity. Amtrak took over the Sunset route in 1971, and later built a smaller station nearby so the original station could become the centerpiece of an entertainment complex.

Tobin Center for the Performing Arts   In July 2010, San Antonio's venerable Municipal Auditorium was renamed in honor of the Tobin family, as the Tobin Endowment's $15 million challenge grant provided a large step toward turning the building into a world-class center for symphony, opera and ballet. The name most associated with the grant is Robert Lynn Batts Tobin (Tobin Park p. 88), but the family has long been associated with the San Antonio cultural scene. His mother, Margaret Lynn Batts Tobin (Margaret Tobin Avenue p. 132), was an arts patron instrumental in establishing the city's symphony orchestra in 1939 and, a few year later, an opera series. Her only son Robert had no heirs, and when he died in 2000, the family fortune was used to create a foundation that has funded many theater and art projects. Municipal Auditorium was completed in 1926 as a memorial to World War I veterans, its planning begun under the administration of Mayor John Wallace Tobin (p. 76), Robert's great-uncle. Ravaged by fire in 1979, the building, restored and modernized, reopened in 1985 and began serving again as the venue for a diverse range of events including opera, ballet, Broadway musicals, rock concerts, Fiesta coronations and boxing and wrestling matches.

Tower Life Building   In 1922, Smith Brothers Properties Company of Dallas acquired the 10-acre Bowen's Island property (p. 85), soon to be turned into ideal commercial property when a river bend defining the "island" was removed during construction of a cutoff channel. Company President J. H. Smith, Vice President F. A. Smith and attorney J. W. Young envisioned a multiple-use complex similar to Rockefeller Center

Sunset Station served Southern Pacific passengers for more than half a century.

in New York. The 30-story **Smith-Young Tower** was to be the flagship building. Construction began in 1927, along with the adjacent Plaza Hotel (p. 14), once connected by an underground tunnel. When completed in 1928, this octagonal skyscraper was the tallest building in the Southwest and remained the tallest in San Antonio for 60 years, until construction of the Marriott Rivercenter Hotel. Known as the **Transit Tower** while headquarters for the city's transit system, it was renamed after **Tower Life Insurance Company** purchased the building for its headquarters in the 1960s.

USS San Antonio The first ship named by the U.S. Navy for the city, the USS San Antonio is the lead ship of a new class of 10 to 12 amphibious transport vessels expected to replace up to 41 existing ships. Not surprisingly, as the prototype USS San Antonio's construction and initial sea trials encountered delays and large cost overruns. Designed to deliver up to 800 marines ashore by landing craft and helicopter, the ship carries a naval crew of 28 officers and 332 enlisted personnel. Its motto, "Never Retreat, Never Surrender," is taken from the words of Alamo commander Col. William Barrett Travis to the people of Texas: "I shall never surrender or retreat. . .Victory or death!" The bow of her sister ship USS New York was built with steel salvaged from the World Trade Center.

Victor Braunig Lake Although this 1,350-acre lake in southeast Bexar County is a popular location for fishing, boating and picnicking, its origin had a more practical purpose. A severe drought in the late 1950s and increasing demand for energy showed the need for more power plants. Convinced that Edwards Aquifer water needed to be conserved for drinking purposes, City Public Service Company General Manager Victor Braunig (1890–82) decided to cool the plant with sewage effluent processed by a San Antonio Water System treatment plant, that water deemed safe for aquatic life and recreational activities. The lake was created in 1964 and its water used to cool Braunig Power Plant when it went on line two years later, helping CPS reduce its use of Edwards Aquifer water by 97 percent and save billions of gallons. Braunig started working at CPS—then San Antonio Gas and Electric Company—immediately after his graduation with honors from Texas A & M and spent 50 years with the company, serving as general manager from 1949 to 1958.

Wonderland of the Americas As the city spread towards the northwest, **Wonderland Shopping City** opened in 1961 in Balcones Heights near the intersection of IH-10 and Loop 410. It was built by a company headed by Charles Becker, Handy-Andy grocery stores owner and mayor of San Antonio in the mid 1970s. The name was picked by mall manager Jack Nicholson with the idea that since three-fourths of mall sales occurred during the Christmas season, the mall could be promoted as a "winter wonderland" to increase sales, though funds to carry out the winter theme never materialized. In 1986, after a $28 million renovation, the center was renamed **Crossroads Mall**. In 2010, new investors chose to restore part of the original name.

Wulff House Built about 1870, this elegant King William District home was restored in 1974 by the San Antonio Conservation Society as its headquarters. Anton Wulff (1822–94) came to Texas in 1848. Like many Germans, he did not join the Confederate cause during the Civil War but returned to Germany with his family for the duration of hostilities. He returned to become a successful businessman running stagecoaches and wagon trains between San Antonio and Chihuahua, Mexico. Wulff loved gardens and planted trees, shrubs, and flowers on public plazas at his expense. In 1885 he was appointed the city's first park commissioner by Mayor James R. Sweet (p. 18), with whom he worked as a $5 per month clerk when he first came to San Antonio. He began the beautification of Alamo Plaza shortly after its paving.

· 7 ·

"LANDMARK" NAMES

Linda Pace created ArtPace.

Artpace Described by the San Antonio Express-News as "arguably the most generous art patron in the city's history," Linda Pace (1945–2007) was also a respected artist and collector, but her greatest legacy to the city and the art world is Artpace. Defining its mission as a laboratory for the creation and advancement of contemporary art, the center has achieved national acclaim for its exhibitions, in-residence fellowships and educational programs. The daughter of Pace Picante founder David Pace (p. 170) and his watercolor artist wife, she and her husband Kit Goldsbury (p. 159) took a leap of faith and bought the company in 1985 for $14 million. When she and Goldsbury divorced, she sold her half interest in the company to him, enabling her in 1995 to establish a private foundation that has funded her ideas. Housed in an abandoned downtown auto dealership building, Artpace has attracted an illustrious list of local, national and international artists ever since. Among her artistic achievements is ChrisPark, designed in honor of her son (p. 73).

Cappy's Cappy Lawton opened Cappy's Restaurant in Alamo Heights in 1977, when he was 30. He had grown up in the Alamo Heights neighborhood and learned cooking skills from his mother and engineering skills from his father, who overhauled airplane engines. During high school and college, Lawton worked in the design departments for Swearingen Aircraft and Dee Howard Company. At San Antonio College and the University of Texas at Austin he studied business and engineering. But he chose not to pursue the aircraft industry, and opted instead to research and begin his own business, a college pub next to SAC called the Quarterhouse. This was the springboard for 29 restaurants throughout Texas, including Mama's, Mama's Café, EZ's, Cappyccino's and La Fonda on Main. Today, Cappy's Restaurant utilizes the skills of wife Suzy, son Trevor and daughter Avery.

Bill Miller Bar-B-Q Using a $500 loan from his father, Bill Miller opened a small poultry and egg business in 1950, and three years later added a small fried chicken-to-go restaurant unique at the time for offering quality food with five-minute service. A second restaurant opened in 1963, and today there are nearly 70 in San Antonio, Austin and Corpus Christi. In addition to working at the restaurant as cashier and hostess and raising four children, Miller's wife Faye (1919–2008) worked night shifts as a registered nurse to provide the family with income while the business was getting off the ground. All three sons and a brother-in-law are involved in the company, having worked together for more than 30 years. All food items—barbecued meats, pies, breads—are cooked in the central commissary in downtown San Antonio and trucked out to restaurants, causing the company to limit operations to sites that can be so serviced daily.

Catering by Rosemary Although now part of a conglomerate known as the RK group, most longtime San Antonians still call the business Catering by Rosemary. When pilot Henry Kowalski returned to the U.S. after World War II, he married his sweetheart Rosemary Hughes, born in 1924, a San Antonio native and graduate of Incarnate Word High School. In 1946 the couple bought a tiny barbeque restaurant on North Zarzamora called Uncle Ben's that served mainly college students in the Woodlawn area. In response to requests from friends, she began to cater private parties, delivering the food herself in a 1953 Buick. In 1961 the company was officially named Catering by Rosemary. It catered the majority of pavilion extravaganzas during HemisFair '68, and soon thereafter became sole caterer for the San Antonio Convention Center. For five decades the company has catered events for Pope John Paul II, six U.S. Presidents, seven Texas governors, several foreign heads of state and countless celebrities. With business operations consolidated on a six-acre site on East Commerce Street and with 500 full-time and 250 part-time employees, the CEO is now son Greg Kowalski.

Earl Abel's Although perhaps not as familiar to newcomers to the city, Earl Abel's has been a San Antonio institution for nearly 80 years. Earl Abel was a successful silent film organist when the Depression hit and he had to look for another line of work. Despite having no experience in the food industry, he bought a small house on Main Avenue and opened a restaurant in 1933. To attract customers, he applied show biz skills by telling jokes and stories, but even that did not bring prosperity. He was about to go broke when Duncan Hines saved the business by mentioning the tiny restaurant in Adventures in Good Eating. In 1940 Abel opened a larger restaurant at Broadway and Hildebrand in 1940, originally as a drive-in with carhops. He eventually expanded to six restaurants (including one in California), but World War II forced him to sell all except the one on Broadway. Serving a broad family-oriented menu including their famous fried chicken, Earl Abel's attracted a loyal customer base. In 2006 the landmark location on Broadway was torn down to make way for a high-rise condominium, and son Jerry Abel sold the restaurant to new owners who moved to a location on the Austin Highway.

Edwards Aquifer It was surprisingly difficult to track down the origin of the name of this huge natural structure, which lies beneath parts of 11 counties, receiving and storing the water so important to the existence of San Antonio. Even Gregg Eckhardt, who has created a well-researched Website about the aquifer (www.edwardsaquifer.net), is not entirely sure. He quotes an 1898 article by two geologists, Hill and Vaughan, who called it "an artesian groundwater system occurring in Edwards limestone," presumably referring to the Edwards Plateau, southernmost unit of the Great Plains. The plateau was probably named for Edwards County, named in turn for Hayden (or Haden) Edwards (1771–1849), a pioneer settler and land speculator whose dispute with the Mexican government over a land grant near Nacogdoches led to the so-called Fredonian Rebellion. But Nacogdoches is in East Texas and Edwards County is much further west, near Del Rio. The Edwards Aquifer Authority's Website (www.edwardsaquifer.org) refers to him as the "impresario of West Texas," but nothing in his biography suggests he traveled to west Texas.

*Florence Butt's grocery store grew from a home
operation financed by $60 in savings.*

Frederick's He was literally born into the restaurant business. Frederick Costa was born in Vietnam in 1954, the year the French were defeated in a 13-year war ending 77 years of colonial rule in Indochina. Of partial French ancestry, his parents were both natives of Vietnam and owned a fine restaurant in the city of Haiphong. When Frederick was two, the family moved to Bayonne in the Basque region of France, where they ran a Vietnamese restaurant in which he began to work at about age six. In 1969, the family moved to Paris and opened the first Vietnamese restaurant to be featured in the Michelin guide. Immigrating to Washington, D.C. in 1978 on a three-month tourist visa, Frederick was hired by one of the capital's French restaurants as a salad boy, bus boy and valet car parker. He stayed long past his legal limit to work his way up from waiter to manager. With limited funds to invest in a new venture, he and two friends picked San Antonio as the place to start a new restaurant and in 1985 opened L'Etoile in Alamo Heights. He became a U.S. citizen in 1986. Eventually he struck out on his own and opened Frederick's (fred-REAKS) in Lincoln Heights in 2000, adding a bistro on N.W. Military Highway in 2008.

H-E-B In 1906 Florence Thornton Butt (1864–1954) risked $60 of her savings to finance a new business: a tiny grocery store on the first floor of the family's two-story home in Kerrville. Her third and youngest son, Howard Edward Butt (1895–1991), returned to Kerrville after a tour in the Navy during World War I and attempted to expand the business. New stores failed in at least seven small towns until in 1928 a store in Del Rio proved successful. The company moved its headquarters to Corpus Christi in the early 1930s and in 1941 opened its first store in San Antonio, where eventually its headquarters would also be located. Howard Butt was a devout Baptist and strongly opposed the sale of alcoholic beverages in his stores. Only after his staff convinced him in the late 1970s that it was necessary to add beer and wine to their shelves to compete with rivals did he finally allow this to happen.

The firm, with sales of more than $7 billion annually, is now run by Howard's youngest son, Charles. Howard E. Butt Jr. runs the H. E. Butt Foundation.

James Avery Jewelry After surviving 44 missions over Germany as the commander of a B-26 in World War II, James Avery, born in 1921, received a bachelor's degree in industrial design from the University of Illinois. After

Jeweler James Avery worked by himself for three years before sending out his first catalog.

teaching a class in jewelry making at the University of Colorado and spending a summer in Kerrville in 1954, he decided to pursue a career in jewelry design. Having spent time in San Antonio during pilot training, he loved Texas and Texans, so moved to Kerrville and started designing and making jewelry in a two-car garage with about $250 in capital. His renewed Christian commitment led him to a new direction in his life, which explains why much of his jewelry has a Christian theme. Working alone for three years, he began to develop a strong customer base, and in 1957 mailed out his first catalog. Eight years later he moved the company to 20 acres not far from his garage in Kerrville. In 1988 he was named San Antonio Entrepreneur of the Year. At the end of 2009, the company had five manufacturing plants—all in the Hill Country—and 54 retail stores in six states. The founder stepped down in 2007, but his two sons now run the business, Chris Avery, M.D. as CEO and brother Paul as executive vice-president.

Jim's Born in 1922 in Shreveport, Louisiana, G. "Jim" Hasslocher, was raised by a single mother who moved her family to San Antonio during the Depression. Although he wanted to attend West Point, World War II broke out and he served as a U.S. Army Corps of Engineers officer doing construction work. While still stationed in the

Pacific, he wrote his mother and asked her to find him a piece of property where he could start his own business. She found a spot on Broadway near the Witte Museum entrance to Brackenridge Park. Stocking up with fifty army surplus bicycles, in 1946 he opened a bike rental shop. When summer came he added ice-cold watermelon slices and, later, charcoal-broiled hamburgers. There he met his wife Veva (1924–2009), who played a major role in the growth and operations of the business. Having an ability to anticipate consumer trends, Hasslocher visited the original McDonald brothers' walk-up hamburger stand in the early 1950s and returned home to create his own version, Jim's Hamburgers. Later he developed Frontier Drive-Ins, introducing car and dining room service. In 1963 he opened his first Jim's Coffee Shop at Broadway and Loop 410, creating the familiar cowboy logo and name that gradually spread across the city. He operated the Tower of the Americas Restaurant from 1968 to 2005 and opened his first Magic Time Machine in 1973. Now 21

Jim Hasslocher started his food empire with a bicycle rental and hamburger stand.

restaurants operating as Frontier Enterprises in San Antonio, Austin, and Dallas, Jim's has stuck to serving quality food at low prices in a family-oriented setting.

Kronkosky Charitable Foundation   The $300 million fortune that supports this foundation had humble beginnings. Albert Kronkosky Sr. quit school in his hometown of New Braunfels at the age of 14 and came to San Antonio with five cents in his pocket. He found a job as bottle washer for the San Antonio Drug Company and eventually became chairman of the board. In addition to other business and real estate interests, he formed the Gebhardt Chili Powder Company. Albert Kronkosky Jr. was born in 1908 and by 1944 had taken over the family businesses, which he sold in 1950. For the next 45 years he compounded his inherited wealth with wise investments. Albert Jr. and his wife, Bessie Mae, had no children. In 1991 they established a trust to fund the Kronkosky Foundation, unique in its stated mission: "To produce profound good that is tangible and measurable in Bandera, Bexar, Comal, and Kendall Counties."

Los Barrios   In Spanish, los barrios means "the neighborhoods," but that is not the origin of the name of this pair of restaurants. When Viola B. Barrios (1932–2008) became a widow in 1975, she had no idea how she would support her family. After two failed business ventures, she turned to what she knew best—cooking—and with $3,000 opened a restaurant in an old downtown garage that had previously housed an outboard motor repair shop. Working seven nights a week until 11 p.m., and with the help of her children and one waiter, Viola soon outgrew the old garage, moved to an old Dairy Queen on Blanco Road, repeatedly expanded it and opened a second location north of Loop 1604. It has been featured on many lists of "Top Mexican Restaurants" and on ABC's Good Morning America. She was described as an exceptionally generous and caring person, freely giving loans—most un-repaid—to needy employees, helping neighbors or gathering clothing and furniture to take to her original hometown of Bustamente in Nuevo Leon, Mexico. It was thus especially tragic that she was killed by her teenage next-door neighbor in a drug-related robbery-arson-murder. The young assailant was sentenced to life imprisonment without parole.

Pace Picante Sauce   Among the most widely recognized grocery products in America is the sauce created by a San Antonio entrepreneur, David Pace (1914–93). Born and reared in Louisiana, Pace attended Tulane University on a football scholarship and played in the first Sugar Bowl. After graduation, he was a coach until the advent of World War II, when he became a test pilot. Settling in San Antonio after the war, he developed a way to keep salsa, already a favorite Southwestern dish, fresh on the shelf and in 1947 began to market his new product. His son-in-law Christopher "Kit" Goldsbury (p. 159) took over the business and in 1995 sold the company to Campbell Soup, but the Pace name remains a prominent label in the salsa aisle.

Red Berry Mansion on the Lake   One of 13 children, Virgil Edward "Red" Berry (1899–1969) was born in a log cabin in Fort Smith, Arkansas. With only a seventh grade education, he went to work for the Union Pacific Railroad and joined the U.S. Army during World War I. First introduced to San Antonio as a military policeman during the war, he returned to this city in 1929 and became a major player in local gambling circles. There were numerous raids on his clubs and he was indicted for murder at least three times, though never convicted. In a game of "pitch" in the late 1940s he won title to an 84-acre tract in southeast San Antonio, and there constructed a 13,000 square foot French chateau mansion and created a 15-acre lake. He moved his casino operations to the basement, which became the haunt of wealthy gamblers until a 1955 police raid shut down the casino and confiscated his equipment. Berry then sought respectability. He pushed for passage—unsuccessfully—of pari-mutuel betting legislation while serving in both the Texas House and Senate from 1964 until his death in 1969. After his death the estate changed hands twice, ultimately purchased by Cardell Cabinetry owner Bill Tidwell, who refurbished the mansion to its original splendor and reopened it as a special events facility.

San Antonio Spurs   Aside from the Alamo, perhaps the San Antonio name most recognizable elsewhere is of the basketball team, winner of four National Basketball Association crowns. In 1971, after four years of struggling in the old ABA as the Dallas Chaparrals, the franchise was bought by a group of San Antonio investors led by Angelo Drossos and B. J. "Red" McCombs (p. 151). A name selection committee chose to honor McCombs's suggestion that it be short and catchy, and settled on the name of McCombs's hometown—Spur, Texas.

Schilo's   The oldest continuously operating restaurant in San Antonio had its origins in Beeville. Fritz Schilo (SHE-low) opened a saloon there in the early 1900s, but in 1914 moved his family and business to San Antonio. The saloon closed when Prohibition came in 1917, but later that year Schilo opened a delicatessen at the corner of South Alamo and Worth streets. Food was prepared by his wife, and customers kept coming for Mama Schilo's original split pea soup and root beer prepared with egg white to give the drink body and head, simulating real beer. In 1943 the delicatessen moved to its present location on Commerce Street. In 1980 the third generation of Schilos sold to another local German family, the Lyons family, owners of Casa Rio next door.

TETCO   For those who appreciate and respect success that comes from hard work, Tom E. Turner Sr. (1913–2001) should be the ultimate role model. An exceptional athlete as a junior high school student in Fort Worth, Turner was forced to drop out of school in the eighth grade for financial reasons when his father died. He moved to San Antonio in 1934 with his wife, Mary, and two young sons and found a job pumping gas at $10 a week for six or seven 12-hour shifts per week. When his boss, Sigfried (Sig) Moore, sold the business, he loaned Turner $350 to buy his own station. Turner named it Sigmor Shamrock in honor of his former employer and benefactor. Turner soon could buy a second station, which his wife ran while he handled the first. In the 1950s Turner and Moore formed a partnership that grew into the largest independent gasoline retailer in America. Turner figured out economic advantages of combining gas stations and convenience stores about a decade before major oil companies caught on. Among other ventures along the way, he created KBUC country-western radio, developed the Sonterra Country Club, bought the San Antonio Dodgers baseball team and quietly gave a great deal of money to various charities and needy individuals. In 1983, Turner sold Sigmor and its 600 stations to Diamond Shamrock. Forced to sit on the sidelines for a while because of sale restrictions, Turner eventually created another company, TETCO, an acronym of his initials.

Tom Turner started out pumping gas at 21.

Texas Cavaliers   Those men in red and pale blue uniforms who ride on the annual River Parade floats during Fiesta are members of an elite social organization begun in 1926 with several objectives, among them to sponsor a Fiesta King (as they have each year since 1927) and to "preserve the Texas tradition of horsemanship in this age of automobiles." The first Cavaliers king was named Antonio IX since kings of eight previous Fiestas had been sponsored by other organizations. The first president ("Grand Seignor") and prime organizer was John B. Carrington, whose family was from Halifax County, Virginia. To an upper class Virginian of that day, the term "cavalier" both denoted aristocracy and implied men on horseback. Their uniforms are essentially unchanged from their appearance in 1928. One early member, Ward Orsinger (p. 83), said the design was roughly patterned after a French officer's uniform he admired during overseas service in World War I. As for preserving horsemanship, a Texas Cavaliers Saddle Club did organize horse-related competitions and social gatherings in the early years as well as exercising military horses in Olmos Basin on weekends.

Valero Energy Corporation   Valero was created on January 1, 1980, at the time the largest corporate spin-off in U.S. history. Its birth was tumultuous. In the 1970s LoVaca Gathering Company, the major subsidiary of Houston-based Coastal States Gas Corporation, was embroiled in lawsuits from municipal customers claiming they had been overcharged for natural gas. In 1973, the Texas Railroad Commission and the attorney general put LoVaca under independent management. As head of the company the new board selected Coastal's young senior vice president of finance, William E. Greehey (p. 177). After six years of litigation, the new Valero company was formed, taking its name from Mission San Antonio de Valero, better known as the Alamo (p. 3).

Woman Hollering Creek   The sign marking this spot on IH-10 in Guadalupe County between San Antonio and Seguin probably piques more curiosity than almost any other in south central Texas. Although the true story behind the name seems unknown, the TexasEscapes. com Website states that the term "woman hollering" is probably a loose and inaccurate translation of the Spanish La Llorna, which means "the weeping woman." Historian C. F. Eckhardt from nearby Seguin reports that a map printed in the Republic of Texas era called the creek "Arroyo de la Llorona." What actually made the woman weep—or holler—is debated, whether from being tortured and killed on that site by Comanches, from warning of approaching Indians or calling for help for her son who had fallen into the creek.

Yanaguana Cruises   The strange name of the company that operates passenger barges on the San Antonio River stems from Spanish times. In 1691 explorers stumbled onto San Pedro Springs (p. 1) in an area called Yanaguana by the Papaya Indians. The word is said to have meant "living waters" or "refreshing waters."

· 8 ·

MEDICAL CENTER

To bring a medical school to the city, the San Antonio Medical Foundation was established in 1947. After more than 20 difficult years, the medical school and teaching hospital were dedicated on July 12, 1968. The only other building on the 200 acres donated to create the Medical Center in then far northwestern San Antonio was Southwest Texas Methodist Hospital, which had opened in 1963. With two exceptions, streets in the South Texas Medical Center are named to honor individuals who helped create the complex.

Audie Murphy VA Hospital Audie L. Murphy (1924–71) was born in Kingston, Texas and joined the Army around his 18th birthday. Having received every medal that the United States gives for valor—two of them twice—as well as decorations from several foreign governments, he is the most decorated combat soldier in U.S. history; David Hackworth and Ernest Edgar Hume were awarded more medals, but Murphy had more citations for heroism in the face of enemy fire. His Medal of Honor was for valor in France, where he was credited with killing or wounding 50 German soldiers and stopping an attack by enemy tanks. After the war he became a movie star, appearing in 45 motion pictures. Not so well known were the lyrics he wrote for 14 songs. He died in a plane crash at the age of 47.

Audie Murphy was the nation's most decorated combat soldier.

Burton and Miriam Grossman Cancer Treatment Center   CTRC Burton Grossman (1908–99) was born in Corpus Christi to Russian immigrant parents. At the University of Texas he met and married his first wife, a native of Tamaulipas, Mexico. Invited by his father-in-law to help run the family Coca-Cola business in Tampico, he expanded the company to 16 bottling plants, sugar mills and other enterprises. In 1970 he married another college friend, San Antonio's widowed Miriam Hyman. Although their names appear on the Cancer Treatment Center, most of his gifts were made anonymously or with so little fanfare that the extent of his giving to cultural, educational, medical and research institutions in his adopted Mexico and in the United States is virtually unknown.

Charles and Betty Urschel Tower   Before the CTRC moved to its present location, it was housed on Medical Drive in the Charles F. Urschel (p. 182) Pavilion, named in honor of the father of its major donor, Charles F. Urschel, Jr.

Charles Urschel Jr., far right, with his mother and three Slick cousins who later became his stepbrother and stepsisters.

(1917–81) and his wife Betty (1917–88). This newer building in the relocated CTRC is named the Charles and Betty Urschel Tower in honor of those original donors, and given by the family foundation. Charles Jr. was first cousin and stepbrother of Tom Slick Jr. (p. 182), with whom he shared interests including oil and gas exploration, ranching, airplanes and automobiles. At one time he was one of two Mercedes distributors in the entire United States, and for several years sponsored cars in the Indy 500 race with his other stepbrother, Earl Slick. He met Betty, born Mary Elizabeth Hails, at Stanford University and they married in 1939. She was a founder, officer and patron of many San Antonio arts organizations.

Chester Todd Drive   This street on private property does not appear on city maps. It is named for Chester L. "Chet" Todd (1921–91), who began as a telephone lineman after high school in Texas and rose to become Southwestern Bell's vice president of customer services for Texas. Todd was active in many civic and charitable activities in San Antonio, including medical research.

Roger and Cherry Zeller Building   This CRTC wing is named for a self-made millionaire and another of San Antonio's quiet philanthropists. After a six-week courtship during his pilot training in San Antonio in 1942, 2nd Lt. Roger Zeller (1917–97) proposed to Laura "Cherry" Dietzel. Shortly thereafter they married, but within a few months he was based in North Africa as a B-26 pilot. On his 19th combat mission, over Sardinia, he was shot down, captured and sent to a prisoner-of-war camp in Italy. He and a comrade escaped and after 24 days made it back to Allied lines. After the war he rose to the rank of brigadier general in the reserves and at 39 became the youngest officer elected president of the National Reserve Officers Association of the United States. After success as an insurance salesman, in 1958 he started Columbia 300 Industries, which became the largest bowling ball manufacturing company in the world, turning out 5,000 balls a day. During their 55 years of marriage the Zellers made numerous charitable contributions in San Antonio.

World War II pilot Roger Zeller, left, named his B-26 for his wife.

Ruth McLean Bowers Drive This street—also on private property and not appearing on city maps—is named for the only child of Marrs McLean (1883–1953), whose oil discoveries on land he purchased around the old Spindletop field in East Texas exceeded production of the original 1901 strike there. In 1937 McLean sold his oil business and moved to San Antonio, where the next year his daughter graduated from St. Mary's Hall. A philanthropist and women's rights activist who assisted with funding of the Roe v. Wade case, Ruth McLean Bowers served on the boards of Denton's Texas Women's University and San Antonio's Trinity University.

Dan Parman Auditorium Long a friend of the Health Science Center, Dan Parman endowed its chair of medicine and donated his home as a residence for the president. In recognition of those gifts, the main auditorium on campus was named for him. He is also known as developer of a large part of northern San Antonio (Parman Library, p. 139).

Dolph Briscoe Jr. Library The son of a prominent and politically powerful rancher father from Uvalde, Dolph Briscoe Jr. (1923–2010) was Texas governor from 1973 to 1979. His wife, Janey Slaughter Briscoe (1923–2000), had more direct involvement with the UT Health Science Center; the children's wing at University Hospital is named in her honor. She served six years on the University of Texas Board of Regents. The decision to name the library for the former governor was made at her last board meeting.

Ewing Halsell Drive The father of Ewing Halsell (1877–1965) owned part of the famous XIT Ranch. In 1942, Ewing Halsell bought the 90,000-acre Farias Ranch in Maverick County and moved his ranching headquarters to San Antonio. For many years he lived in the St.

Rancher Ewing Halsell established a major charitable foundation.

Floyd Curl was a Methodist clergyman whose son won the Nobel prize for chemistry.

Anthony Hotel with his wife and "unadopted daughter," ranch secretary Helen Campbell. In 1957 the Halsells established the Ewing Halsell Foundation, which made substantial contributions to the Medical Center, though Halsell was never involved directly with the work of the foundation or the Medical Center. Long instrumental in distribution of foundation funds was its board chairman Gilbert Denman.

Floyd Curl Drive   Robert Floyd Curl (1897–1971) was a Methodist clergyman for nearly 55 years, serving as pastor, district superintendent, administrator and professor at Perkins School of Theology. As executive secretary of the Southwest Texas Conference, Dr. Curl, on January 24, 1955, presided over the first meeting of trustees for Methodist Hospital. When one of the first streets in the Medical Center was named for him, the only building on the street was Methodist Hospital. When his son, Robert F. Curl Jr., was nine years old, his father gave him a chemistry set. The younger Dr. Curl went on to win the Nobel Prize in chemistry.

Frank Harrison Memorial Walkway   The enclosed walkway spanning Merton Minter Drive and connecting University Hospital with the VA Hospital honors Frank Harrison, M.D., Ph.D., first president of the University of Texas Health Science Center at San Antonio when various biomedical units were brought together under a single organization. He originally planned to join his father, a Dallas neurologist, in practice, but while he was in Chicago for graduate work his father died. Harrison then chose an academic career, becoming president of the University of Texas at Arlington before coming to San Antonio, where he remained until 1984. Harrison was instrumental in creating the Northside School District's Health Careers High School and the Southwest Research Consortium.

Frank Tejeda VA Outpatient Clinic   Although not in the Medical Center, this nearby facility associated with the Audie Murphy VA Hospital is named for decorated Vietnam marine, congressman, and veterans rights advocate Frank M. Tejeda (p. 98).

Greehey Children's Cancer Research Institute   A $25 million donation from the Greehey Family Foundation made possible this facility plus scholarships for deserving student and research fellows. In recognition of this support, the north campus of the Health Science Center has been designated the Greehey Academic and Research Campus. There is hardly a major charitable organization or civic project in this city that Bill Greehey has not been heavily involved with. A self-made man who was the first person from his hometown of Fort Dodge, Iowa to attend college, he came to San Antonio for a tour of duty at Lackland AFB. He later earned an accounting degree from St. Mary's (Greehey Arena, p. 120) in two and a half years, working nights and weekends to support his wife and two small children, and later began his meteoric rise to become CEO of Valero Energy. High on the list of his charitable endeavors is the city's effort to deal with homelessness, Haven for Hope (p. 12) for which Greehey was the largest financial supporter and major driving force.

One of Bill Greehey's major donations made possible the Children's Cancer Center.

Hartman Pavilion   The 12th floor "private wing" of University Hospital was named in honor of a highly respected local surgeon, Dr. Albert Hartman Jr. (1907–83). Long before San Antonio had a medical school or university-based teaching program, there was a surgical training program at the Robert B. Green Hospital (p. 149). That hospital was closed in the late 1940s because of financial and staffing problems. Dr. Hartman played a leading role in reopening "the Green" in 1950 and in establishing a surgical residency program there. A strong supporter of medical research, he was a driving force behind the Southwest Foundation for Research and Education and served as its board chairman for nine years. He later worked hard to help bring a medical school to this city, but was on the losing side, favoring locating it downtown near the Robert B. Green (Von Scheele Drive, p. 183).

Jim Hollers Drive   This street does not exist yet¬—but it should. James P. Hollers, D.D.S. (1899–1976), a past president of the American Dental Association, was a key force behind creation of the Medical Center. In 1956, while president of the San Antonio Chamber of Commerce, he was elected to replace one of two foundation directors who had resigned because of disagreement over the proposed site. Taking over as chairman in 1957, he served until 1970, when he was given a five-year contract as executive director. He was instrumental in securing creation of the Audie Murphy VA Hospital adjacent to the new medical school. In 1983 the foundation board discussed appropriate memorials to Hollers; among the recommendations were that a street in the Medical Center be named for him. This has not happened yet, but perhaps Jim Hollers will turn out to be the only name listed in this book before a street is named for him.

Joe R. and Teresa Lozano Long Campus   In 2008, San Antonio's main Health Science Center campus was named in recognition of a $26 million gift by a pair of self-made millionaires. Both were raised in small Texas towns, Joe in Centerville and Teresa in Premont. They met when both were teaching school in Alice, and from there embarked on divergent but equally impressive careers. Joe earned a law degree at UT-Austin in 1958 and entered private practice in 1965, specializing in banking law. Within a few years he was part of a group that bought two Austin banks and later added seven more, creating First State Bank, of which he was CEO. He continued to expand the bank and sold his holdings to Norwest Corporation in 1998. Teresa received her Doctor of Education at UT in 1965 and went on to serve in several governmental capacities, including as a consultant for the U.S. Office of Education on Migrant Education and the Head Start Program. The emphasis of their giving has been to provide scholarships, favoring students from the Valley and border regions who intend to return home and practice in South Texas.

John E. Hornbeak Building   As the person most responsible for negotiating the transformation of Methodist Hospital into the Methodist Healthcare System in the 1990s (p. 180), John Hornbeak, born in 1947, deserves a permanent place in the Medical Center. Born in Miami and raised in Birmingham, as a high school debater he won the Alabama VFW's "Voice of Democracy" contest. He worked his way through college in a hospital laboratory and graduated from Infantry Officer Training School at Fort Benning, Georgia. After transferring to the Medical Service Corps, he was sent for further training to San Antonio, where he met his wife of 39 years. After working his way up the hospital administrator ladder, he was named CEO of Methodist Hospital in 1987. In the following years, Hornbeak led what turned out to be an exceptionally complex social, political, and financial makeover that lasted about five years. When the new organization was established in 1995, he became CEO of the Methodist Healthcare System. Upon his retirement in 2007 he joined the faculty of Trinity University's Graduate Program in Healthcare Administration as executive-in-residence.

John Smith Drive   As spokesman for the Bexar County Medical Society in 1955, John M. Smith Jr., M.D. (1914–2003) presented a plan to the bishop of the Methodist Church's Southwest Conference asking the conference to administer a new hospital in San Antonio. Having set in motion creation of the first occupant of the South Texas Medical Center, Smith's efforts in securing and co-coordinating support from the Texas legislature, UT Board of Regents and other bodies were pivotal in developing the new medical center. As a Texas Department of Health board member, Smith was also instrumental in obtaining Hill-Burton matching funds to make up the shortfall in construction costs for the Teaching Hospital that had been approved by Bexar

Dr. John Smith played a major role in creation of the South Texas Medical Center.

County voters. Smith was active in medical politics for his entire career, serving as president of both the Bexar County Medical Society and the Texas Medical Association. His son, Dr. Marvin Smith, a cardiovascular surgeon, later became president of the County Medical Society, making them the only father and son to fill that chair.

L. E. Fite Drive   Lewis E. Fite worked closely with Sid Katz and Melrose Holmgreen to acquire an additional 400 acres for the Medical Center. A modest man, he resisted efforts to name a street for him during his lifetime, but after his death the San Antonio Medical Foundation put his name on the short street between what is now St. Luke's Baptist Hospital and Methodist Plaza, connecting Ewing Halsell and Floyd Curl drives.

Louis Pasteur Drive   Louis Pasteur (1822–95) was the 19th-century French chemist and biologist who proved the germ theory of disease and founded the science of microbiology. Although best known for his pasteurization process for milk, his discoveries also solved the problem of souring wine and beer, very prevalent in his native France. He also discovered the cure for rabies. Pasteur's writings encouraged Edinburgh's Lord Lister to develop sterile techniques for operating rooms.

McDermott Clinical Sciences Building   This Health Science Center research facility on Floyd Curl Drive, west of the main Medical Center area, was named for Gen. Robert F. McDermott, former CEO of USAA (p. 64).

Melrose Holmgreen Drive   In 1878, Prussian native George Holmgreen (1822–99) bought a struggling foundry and built it into one of San Antonio's longest lasting businesses, Alamo Iron Works.

As company president, descendant Melrose Holmgreen (1890–1975) was one of the original seven trustees of the San Antonio Medical Foundation, in addition to serving for 30 years as a Chamber of Commerce director and helping establish the San Antonio River Authority and the United Way. In the 1960s he was on the land acquisition committee that gradually purchased 400 acres of adjacent land. A nephew, John C. Holmgreen, was later foundation president (p. 111).

Melrose Holmgreen was an original trustee of the San Antonio Medical Foundation.

Merton Minter Drive   Merton Melrose Minter, M.D. (1903–77), a key supporter in establishing a medical school in San Antonio, opened the Minter Clinic in San Antonio in 1932 and was chairman of the University of Texas regents (1959–61), a Texas Medical Association trustee (1951–52), and San Antonio Medical Foundation chairman (1971–76).

THIS BUILDING IS DEDICATED
THIS 22nd DAY OF MAY 2007
Honoring
JOHN E. HORNBEAK, FACHE

This plaque recognizes the leadership role of John Hornbeak at Methodist Hospital.

Methodist Hospital   The first and at one time the only hospital in the Medical Center was Methodist Hospital. Although the Methodist Church lent its name to and established the social mission of the hospital when it was chartered in 1955 (Floyd Curl, p. 176), the church provided no financial aid. In the tumultuous 1990s Methodist Hospital leaders (John Hornbeak, p. 178) considered alternative pathways to delivery of health care, through partnerships with the other major hospital systems in the city or by developing a Scott and White type of doctor/hospital relationship. The ultimate decision was to form a partnership with a nationwide hospital system known as Columbia/HCA, now Hospital Corporation of America. HCA had acquired the four San Antonio hospitals previously owned by Humana when it chose to concentrate solely on healthcare insurance. The resulting Methodist Healthcare Ministries had two major divisions: a for-profit group of hospitals, including Methodist and the four former Humana hospitals, and a charitable arm that would administer half the profits from the hospitals to aid the underserved.

Reeves Rehabilitation Center   As a recent graduate of Jefferson High School and an 18-year-old Marine on Okinawa, Blair "Bruzzie"

County Judge Blair Reeves, paralyzed by a sniper's bullet in World War II, got around in a specially constructed motorcycle.

Reeves (1925–97) took a Japanese sniper's bullet in his spine. It left him a paraplegic for the next 50 years. Unable to become a coach, he went to law school. In 1966 he was elected Bexar County judge. The following year he cast a tie-breaking vote to double the hospital tax rate to build and maintain the teaching hospital, overriding the wishes of voters who had rejected such a proposal in a previous election. This act of political courage is considered to have saved the teaching hospital and Medical Center. Reeves was later chief justice of the Fourth Court of Appeals, and the new Justice Center was named partly in his honor (p. 150).

Salk Drive   Louis Pasteur's research was a global war against all bacteria, but Jonas Salk (1914–95) focused his efforts on a single microorganism—the poliomyelitis virus. In developing the first vaccine against polio, Salk essentially eradicated a crippling or fatal disease, but never profited from his remarkable discovery. When asked who owned the vaccine, he replied, "the people." He did his landmark research at the University of Pittsburgh, and in 1963 he became director of the Salk Institute for Biological Studies in San Diego, California.

Sam and Ann Barshop Institute for Longevity and Aging Studies
Located in the Texas Research Park rather than in the Medical Center,

this multi-disciple research facility to study the aging process was founded in part by contributions from the Barshop family. Sam Barshop, born in 1929, and his siblings borrowed money to open their first La Quinta Inn in 1968 in anticipation of the need for hotel space to accommodate visitors to HemisFair '68. Based in San Antonio for 34 years, the low-cost chain grew rapidly and in 1991 was purchased by the Bass family, who moved its headquarters to Dallas. Barshop, a former member of the University of Texas Board of Regents, has been inducted into the San Antonio Business Hall of Fame and the Texas Philanthropy Hall of Fame.

Sid Katz Drive   Born of Jewish immigrant parents from Lithuania, Sid Katz (1893–1968) spent his earliest years in Clinton, Kentucky. There was no synagogue in which the family could worship, so they attended the local Methodist church—which could explain why Katz was a dedicated fundraiser for planning and construction of Southwest Texas Methodist Hospital. He was also chairman of the Medical Foundation's land acquisition committee. His son Charles succeeded him as a trustee; the continuation of this street from Ewing Halsell to Floyd Curl is called Charles Katz Drive.

Tom Slick Drive   Thomas Baker Slick Jr. (1916–62), best known as founder of the Southwest Research Institute and the Southwest Foundation for Biomedical Research, was also a millionaire oilman, rancher, philanthropist, adventurer, author, art collector and inventor. With New York architect Philip Youtz in the 1970s, he developed the Youtz-Slick construction method, which used hydraulic jacks to lift precast concrete slabs into place. Many buildings at Trinity University, as well as the Tower of the Americas, were built with this technique. Slick was an original Medical Foundation board member who died at the age of 46 in a private plane crash just as the Medical Center was beginning to develop. He was cousin and stepbrother of Charles Urschel Jr. (p. 174).

Groom, Tom Slick Jr., left, and his best man, Charles Urschel Jr.

Urschel Memorial Research Laboratory Charles F. Urschel (1888–70) was partner in the oil business with Tom Slick and was married to Slick's sister Flored. Charles and Flored had one child, Charles Jr. (p. 172), who was thus a first cousin of Tom Slick, Jr. (above). The elder Tom Slick died in 1930, shortly after Flored's death. Charles Urschel then married Slick's widow Berenice, making cousins Charles F. Urschel Jr. and Tom Slick Jr. stepbrothers as well. This laboratory in the Southwest Foundation for Biomedical Research is named after Charles and Berenice, in recognition of the gifts of the Urschel and Slick families to the building. Charles Urschel has a footnote in history as the man who made "Machine-Gun" Kelly a household name. In 1933, two men, one toting a "tommy-gun", kidnapped millionaire oilman Urschel and demanded $200,000. When the ransom was paid a week later, Urschel was released. His phenomenal memory under very stressful circumstances led to the FBI's discovery of the hideout and capture of the kidnappers after a manhunt through several states. George "Machine-Gun" Kelly and his conspirators were the first in the nation to be tried under the new federal kidnapping law, the Lindbergh Act, and received life sentences.

Von Scheele Drive In the late 1950s and early 1960s, a bitter fight was waged over whether to put the medical school downtown or at the edge of the city. Edgar Von Scheele was one of four investors who owned the 200 acres of Oak Hills land in northwest San Antonio donated to the Medical Foundation and Methodist Hospital once the site was selected.

MILITARY BASES

Brooke Army Medical Center (BAMC)   This world-renowned facility with its noted burn center was called simply the post hospital in the post's early years. A structure built on the northern end of the parade ground in 1938 was named Brooke General Hospital in 1942 in honor of Brig. Gen. Roger Brooke (1878–1940), an infectious disease specialist who was chief of the hospital's medical service. From 1928 to 1933 Brooke commanded Fort Sam's station hospital. In 1996 a new Brooke Army Medical Center was built at the eastern edge of Fort Sam Houston on George C. Beach Avenue.

Beach Pavilion   The influx of casualties in World War II necessitated expansion of Brooke Army Medical Center. In 1944 three buildings were joined as a single structure and named Annex IV of Brooke General Hospital. In 1959 it was named for Brig. Gen. George Corwin Beach Jr., hospital commander early in World War II. The Beach Pavilion remained in use until the move to the new medical center in 1996.

Center for the Intrepid   The world's finest rehabilitation facility, the Center for the Intrepid on the grounds of BAMC was a gift from the American people to its wounded warriors. It is the first Department of Defense medical treatment facility built and paid for strictly through private donations. More than $60 million was raised in less than one year by the Fisher Foundation and the Fallen Hero's fund. The Center was the vision of Arnold Fisher (nephew of Zachary Fisher, below), a Korean War veteran who spearheaded the fund-raising and emphasized that the facility be the best possible, regardless of cost, for those who sustain amputations, burns and severe extremity injuries. The word intrepid means fearless or dauntless, which is intended to honor the patients. The name was probably also chosen because in 1978 Fisher founded the Intrepid Museum Foundation to save the historic and battle-scarred aircraft carrier of that name. Four years later, the USS Intrepid opened as the Intrepid Sea-Air-Space Museum in New York City, now the world's largest naval museum.

Fisher House   The Fisher House program is one of the most remarkable philanthropic efforts in our nation's history. Zachary Fisher (1910–99) started in the building business at age 16 with his brothers Martin and Larry. He sustained a severe leg injury in a construction accident as a young man, which disqualified him from enlisting when Pearl Harbor was attacked. During the war he built coastal fortifications for the Corps of Engineers and afterward he and his brothers created what would become one of the nation's largest construction and real estate companies. He and his wife Elizabeth created the Fisher House program in 1990, opening the first two at Bethesda Naval Hospital and Walter Reed. Brooke Army Medical Center and Wilford Hall got their Fisher Houses two years later. There are now 45, each adjacent to a military or VA hospital, and another 16 planned. Houses are built with Fisher Foundation money and given to the U.S. government, and suites and amenities are provided free of charge for families of injured servicemen and women. The program has expanded to include airline tickets and cash grants, since the government is prohibited from providing such services. In 1998 Fisher was awarded the Presidential Medal of Freedom by Bill Clinton, who also wanted Congress to make Fisher an honorary veteran. But the bill did not pass, and Bob Hope remains the only person accorded that honor.

Brooks City Base Although no longer a military facility, Brooks has a long heritage of service to the nation's defense. In 1917, the army established a San Antonio base to train flight instructors in the Gosport System, developed by the Royal Air Force, in which an instructor spoke to a student pilot through a tube and corrected the trainee in flight. Initially named **Gosport Field**, the site had its name changed to Signal Corps Aviation School, Kelly Field No. 5, and then to **Brooks Field** in honor of Cadet Sidney Johnston Brooks Jr., first San Antonio native to lose his life in a World War I-related activity. Brooks died making a landing attempt in his Curtiss JN-4 at nearby Kelly Field. Brooks was made headquarters for aerospace medicine

Cadet Sidney Brooks was the first San Antonio native to lose his life in the crash of a military plane.

in 1959. In 2002, ownership of Brooks passed from the Air Force to a quasi-municipal entity known as Brooks Technology and Business Park, although 1,500 military personnel and a like number of civilian scientists have continued to work there.

Camp Bullis Camp Bullis was established in 1917 as a troop training site on 16,000 acres of the **Leon Springs Military Reservation** in northwest Bexar County. It is named for Brig. Gen. John Lapham Bullis (1841–1911), an enlisted man in the Civil War who was cap-

tured at Gettysburg and spent 10 months as a Confederate prisoner in Virginia. Later he was commander for 15 years of the black Seminole Scouts in the Indian Wars, which included the capture of Apache Chief Geronimo. He also was paymaster at Fort Sam Houston. After the death of his first wife, the former Alice Rodriguez, member of an old San Antonio family, he married another San Antonian. His mansion at the corner of Grayson and Pierce streets near Fort Sam Houston was built with proceeds of his frontier land investments and is now Bullis House Inn, a bed-and-breakfast facility.

Gen. John Bullis built his retirement home in San Antonio.

Camp Stanley Military maneuvers had been conducted at the Leon Springs Military Reservation in northwestern Bexar County for nine years when the facility was named **Camp Funston** in honor of Maj. Gen. Frederick Funston (p. 25), who died while serving at Fort Sam Houston as commanding general of the Southern Department, then the Army's largest and most important command. Gen. Funston was a native of Kansas. When a base in that state was named for him, the local camp was renamed in honor of Brig. Gen. David Sloane Stanley (1828–1902), a West Point graduate awarded the Medal of Honor during the Civil War. Much of Stanley's postwar duty was in Texas, including his last position as Department of Texas commander. He lived longer (1884–92) in the Commanding General's Quarters at Fort Sam Houston than any other officer.

Fort Sam Houston In 1876 construction of a permanent military installation began on 93 acres donated by the city. By 1900 it was the largest army base in the nation. First called **Post San Antonio**, the name was changed in 1890 to honor one of the state's most revered heroes. Samuel Houston (1793–1863) represented Tennessee in Congress and later served as governor of that state. As commander at the Battle of San Jacinto, General Houston routed Santa Anna's Mexican army and avenged the Texians' defeat at the Alamo. This battle resulted in independence from Mexico. He served as the first (and third) president of the Republic of Texas and, after Texas joined the Union, as its first U.S. Senator. In 1859 he was elected governor, but in 1861 when he refused to take the oath of loyalty to the newly created Confederate States of America he was removed from office. Fort Sam Houston tenants now include Fifth U.S. Army headquarters, the Health Services Command, the Academy of Health Services and Brooke Army Medical Center.

Cole Junior and Senior High School This school is named for Robert George Cole, born in the Station Hospital at Fort Sam and a graduate of Jefferson High School. Beginning his career as a private, Cole graduated from West Point in 1939. As Lt. Col. Cole he was a battalion commander in the 101st Airborne Division, landing during the early hours of D-Day in 1944. He was one of two camouflaged paratroopers photographed speaking with Gen. Dwight Eisenhower before the D-Day jump. Several days later he led a bayonet charge under heavy fire to seize a causeway over the Douve River, for which he was awarded the Medal of Honor.

He was killed by a sniper in September 1944 while leading his battalion in an ill-fated attempt to break through German defenses before winter. Cole High School won the 3-A state basketball championship in 1989 with a 36-0 undefeated season; the star of the team was its center, Shaquille O'Neal.

Paratrooper Robert Cole, right, spoke with Gen. Dwight Eisenhower before D-Day.

Kelly Air Force Base What was the nation's oldest continually operating flying base when it closed in 2000 was first renamed **Kelly USA** and is now named **Port San Antonio**, a privately run industrial park at the southwestern edge of the city utilizing the former base's extensive facilities. The site was selected in 1916 by Gen. Benjamin Foulois, "father of military aviation," to expand the fledgling Aviation Section of the U.S. Army. First designated **Aviation Camp**, the name was changed in 1917 to Camp Kelly in honor of Lt. George E. M. Kelly (1878–1911), killed in a crash at Fort Sam Houston on May 10, 1911, the first American military pilot to be killed while flying a military aircraft. As Lt. Kelly came in for a landing in a recently repaired Curtiss biplane, he hit the ground hard, bounced into the air and careened toward nearby troop tents. An eyewitness said Kelly deliberately crashed away from the tents to avoid hitting people on the ground. By 1917 **Kelly Field** was home to 1,100 officers and 31,000 enlisted men. Later trainees included Lt. Charles Lindbergh (p. 79). As Kelly Air Force Base it had 25,000 military and civilian employees, making it San Antonio's largest single employer.

Lackland Air Force Base Originally part of Kelly Field, this was once a bombing and gunnery practice range. When Brig. Gen, Frank Dorwin Lackland (1884–1943) was Kelly commander in 1938, he envisioned a major training base overlooking Kelly's runways. Construction began in 1941 on what was initially called the **San Antonio Aviation Cadet Center**. Its role in training troops became increasingly important during World War II. It was named **Lackland Army Air Field** in 1947 and the next year, after creation of the U.S. Air Force, became Lackland Air Force Base, the training facility known as "the Gateway to the Air Force."

Wilford Hall Medical Center Completed in 1957 on the grounds of Lackland Air Force Base, this specialty and critical care referral center is the only U.S. Air Force hospital named for a person. Maj. Gen. Wilford F. Hall (1904–62) was a military medical officer from the time of his graduation from medical school in 1928 until his retirement in 1959. A founder of the American Board of Aviation Medicine, his most significant contribution was developing and promoting procedures and aircraft for patient air evacuation in both peacetime and in war. The hospital was named in his honor the year after his death.

Capt. William M. Randolph, member of a new field's naming committee, was killed in a plane crash in 1928.

Randolph Air Force Base As growth of San Antonio encroached on Kelly Field, the military began to look for a less congested site for a new flight training facility. Fearing this would be located in another city, San Antonio officials scrambled to put together such a property. Their first package was a site east of town belonging to several German farm families. This fell through when one farmer, William Rittimann, decided not to sell. Thanks mainly to the efforts of Ernest J. Altgelt, who spoke fluent German, a 2,300-acre site in northeastern Bexar County was put together successfully and given by the city to the government in 1928. It took more than five years to build 500 Spanish Renaissance revival-style buildings and 30 miles of roadways in a unique design divided by a circle into functional quadrants by 1st Lt. (later brigadier general) Harold Clark. As a Corps of Engineers project it was exceeded in scope only by construction of the Panama Canal. It was named for Capt. William Millican Randolph, a native Texan and graduate of Texas A & M University killed when his AT-4 crashed on takeoff from Gorman Field. He had been a member of the committee that selected a name for the new field. Randolph's son, William Read Randolph, also died in a plane crash in March 1941 while on a recreational flight with the St. Mary's Flying Club.

Mickler Memorial Field During the 2001 football season, Randolph High School named its football stadium in honor of the man who coached the Ro-Hawks to 17 playoffs in 25 seasons. Navy veteran Bob Mickler (1927–92) became the school's first coach in 1962 and took his 1967 team to the Class 3-A state finals. He was the grandson of William Wurzbach (page 45).

Dozens of streets, buildings, fields and facilities on San Antonio military installations are named for military heroes. One compilation of such names is Surrounded by History: How Fort Sam Houston's Built Environment Embodies the Values of Distinguished Soldiers *by John Manguso, director of the Fort Sam Houston Museum; the book is available at the museum.*

· 10 ·
SUBURBAN NEIGHBORHOODS

INCORPORATED SUBURBS

Alamo Heights   In 1852, San Antonio city council sold public land at the headwaters of the San Antonio River to a city alderman, James R. Sweet, who built the first permanent home in this area. Seventeen years later 108 acres were sold to Isabel Brackenridge and her 37-year-old son, George. Naming the property Alamo Heights, they lived in the Sweet home until completion of their nearby mansion, Fernridge, also called Head-of-the-River. George Brackenridge, increasingly affluent and influential, acquired adjacent land (p. 70). After his mother's death in 1896, Brackenridge sold his home and 280 acres to the Sisters of Charity of the Incarnate Word, who established what is now the University of the Incarnate Word (p. 132). Other than the 1859 home that became the Argyle Hotel (p. 149), there was little development until the Denver-based Alamo Heights Land and Improvement Company bought ranchland around the Argyle in 1890. Development struggled until about 1908. Growth increased in the 1920s under Clifton George Sr. In 1922 the 1.9-square-mile City of Alamo Heights was incorporated and the next year the 9.4-square-mile Alamo Heights Independent School District was formed.

Balcones Heights   The Balcones Escarpment, a geologic fault zone several miles wide, extends in a broad arc across Texas from Del Rio eastward to the Red River. Through the San Antonio area it rises some 300 feet, giving the area a panoramic view of the downtown city. In 1756, a Spanish explorer, Bernardo de Miranda y Flores, named the escarpment Los Balcones because the stair-stepped line of hills he encountered as he rode north from San Antonio reminded him of a rising series of balconies. The opening of Jefferson High School in 1931 spurred creation of nearby residential developments, of which Balcones Heights was one of the most aggressive. Development was slowed by the Great Depression, and it was not until after World War II that homebuilding began. Despite a concerted effort by the City of San Antonio to annex the community, Balcones Heights was successfully incorporated as an independent city in 1948.

Cassin This small community south of Mitchell Lake in southern Bexar County was settled before 1900 and was named for local landowner and rancher William Cassin. An artificial lake was created in 1907 and apparently also named for the same person. William's daughter Elizabeth married Terrell Bartlett, an engineer with Cassin on the Medina irrigation project (p. 21).

Castle Hills The Lodge Restaurant of Castle Hills occupies the former residence of Chester A. and Helen Slimp. The two-story rock house was begun in the 1920s and completed in 1931 on a 35-acre site far from town. It is said that the house had a grand view of downtown San Antonio, and that local residents called the house the Castle on the Hill, from which the municipality took its name when incorporated in 1951.

China Grove This southeastern Bexar County town, incorporated in 1960, was probably named for chinaberry trees on John Henry Robertson's farm.

Converse The chief engineer of the Southern Pacific railroad, a Major Converse, bought land, including the town site, some 13 miles northeast of San Antonio in 1877. Originally settled by German farmers, it is said to have the oldest 4-H Club in Texas, and was incorporated in 1961.

Elmendorf Carl Alexander "Charles" Elmendorf (1820–78) was among the steady wave of German immigrants who arrived in Texas in the mid-19th century. First settling in New Braunfels, he later moved to San Antonio and became a prosperous merchant. Most German-Americans in the area were opposed to slavery, an uncomfortable if not dangerous attitude in a Confederate state. Therefore Carl took his family first to Mexico and then back to Germany during the Civil War. Returning to San Antonio in 1866, he opened a hardware store on Main Plaza and invested in other business ventures. One was a brick company south of town on Roland Street toward an area where the soil had clay suitable for pottery. Although the town of Elmendorf was not established until 1885, some seven years after Carl's death, it is presumed to have been named in his honor because he owned most of the land in that vicinity. Some accounts suggest the town, incorporated in 1963, was named for his eldest son, Henry (1849–1918), mayor of San Antonio in 1895.

Harlandale This name of this subdivision in the southeast part of town was one of the most elusive to uncover. It turns out that B. B. Harlan, a California investor and a local attorney named Ramsay Bogy purchased a block of land in 1909 and platted it out into some 129 home sites. A 1912 Express-News advertisement for the Harlandale Realty Company listed H. J. Benson as president and B. B. Harlan as vice president. Around 1920 this land was purchased by the Barrett family, and Marcus Thurman Barrett became primarily responsible for developing Harlandale and other south side areas. His descendants report that in the 1920s, Barrett had 100 salesmen selling land and housing in this suburban area, San Antonio, which had its own trolley line from downtown.

Helotes   This area was settled about 1856 by Mexicans who intermarried with Apache Indians. Helotes in Spanish means "roasting green ear of corn," referring to the entire cob. The area around John T. Floore's Country Store is thought to have been where Lipan Apaches had sacred cornfields. It is said that the people of Helotes supported the cause for Texas independence by supplying corn for both soldiers and horses. As development surged toward the community, Helotes was incorporated in 1981.

John T. Floore Country Store   Visitors to this Helotes landmark soon after it opened in 1945 would have no trouble feeling at home there today. Little has changed since a former manger of the Majestic theater, John T. Floore, who died in 1975, bought a plot of land and built an authentic country store and dance hall behind high walls on Bandera Road. Many of the greatest country stars performed there, including Bob Wills, Hank Williams, Patsy Cline, Ray Price, Johnny Cash and even Elvis Presley, though Floore's will always be most associated with Willie Nelson. Early in his career, Willie developed an almost father/son relationship with Floore. In the early years they had a contract stipulating that Willie would perform regularly at the Country Store and nowhere else in San Antonio. Long after Willie because world famous, he continued to perform at Floore's. A clever promoter and sound businessman, Floore was also civic minded and was instrumental in organizing the Helotes Volunteer Fire Department, the Helotes Lions Club and encouraged consolidation of the Northside Independent School District. In 2005 the John T. Floore Country Store was recognized by the state as a historical landmark.

Kirby   Kirby became a station on the new Galveston, Harrisburg & San Antonio Railway in 1877. According to a book by Clara Weller, a former Kirby city councilwoman, the railroad's Kirby Yard was originally a stockpile of ties used by the Southern Pacific to construct and repair tracks. The apparent source of those ties was Kirby Forestry of South Carolina. This operation does not seem to have been owned by the East Texas and Louisiana lumber magnate John Henry Kirby, for whom Kirby Drive in Houston was named. Kirby was incorporated in 1955.

Leon Springs   About seven miles northeast of the town of Leon Springs are natural springs that supply Leon Creek. Once vital to the survival of Comanche, Tonkawa and other Indian tribes, they attracted settlers as well. In the mid-19th century the settlement was the first stagecoach stop northwest from San Antonio. It saw growth spurts during the two world wars because of its proximity to the Leon Springs Military Reservation, 21,818 acres including camps Bullis and Stanley (p. 185). The origin of the name Leon Creek is debated. Some say that it was named for large wild cats that lived in the Hill Country, león being Spanish for lion. Jeanne Dixon and Marlene Richardson in their history of Leon Springs conclude that it was named for the Spanish explorer Alonso de Leon (1639–91), a former governor of Coahuila who led four expeditions across Texas in 1686–89, or for his son, also an explorer.

   Rudy's Country Store and Bar-B-Q   Between 1847 and 1881 stage lines ran from San Antonio to Fredericksburg and on to El Paso, and contracts were given to businessmen to provide the stage lines with fresh horses, feed, and water, and to be a rest stop for passengers. German immigrant Max Aue (1829–1903) settled in Leon Springs on the 640 acres he was awarded in 1852 for his service with the Texas Rangers, and later bought another 20,000 acres from the State of Texas for 25 cents an acre. He built a small store that served as the post office and stage stop and in 1879 built a two-story hotel. When the railroad came through in 1887 his stage stop became the train depot. As the military moved into Camp Bullis and Camp Stanley nearby, and more autos were on the roads, business became even more brisk, and in 1927 Max's son Rudolph (Rudy) built a new store and gas station. Subsequent owners kept involved in the food business, and in 1989 barbeque was added. In 1992, food guru Phil Romano bought the property and turned Rudy's grocery and gas station into Rudy's Country Store and Bar-B-Q. There are now nearly 30 stores, mostly in Texas but also in Colorado Springs, Albuquerque, and Norman, Oklahoma.

Leon Valley   Not to be confused with Leon Springs, Leon Valley, also in northwestern San Antonio but closer to downtown, was settled in the mid-1850s by ranchers well armed for protection against Indian raids. Leon Valley was a stagecoach stop (Huebner Road, p. 39) and was incorporated in 1952 (Raymond Rimkus, p. 84). It was named for Leon Creek, which runs along its western border but not actually through the town. A tributary, Huebner Creek, which passes through city limits, originates seven miles northeast of Leon Springs (see above) and meanders through western San Antonio until joining the Medina River in south Bexar County.

Macdona. Macdona was first a stop on the newly built Galveston, Harrisburg, and San Antonio (later Southern Pacific) Railway in 1886. It was named for George Macdona, an Englishman who owned the town site.

Monte Vista Historic District   This was never a separate town but is included here for its important role in San Antonio's growth. The designated 100-block historic district two miles north of downtown includes Laurel Heights and several other separate real estate developments, among the city's most prestigious early neighborhoods. Impetus to preserve the area came from Trinity University Professor Donald Everett's visit to the decaying neighborhood surrounding Northwestern University's Chicago campus, prompting him to urge preservation of the area beside Trinity. The name Monte Vista, chosen to represent the collection of neighborhoods, means "mountain view" in Spanish. In 1920 it won from 5,000 entrants in a statewide contest, even though the area was only 165 feet higher than Houston Street.

Olmos Park   In the late 19th century, this 1,600-acre area was owned by Ladislaus Uhjazzi, an Austrian count who built a mansion surrounded by landscaped grounds. His fortune came from rental income in his native Austria. When Austria passed legislation to prohibit profiteering by absentee landlords, Uhjazzi was forced to return. Not long after, his home burned down, and the property lay vacant. In 1918 it became the site of Camp John Wise, the U.S. Army Balloon School, which moved to Brooks Field after World War 1. The flood of 1921 prompted start of construction in 1925 of a dam across the usually dry Olmos Creek. Developer Herman Charles Thorman immediately bought a large piece of property just west of the site. The dam was not as important to Thorman as the road that would run across it, for until then there was no direct connection between Laurel Heights/Monte Vista on the west and Alamo Heights on the east. Beginning in 1927, Thorman created a rigidly controlled residential community, incorporated in 1939 to prevent annexation by the City of San Antonio. The name presumably was derived from the Spanish word for elm tree.

Shavano Park   Shavano Post Office opened in 1881, with Augustin De Zavala as postmaster (p. 36). Shavano may have been the name of an extinct Indian tribe or the phonetic misspelling of a Frenchman named Charbonneau who lived in the area. In the late 1800s Shavano and Locke Hill (p. 41) were used interchangeably. Stagecoaches ran between Shavano, San Antonio and Boerne, but Shavano did not develop and the post office closed in 1903. The land was eventually bought by furniture magnate George Arthur Stowers. What is now Shavano Park was sold in 1947 to Wallace Rogers and Sons for residential development. The city was incorporated in 1956.

Somerset The town of Old Somerset was founded in 1848 in northern Atascosa County by Baptists from Somerset, Kentucky. In 1909, the town was bypassed by the railroad, so the same residents moved their town three miles north into the early oilfields of southern Bexar County and named it Somerset. It was incorporated in 1970.

St. Hedwig The original settlers of this town came in the mid-19th century from the predominantly Polish region of Silesia in Central Europe. A post office called Cottage Hill opened here in 1860, but the name was changed in 1877 to St. Hedwig in honor of Silesia's patron saint. Married to the Duke of Silesia in the 13th century, Duchess Hedwig was later canonized for her charitable works, mainly supporting the existence and expansion of monasteries in Silesia. St. Hedwig became incorporated in 1957.

Terrell Hills About 1880, Brig. Gen. Charles Milton Terrell (1832–1904) acquired 640 acres while stationed as paymaster at nearby Fort Sam Houston. He made it the family farm. His son, Dr. Frederick Terrell (1856–1940), a graduate of Harvard Medical School and a respected San Antonio physician for some 20 years, gave up his practice to pursue business interests, including presidency of City National Bank. He was also president of the San Antonio school board and for three months in 1903 was mayor pro tem of San Antonio. In 1920 Dr. Terrell began selling his farmland, named Terrell Hills, as his daughter Sarah Terrell Engelke continued doing after his death. Terrell Hills was incorporated in 1939, gaining as its city hall the fire station built by the city of San Antonio during an unsuccessful annexation attempt.

Dr. Frederick Terrell's farmland became part of Terrell Hills.

Universal City As soon as Randolph Field (p. 188) opened nearby in 1931, development began here, first in a Depression-doomed development platted as Airport City. Universal City was incorporated in 1960. Its name may have come from its first developer, A. Milner, to indicate universal importance of Randolph Field, or from the idea that pilot trainees from around the world made it a universal city. Despite reports that the name comes from a Universal Studios camp outside the base during filming of West Point of the Air in 1935, that film was made not by Universal Studios but by M-G-M. Randolph-based I Wanted Wings was by Paramount; Air Cadet (1951) was by Universal-International Studios.

Von Ormy This was settled after the Civil War as a crossing on the Medina River. In 1879 a post office was named Mann's Crossing for the family operating the ferry. In 1886 it was changed to honor an Austrian—or Russian, or Hungarian—nobleman who lived for a short time on a nearby estate. In 1885, Count Adolph von Ormy (or Norbert Von Ormay) bought 2,300 acres, including a mansion built by San Antonio merchant and entrepreneur Enoch Jones (p. 14). The countess returned to Europe after a year. The count disappeared under mysterious circumstances a year later. In 2006, on the 120th anniversary of the renaming of Mann's Crossing, local citizens designated December 4 as Von Ormy Day and crowned a Count and countess Von Ormy.

Murray and Barbara Winn developed Windcrest.

Windcrest In 1953, Murray and Barbee Winn bought 77 acres at Austin Highway and the future Loop 410. His father came from Memphis to manage a chain that became Winn's Stores, but when he died in 1947 Murray sold the stores. The Winns did most of the early development. The name "sort of came to them" one evening as they stood in a stubby cornfield watching a water well being drilled, with a gentle breeze blowing over the stalks. Incorporated in 1959, Windcrest is known for elaborate outdoor Christmas lights and decorations. These began when the Winns purchased 400 strings of lights and distributed them to the dozen residents as a way to attract people to the new community. Developed during the Cold War when Americans feared a Soviet nuclear attack, one of Windcrest's most unusual amenities was a community bomb shelter big enough to hold 300 people.

SAN ANTONIO SUBURBAN NEIGHBORHOODS

Many interesting, historical and quirky names can be found among streets within San Antonio city limits. Some neighborhoods include the name of the subdivision in virtually every street—Whispering Oaks, Forest Oaks, Bluff View, Hunter's Creek, Knollcreek, Windcrest, to name a few. Others have some sort of theme or commonality among their street names. A few of these are listed below.

Alamo Ranch   In addition to **Defenders Parkway** and **Volunteer Parkway,** this neighborhood has streets named for men who fought at the Alamo. A few are well known, such as **James Bowie** (p. 7) and **Albert Martin** (p. 16), but most are obscure names history has long since forgotten, such as **William Carey, Amos Pollard, Isaac Ryan** and **Jacob Walker.**

Churchill Estates   This subdivision is not named for Winston Churchill but rather for Churchill Downs, site of the Kentucky Derby at Louisville, Kentucky. Thus at least 18 of its streets are named for former winners of this classic race plus famous horses that were not Derby winners. Others recall the other two races of the Triple Crown—**Belmont** and **Preakness**—plus **Runnymede,** named for the noted Kentucky horse breeding farm in the same family since its founding in 1867.

Colonies North   Developers of Colonies North intended to commemorate Revolutionary War era names in the original 13 colonies, such as **Ticonderoga, Northampton, Litchfield, Nantucket, Betsy Ross, Steuben** and **Quakertown.** One major thoroughfare is Tioga, which may have a colonial ring but has nothing to do with that era of history (p. 44). Nor does **Bull Run,** a battle name from the Civil War, not the Revolutionary War.

Harmony Hills   One developer of this subdivision, Jim Uptmore, reports that names were chosen for it that had a direct musical meaning or came from songs popular in the 1940s and 50s. Streets easily recognized as musical terms include **Serenade, Sonata, Finale, Sonnet, Ballet, Tango, Nocturne** and **Minuet.** Others reflects songs of that era: **Raindrops** Keep Falling on my Head, written for the movie *Butch Cassidy and the Sundance Kid*; Mr. **Sandman,** by The Chordettes; **Lida Rose,** a popular barbershop song; **Temptation,** from the 1952 movie *Singin' in the Rain* and popularized by Perry Como; Wake up little **Susie,** by the Everly Brothers; **Fantasia,** the Walt Disney animated musical; **Tammy,** Debbie Reynolds; **Summertime,** George Gershwin; **Rhapsody** in Blue, also Gershwin); Some **Enchanted** Evening, Rodgers and Hammerstein; Mood **Indigo,** Duke Ellington; Friendly **Persuasion,** Pat Boone; **Patricia,** Perry Como; **Moonglow,** Benny Goodman Quartet; **Granada** (Spanish); and **Verdadero** (Peruvian). A few others relate to popular vocal groups: The **Limelighters** and The **Intrigues.**

Los Angeles Heights   This post-World War II subdivision lies between Fredericksburg Road and IH-10 in near northwest San Antonio. Most street names recall familiar California cities—**Hollywood, Fresno, Pasadena, Sacramento, Santa Anna, Santa Barbara, Santa Monica.** Others are named for less well-known localities—**Hermosa** (Beach), **Ridgewood, Catalina** (Island) and, possibly, Gardena, misspelled **Gardina.** There is also a tiny **Catalina Park** in the neighborhood.

Marshall Meadows   Across Eckert Road from Marshall High School, the streets in this subdivision are named for illustrious sports stars from baseball—**Babe Ruth, Mickey Mantle, Joe DiMaggio, Lou Gehrig, Connie Mack, Jimmy Foxx;** football—**Bart Starr, Knute Rockne;** golf—Ben **Hogan, Sam Snead,** Bruce **Devlin;** tennis—Don **Budge,** Chris **Evert.**

Oak Hills Terrace   Many streets in this subdivision are named for well known entertainment figures: TV—**Gomer Pyle, Edie Adams, Ben Casey, Ponderosa** from Bonanza, **Desilu,** Walter **Cronkite, Alan Hale** from Gilligan's Island, **George Burns;** Hollywood—**Gary Cooper, Cary Grant,** Humphrey **Bogart, Dan Duryea,** Stewart **Granger, Steve McQueen,** Jimmy **Gleason, Danny Kaye, Charlie Chan, Lon Chaney,** Eva and Zsa Zsa **Gabor, Angie** Dickinson, Paula **Prentiss, Errol Flynn** and Mia **Farrow;** and a few singers—Elvis **Presley, Dean Martin, Brenda** Lee. Several streets are named for sports figures—tennis stars Bjorn **Borg, Billie Jean King** and John **Newcombe;** two from football—San Antonio native **Kyle Rote** and University of Texas coach **Dana Bible;** and one golfer,—**Gary Player.** The only name that does not fit the pattern is of a Lutheran minister, **Merkens** (p. 41).

Sonoma Ranch   Sonoma County is in California, but many of these streets are named for New Mexico cities: **Alamogordo, Artesia, Dona Anna, Española, Portales, Raton, Ruidoso, Santa Fe, Sandia** and **Socorro.**

Tobin Hill   Although never officially designated as such, Tobin Hill, between downtown and Monte Vista (p. 194), acquired that name from a home built on an eminence in 1883 by William G. Tobin, father of Mayor John Tobin (p. 76). The neighborhood's history dates back to the 1870s, as it was becoming home to many prominent citizens who worked downtown. During the following decades came more surges of development, in the 1920s after World War I and again in the 1940s after World War II. With the subsequent decline of downtown businesses and suburban growth, the area deteriorated until spurred toward recovery by an active neighborhood association representing some

6,000 residents and energized in the early years of the 21st century by the nearby extension of the River Walk and redevelopment of the Pearl Brewery.

Walker Ranch This gated community was once part of the sprawling Walker Ranch, connected to what is now the Walker Ranch Historic Landmark Park. Those familiar with its history (p. 91) will recognize the street names: **Ganahl Court** and **Walkers Way** are family names of the ranch owners; Edward **Higgins**, who owned the land in 1858; Ricardo **Salazar** a midget Hispanic born on the family ranch in Kerr County who was a ranch foreman for Ganahl Walker; and **Charlisa** Ganahl, Walker's mother.

· 11 ·

SURROUNDING COUNTIES

ATASCOSA COUNTY

Atascosa County takes its name from the Atascosa River. The word Atascosa comes from a Spanish word meaning "clogged up" or "bogged down." "Boggy" may refer to an abundance of water, which makes it good farming country, but that may also have created problems for early travelers.

Benton City   Although the exit signs on IH-37 suggest a "city", this is in fact only a ghost town. Once a thriving community and site of the Benton City Institute, the largest "college" between San Antonio and Laredo, the town was bypassed by the Galveston, Harrisburg, and San Antonio railroad (between San Antonio and Laredo) in 1881 and the population melted away. The town is thought by some to have been named for U.S. Senator Thomas Hart Benton of Missouri, a friend and colleague of Sam Houston. A more likely origin is Alfred Benton, a Kentuckian whose heirs were granted some 1,400 acres near here by the State of Texas for his service at the Battle of San Jacinto.

Campbellton   John F. Campbell (1835–1911) came here from Ireland in 1855 to establish a ranch. He also founded this town, where he was the first postmaster, ran a general store, opened the first school and hosted Catholic services in his home.

Charlotte   Around 1910, an entrepreneur from Missouri offered to construct a railroad through Atascosa County. Several landowners donated land to help finance the project, among them Dr. Charles F. Simmons. He built the Artesian Belt Railroad and had towns in the county named for all three of his daughters: Charlotte, Christine, and Imogene, which never got beyond the planning stage. His Artesian Belt Railroad extended 42 miles from Macdona in Bexar County—where it linked with another railroad into San Antonio—down to **Christine**.

Fashing   The 5,500-acre Hickok Ranch was subdivided into farms in 1916. Among the initial communities was a town first called Hickok, then Hindenburg and finally Fashing. The name, probably derived from

the German carnival known as Fasching, reflects the predominately German population that settled here.

Hindes George F. Hindes was a rancher who settled in this area in 1856. In 1912 he donated land for the San Antonio, Uvalde, and Gulf Railroad right-of-way and for a town on the line.

Jourdanton The son of John Campbell (Campbellton, above), Jourdan Campbell, born in 1867, in 1909 founded this town, pronounced JUR-dun-tun. Having been raised in the fertile farmlands of Atascosa County, Campbell spent most of his life in the real estate business and in acquiring his own land for agriculture and investment, eventually owning some 7,000 acres for raising corn and cotton. Among his properties was the 40,000-acre Toby (or Tobey) ranch, owned jointly with T. H. Zanderson, which they subdivided into lots and farms to create the town of Jourdanton. With a donation of land and a $50,000 cash bonus, they enticed the Artesian Belt Railroad to make Jourdanton a stop in 1909. Jourdan Campbell never lived in Jourdanton, preferring to live instead in his native Campbellton.

Leming The first post office when the town was founded in 1880 was named Las Gallinas, Spanish for "the hens." About 1900, P. B. Leming moved here from Missouri to take charge of construction of the San Antonio, Uvalde, and Gulf Railroad. When it was completed in 1902, the 25 residents petitioned the postal service to change the name to Leming.

Lytle Established in 1882 as a station on the International and Great Northern Railroad, Lytle was named for rancher and trail driver John Thomas Lytle (1844–1907). In 1871 he formed a partnership with a cousin, Thomas M. McDaniel, to drive herds from area ranches to northern railheads and ranges. He led several drives to Kansas but later devoted his energies to development of his ever-expanding cattle operations. He and some associates established the Union Stock Yards in San Antonio.

McCoy McCoy was named for rancher W. A. McCoy, who donated land to the railroad for a right-of-way in 1913.

Peggy Developed in the early 1930s by H. R. Smith and John Mowinkle, who hired several hundred laborers to clear mesquite and brush for farmland, this was first known as Hollywood. Later a post office opened with the name Peggy, after a niece of Mowinkle.

Pleasanton Pleasanton was established in 1858, when conflicts with Indians forced settlers to move the county seat to this site at the mouth of Bonita Creek. John Bowen (p. 85) donated five square miles of land for development and later named it after settler John Pleasant. Many claim this to be the birthplace of the cowboy. Cowboy Homecoming celebrations have been held annually since 1966 to recreate the days when Longhorn cattle passed through on up the Chisholm Trail.

Poteet The Strawberry Capital of Texas owes its development to the Artesian Belt Railroad that passed nearby and to artesian wells that allowed strawberries to be grown on irrigated land. It was named for the first postmaster, Francis Marion Poteet, who operated the post office out of his blacksmith shop beginning in 1886.

Rossville Virtually nothing remains of this once prosperous community eight miles west of Poteet, but its origins have strong connections to old San Antonio. Texas Declaration of Independence signer Jose Antonio Navarro (p. 16) gave tracts on either side of the Atascosa River to his son J. A. George Navarro. The younger Navarro's daughter Maria Antonia Navarro married Scottish immigrant John C. Ross, who had come to the U.S. as a blockade runner during the Civil War. Ross and his brother William F. M. Ross, who drove the mail stage from San Antonio to Laredo, founded Rossville in 1873. Toward the end of the 1890s the town had more than 300 inhabitants, but when bypassed by the railroad it withered and died.

BANDERA COUNTY AND BANDERA

County and town are named for nearby Bandera Pass. There are at least three accounts of the name's origin. One is that a Spanish general named Bandera led a punitive expedition in the area against the Apaches. Others relate the name to the Spanish word for flag—*bandera*—referring to a flag placed by Spanish soldiers pursuing Apaches to Bandera Pass to warn against future raids. Another says that a red flag was placed on the pass's highest peak as a symbol of a treaty between the Spanish and the Indians following a battle in 1732. The Apaches agreed not to come south of the pass and interfere with the settlements in San Antonio de Béxar and the Spaniards agreed not to go north and intrude on Indians' hunting grounds. In any case, the name was long in existence when the town was established in 1853. A sawmill on the Medina River created a need for workers to cut the huge cypress trees that grew there. Polish immigrants from nearby Karnes County were recruited and given land. After the Civil War the town was a staging area for cattle trail drives. Bandera is termed the dude ranch capital of Texas.

Lakehills Improvement of county roads to this community, also known as Upper Medina Lake, began in the 1930s but was delayed by World War II. The area did not develop until the 1950s.

Medina As early as 1865 a sawmill had been built here on the Medina River. In 1880 a post office taking the name of the river was established (Medina County p. 210).

Pipe Creek Most stories concerning this name center around O. B. Miles (other accounts have him as Thomas Odem), who lost his smoking pipe in the creek and later retrieved it. Whether or not he was being pursued by Indians has been debated.

Tarpley The post office established here in 1899 was named after Tarpley Prickett, son of postmaster John Prickett.

Vanderpool The first Anglo settlers, who arrived in the 1850s, were forced to leave in the 1860s because of Comanche raids. A post office established in 1886 was named for the first postmaster, L. B. Vanderpool, replacing the town's former—Bugscuffle.

COMAL COUNTY

The county is named for the Comal River, said to be the shortest river in the United States. It originates from the largest natural springs in Texas, filters through the Edwards Aquifer and flows southeast for three or four miles to join the Guadalupe River—all within the city limits of New Braunfels. Comal means "flat dish" in Spanish, thought to describe the landscape along the riverbed. A number of communities settled mostly by Germans, have appeared on the county map since the mid nineteenth century, but only a few have survived.

Bulverde   In the late 1840s, an Indian trail was used to haul freight and passengers by ox wagon along Cibolo Creek between the new German communities of New Braunfels and Fredericksburg. The first settlers along the trail were German wagoneer August Pieper and his bride, who came in 1851. Later pioneers called the community Pieper's Settlement. A post office opened in 1879 was named for an early landowner, Lorenzo de Bulverde (or Luciano Bulverdo). Legend has it that for helping survey the road from Texas to California he was awarded a 320-acre land grant by the Texas governor, though Bulverde never lived on it.

Fischer   In 1853 Hermann Fischer built a log trading post to serve the frontier community. It was reported in the 1960s that the Fischer family had held the postmastership continuously since 1876. The town was called Fischer's Store in the early twentieth century, but was changed back to Fischer in 1950.

Gruene   Once a thriving transportation, business and social hub located at a crossing on the Guadalupe River, Gruene (pronounced GREEN) is now within New Braunfels city limits. In 1872 Ernst Gruene settled his family on 6,000 acres around a small German town originally called Goodwin Community. Son Henry D. built a store to serve families sharecropping the Gruene property. The town was on the stage route between San Antonio and Austin, and soon Henry added a cotton gin and dance hall. In the early twentieth century Gruene Hall was the town social center, and all night dances were held regularly on Saturdays. In 1925 a boll weevil infestation wiped out the cotton crop, the Great Depression completed the financial ruin and by 1950 Gruene was a virtual ghost town. In 1972 a local architect convinced local authorities of the historical value of Gruene Hall, and in 1975 it was added to the National Register of Historic Places. Now the town is crammed with visitors on a nice weekend day, and Gruene Hall—looking pretty much as it did 100 years ago—hosts Country and Western entertainers on Saturday nights.

New Braunfels   In 1842, twenty-one German noblemen organized a society to relieve the overcrowded German states by assisting emigration to Texas. One member, Prince Carl of Solms-Braunfels (1812–75), commissioner-general for the first colony, made an inspection tour of Texas in 1844. He purchased property on the Comal River and signed a peace treaty with its inhabitants, a tribe of Lipan Apaches. After establishing a port on Matagorda Bay called Karlshafen—later renamed Indianola (p. 13)—he led the first wagon train into the Texas interior. Reaching a fertile tract near the confluence of the Comal and Guadalupe rivers on March 21, 1845, he named it for his ancestral estate on the Lahn River in Germany-Braunfels. He laid the cornerstone for Fort

Prince Carl of Solms-Braunfels led a major group of German immigrants into Texas.

Sophia (Sophienburg), named in honor of his wife, Princess of Salm-Salm. The Sophienburg Memorial Museum stands on the site where the fort was to have been built.

Sattler   Variously known also as Mountain Valley and Walhalla, the post office was named for Wilhelm Sattler when opened in his home in 1856. The town was virtually deserted in the 1950s, but it enjoyed some semblance of a resurrection upon completion of a dam in the 1960s that filled the valley above to create Canyon Lake.

Smithson Valley   Although this town 15 miles northwest of New Braunfels no longer appears on most maps, its name is preserved by the athletic teams of its namesake high school, built in 1976. In 1856, former Texas Ranger Benjamin F. Smithson settled in the area and became the first postmaster, but, having come from Alabama, was one of the few settlers not German. He learned the language to speak not only to his neighbors but also to his German wife, Auguste Vogel. By the 1880s the town had become a supply and social center and had a cedar post-cutting industry. A Smithson Valley school opened in 1860, but closed in 1944—four years after the post office closed—and was combined with Sherwood Rural High School.

Spring Branch   Not to be confused with the much larger Spring Branch near Houston, this town was named for a creek originating in a cavern in far northwest Comal County and flowing as a waterfall into the Guadalupe River. The creek is said to have been named by early German immigrants who settled the area in 1852. Like Sattler, Spring Branch was revitalized by recreation seekers after creation of Canyon Lake.

Startzville The Startz family built a small store here in 1935. The community grew after completion of nearby Canyon Dam in 1964.

GUADALUPE COUNTY

Guadalupe County was named for the Guadalupe River, named in 1689 by Capt. Alonso de Leon in honor of Our Lady of Guadalupe, patron saint of Mexico. In 1531 the Virgin Mary is said to have appeared to an Indian peasant in Mexico, leaving her image on his tilda, a poor-quality cactus cloth that should have disintegrated in 20 years but is still intact more than four centuries later. The image was called Our Lady of Guadalupe, and a sanctuary was built in her honor shortly thereafter. The church has been rebuilt several times, most recently being rebuilt in 1976. This New Basilica of Our Lady of Guadalupe, which is four miles from central Mexico City, is the second most frequently visited Catholic site in the world, topped only by St. Peter's Basilica in the Vatican City.

The origin of why this name was designated for the Virgin Mary has always been a matter of uncertainty. One of the most reasonable explanations is that it resulted from translation from the Indian language Nahuatl to Spanish. The Aztec word *coatlaxopeuh* is pronounced *"quatlasupe,"* which sounds like the Spanish word Guadalupe. *Coatha* means "the serpent" and *xopeuh* means "to crush or stamp out." Since the serpent was a symbol of the Aztec religion, it has been thought that the Virgin Mary was the one who would destroy the Aztec religion and its human sacrifices, and replace it with Christianity.

Cibolo The Indian name for buffalo is said to have been cibolo. Folklore has it that the high banks of Cibolo Creek were a favorite hunting ground of Indians, who killed herds of buffalo by driving them over the creek banks.

Fentress Originally Riverside, this San Marcos River settlement was renamed in 1892 for James Fentress, the town's first doctor and a large landholder. Dr. Fentress fought in the Battle of Plum Creek, a decisive victory of Texans over the Comanches, in retaliation for a raid in the Guadalupe Valley in the summer of 1840.

Geronimo This town is named not for the Apache warrior who lived and fought in Arizona but for St. Jerome, a prolific 4th-century priest and scholar best known for having translated the Bible into Latin. In the mid-1500s, the king of Spain awarded the San Geronimo Grant, including much of present-day Bexar, Comal, Guadalupe and Hays Counties. As was the custom, all creeks and rivers originating within the grant took the name of the grant, explaining why there is another San Geronimo Creek in northwest Bexar County. By the time Prince Carl of Solms (New Braunfels, p. 205) brought Germans to the area, "San" was already dropped and the town took the name of the creek. The town's high school is named for José Antonio Navarro, who lived on a ranch along the creek until he moved to San Antonio (Casa Navarro State Historical Park, p. 72).

Kingsbury In 1875, the Galveston, Harrisburg and San Antonio Railway came through and a post office was opened, named for railroad official William Kingsbury.

Marion Before the town site was laid out, this was a camp for railroad workers on the Galveston, Harrisburg and San Antonio Railway. It was named for Marion Dove, whose grandfather Joshua W. Young owned a plantation the railroad passed through in 1877.

McQueeney When the railroad was built through the area in 1876, one stop was named Hilda. The enterprising C. F. Blumberg built a store a mile east of the rail stop, hoping to persuade the railroad to move from Hilda by naming his site McQueeney, in honor of the railroad's superintendent. The stop, however, apparently was never moved.

New Berlin As might be anticipated, this was settled in the 1870s by German immigrants to Texas and named for the German city by that name.

Schertz Sebastian Schertz (1822–90) came from Germany with his parents in 1843 and farmed along the Guadalupe River in Comal County. Like many immigrants he was opposed to slavery, and he was forced to hide during the Civil War. His wife brought provisions to his hiding place, and he managed to escape being drafted into Confederate service. Later the couple moved to Missouri before coming back to Texas, where he established the area's first business enterprise, the Schertz Cotton Gin. He donated land for a depot for the new railroad, and the town was named for him. The town now spills into Bexar and Comal counties.

Thulemeyer Park Starting his fifty-year career with Schertz State Bank as a cashier, World War I veteran Herbert Paul Thulemeyer (1893–1970) worked up to become fourth president of the bank, established in 1913, in the late 1950s. He is credited with making the greatest impact on its growth due to his friendship with many colonels and generals at nearby Randolph Air Force Base. He was also the first mayor of Schertz. The park was dedicated in May 1971.

Juan Seguin was the only Tejano in the senate of the Republic of Texas.

Seguin It is uncertain whether the seat of Guadalupe County is named for Juan Nepomuceno Seguin or his father, longtime San Antonio postmaster Erasmo. Most favor Juan, despite his checkered background. Both were Tejanos—Mexicans living in Texas—and contributed to the Texas revolution. Juan entered the Alamo, but before the battle he was sent out as a courier and thus lived to fight at San Jacinto. Later he was the only Hispanic Texan in the republic's senate, then military commander of San Antonio and its elected mayor. In 1839 the one-year-old town of Walnut Springs changed its name to Seguin. Juan Seguin fled with his family to Mexico in 1842 after his loyalties were questioned, and served in the Mexican army when it invaded Texas in 1842 and in the Mexican War against the United States. He wrote that he was forced to take up arms against Texas or remain indefinitely in a Mexican prison.

Selma The city hall of Selma is in Guadalupe County, but the town spills into Bexar and Comal counties. Settled in 1847, in the late 1880s its population grew with the influx of German and Polish immigrants. Its name is a mystery. Even in the 1930s the town's unofficial historian—a man in his 90s—did not know its origin.

Staples Near a cotton gin powered by the San Marcos River, in 1871 Civil War veteran Col. John Douglas Staples opened a country store that housed the post office; it was designated Staples Store until the Post Office Department dropped "Store" from the name.

Zorn Joseph Zorn had a store here in the 1850s.

KENDALL COUNTY

Kendall County was named in honor of George Wilkins Kendall (1809–67), who helped establish sheep farming in the Texas Hill Country in the mid-nineteenth century. Earlier, Kendall accompanied an ill-fated Texas expedition to Santa Fe that surrendered to the Mexican army, and he was imprisoned in Mexico City. Later his newspaper, the New Orleans Picayune, was a powerful advocate for war with Mexico and annexation of Texas. Kendall served as a volunteer with Capt. Ben McCullough's Texas Ranger Company in the Mexican War. His well-read reports from the field gained him fame as the nation's first war correspondent.

Bergheim   In 1900, Austrian-born Andreas Engel bought three acres of land on the site of present-day Bergheim, which means "mountain-home" in German.

Boerne   In 1849 German colonists camped on the north side of Cibolo Creek, a mile west of the present town of Boerne (BURnee). They called their community Tusculum, after Cicero's home in ancient Rome. A few years later, the present town site was laid out and the named changed to honor Ludwig Boerne. Originally Lob Buruch, he fled to Paris from Germany, changed his last name to Borne and then to Boerne and converted from Judaism to Christianity. By the time of his death in 1837 he had become a prolific and well-known writer as well as reformer and hero to the sort of young German intellectuals who settled here.

Comfort   The town of Comfort was surveyed in 1854 by E. Hermann Altgelt (King William Street, p. 14) on property owned by John Vles. Soon German freethinkers from New Braunfels and Fredericksburg began to settle in the area. One theory of its naming is that the settlers concluded that this confluence of Cypress Creek and the Guadalupe River was a great "genutlicher platzt," or comfortable place, to settle. Or it may have been derived from the "Komm fort," or "come forth," the plea for fellow Germans to emigrate to Texas.

Kendalia   This community was presumably named for George Wilkins Kendall, who established a ranch and introduced sheep ranching in the area in the 1840s (Kendall County, p. 206).

Sisterdale   Founded by German freethinkers in the idyllic valley of Sister Creek in 1847, this community became a hotbed of German abolitionism and Unionism before and during the Civil War. The name is said to come from its location in the valley of Sister Creek, formed by two parallel running brooks, the "Sisters." Sisterdale apparently attracted the most educated and intellectual colonists. A library of the ancient and modern classics was to be found in nearly every home, and weekly philosophical discussion sessions were common.

Waring   Waring was founded in 1888 as a stop on the Kerrville line of the San Antonio and Aransas Pass Railroad. Originally known as Waringford because R. P. M. Waring from Waringford, Ireland, provided the right-of-way through his property for the railroad, the name was shortened to Waring in 1901.

Welfare   Welfare also developed along stagecoach and railroad lines. Once Bon Ton or Boyton, its name was changed to Welfare perhaps for the German word Wohlfarht, meaning "pleasant trip."

Don Strange Ranch   When Don Strange (1940–2009) was still in high school, his parents owned a small party house on Bandera Road in northwestern San Antonio. Strange thought he could do something bigger and better, and indeed he did. Over the next 50 years he parlayed his personal charm, creative skills and indefatigable work ethic into establishing a catering business that would take him even to Hollywood and the White House. Specializing in Mexican and South Texas cuisine, he came up with new ideas and relied on others to do the culinary feats. In 1982, Strange found a piece of property near Welfare, Texas, on which stood a ramshackle stone farm house and through which trickled a barely perceptible creek. He ignored advice to tear down the house, but instead he restored it to a cozy cottage far nicer than its original state, dammed up the creek to create a small pond and added first one "barn," then other buildings. The ranch has hosted hundreds of parties, weddings and celebrations, including an event for ninety-three busloads of attendees at the 2001 International Rotary Convention.

Caterer Don Strange expanded to a ranch near Welfare.

Po Po's   Just off IH-10 at the Welfare exit is this eating establishment with an unusual name. Edwin Nelson, a rancher and dairyman, opened a gas station at this spot in 1929 and later added a dance hall. During Prohibition, you could buy a hamburger for a nickel, but alcoholic beverages were not allowed to be served inside the dance hall. But no problem, bootleggers peddled moonshine outside for 25 cents a shot. In 1932, another local rancher, Edwin "Ned" Houston, bought the place and is credited with giving the dance hall the unique name Po Po's. Houston had a large export operation of cattle to Latin America, and it is generally accepted by local residents that the name was derived from the great Mexican volcano Popocatepetl. The business has since changed hands several times. A unique feature of the interior décor is a collection of more than 2,000 commemorative plates from all over the world.

MEDINA COUNTY

Medina County was created by the legislature in 1848, with the Medina River as its eastern boundary. The river was named in 1689 by Alonso De Leon, governor of Coahuila, who was leading an expedition across

Texas against the French. He named the river for Pedro Medina, an early Spanish engineer whose navigation tables he was using.

Castroville Henri Castro (1786–1865), a descendant of Portuguese royalty, was responsible for settling the land west of San Antonio. In 1827 he was sent to New England as a political envoy from the Kingdom of Naples, became an American citizen and developed wide-ranging commercial interests connecting France with the United States. In 1842, Texas President Sam Houston appointed Castro as consul general representing Texas in Paris. His primary charge as ambassador to France was to bring French money and people to Texas. This he did with vigor, importing some 2,000 persons, primarily from the Alsace and Lorraine regions. After hardships and delays, Castro inaugurated his colony on September 3, 1844. It was named Castroville

Henri Castro was responsible for settling land west of San Antonio.

by colonists' unanimous vote. Castro died in Mexico while returning to France during the American Civil War, having exhausted his strength and fortune in his colonization efforts.

D'Hanis The original D'Hanis was the third settlement established by Henri Castro when 29 Alsatian families arrived here in 1847. Castro named the town for Guillaume (William) D'Hanis, Antwerp manager and principal administrative agent of his colonization company. In 1881 the railroad bypassed D'Hanis; a new town with the same name grew up a mile and a half west. The existing town is sometimes called New D'Hanis.

Devine In 1881, the International and Great Northern Railroad was extended from San Antonio to Laredo. This town on the line was named for Judge Thomas Jefferson Devine (1820–90), who happened to be the railroad's attorney. He was one of only three persons (another was Jefferson Davis) charged with treason by the Union during the Civil War, perhaps because the Confederacy sent him to negotiate with Mexico. Devine was pardoned without a trial and went on to a distinguished legal and judicial career, including a seat on the Texas Supreme Court.

Thomas Jefferson Devine's career included a judgeship on the Texas Supreme Court.

Dunlay Also developed as a railroad town, this was named for train conductor Jerry Dunlay. When Medina Dam was built in 1911, a railroad spur was laid from Dunlay to the construction site.

Hondo Hondo means "deep" in Spanish, a name given not only to the town but earlier to the creek and to a pass. When the railroad expanded west from San Antonio in 1881, Castroville was the twelfth largest city in Texas. Its citizens refused to pay the railroad a bonus, so Castroville was bypassed and Hondo City was established, displacing Castroville as county seat in 1892.

LaCoste Originally known as Fernando, the name was changed in 1898, for Lucian Jean Batiste LaCoste (1823–87), a prominent San Antonio businessman and a native of France. He owned the first ice plant in San Antonio and the first city water works, later purchased by a group led by banker George W. Brackenridge (p. 70).

Mico A small fishing resort east of the main dam on Medina Lake, Mico is an acronym for the Medina Irrigation Company (Natalia, below).

Natalia Englishman Frederick Stark Pearson (1861–1915) was a prime backer of the Medina Irrigation Company, which established— mostly with British investments—an irrigation district of more than 35,000 acres in Bexar, Medina and Atascosa counties. He was also chief engineer for the Medina Dam. Natalia was founded by Pearson and named for his daughter Natalie, though her name was misspelled. He and his wife died while traveling to England on the Lusitania, sunk by a German submarine in 1915. The irrigation company went into receivership two years later.

Quihi Laid out by Henri Castro in 1845, this community is said to have been named for the white-necked Mexican eagle buzzard, the "quichie" or "keechie."

Rio Medina Rio Medina is named for its location between the two main branches of the Medina River.

Yancey Once known as Tehuacana and also as Moss, this community was named for Yancey Kilgore and Yancey Strait, sons of owners of the town site.

WILSON COUNTY

Wilson County is named for James Charles Wilson (1818–61), an Oxford-educated Englishman who came to Texas in 1837. Although he spent seven months in a Mexican prison after the Mier Expedition and became a state senator, nothing in his biography suggests why this county bears his name. In his later years, he lived near Gonzales, but he apparently never lived in the county that was named for him in 1860, one year before his death.

Dewees The town was named for Thomas Dewees, who settled in the area about 1870. In partnership with Jim F. Ellison of Lockhart, Dewees and his brother John ran a successful cattle-driving business, during the 1870s averaging between 20,000 and 40,000 head of cattle per year and peaking at 100,000 in 1874.

Floresville Canary Island immigrant Don Francisco Flores de Abrego built a hacienda and ranch headquarters six miles northwest of the present site of Floresville around 1832, and the community was called Lodi. When Wilson County was formed in 1867, Floresville was created and named for the Flores family. Floresville's reputation as Peanut Capital of Texas dates to Andrew G. Pickett, who owned one of the original plots in the early 1870s. Said to have been the first in the county to have irrigation, Pickett started raising peanuts on it.

Kosciusko Established about 1890 as a supply point for Polish and German settlers, this town was named for Gen. Tadeusz Kosciuszko (1746–1817). Born in Poland, he studied philosophy in France and in 1776 joined colonial forces in the American Revolution, rising to the rank of brigadier general and being granted American citizenship, a pension and property. Returning to Poland, he led an unsuccessful revolt for independence against Russia. Shortly before his death, he freed serfs on his Polish estates and sold his Ohio property to provide education funds for black Americans. Texas settlers dropped the "z" from his name, presumably because the sound is difficult for English-speaking people to pronounce.

La Vernia First settled about 1850, this was originally called Live Oak Grove and then Post Oak. Local historians believe one of the original settlers, W. R. Wiseman, suggested the name be changed to La Verdear after a nearby grove of evergreen oaks. Verdear is Spanish for "to grow green." The name evolved to La Vernia.

Pandora Like many of its neighboring small towns, Pandora was established in the late 1890s as a stop on the San Antonio & Gulf Railroad. Two half-brothers named Montgomery and Sikes owned most of the land where the town was platted, and each wanted the new community to be named in his honor. The railroad officials settled the argument by conferring a named that referred to the box in Greek myth containing unforeseen troubles and problems, released when the box was opened by the mythical Pandora.

Poth Originally Marcelina when established in 1886 as a San Antonio and Aransas Pass Railway siding, the town was renamed in 1901 for A. H. Poth (POWeth), who built a cotton gin and applied for a post office. Poth submitted three names; two were rejected for being already used in Texas, so his name won.

Saspamco This is an acronym for San Antonio Sewer Pipe Manufacturing Company, which about 1901 began using the red clay of the area for manufacturing tile products.

Stockdale Fletcher Stockdale (1823–90) was lieutenant governor of Texas during the last days of the Confederacy. By 1871, when the town was named, Stockdale had become an attorney for the railroad. Use of his name may have been an enticement for rail service to the town.

Sutherland Springs John Sutherland Jr. (1792–1867), a physician who moved to San Antonio in 1835, was hired by the Alamo garrison for medical services. Injured in a fall from a horse, he could not fight and was sent to bring help from Gonzales. He returned with a contingent of men, but they were too late. In 1849 he purchased land on Cibolo Creek near hot sulfur springs. There he built the 52-room Sutherland Springs Hotel, offering 27 varieties of hot and cold mineral baths and earning a reputation for being able to cure cholera and other maladies. He had the town platted, sold lots, served as justice of the peace and postmaster, and sponsored the construction of a school and a Methodist church.

ACKNOWLEDGMENTS

By far the best part about writing this book has been getting in contact with many interesting and interested people. Help in the form of family histories, clues, leads, photos—and some hearsay—has come from a great number of people. I have tried to be diligent in recording the sources of information, but if I have missed a name, it was purely unintentional, and I apologize. In addition to those recognized in the first and second editions, those I do remember who have been helpful in preparing this third edition include:

Paula Allen; Dixie Anderson; Chris Avery, MD; Mark Bagg, MD; Tim Bannwolf; Gilbert Barrera; Arthur H. Bayern; Joseph Bitter, DVM; Amy Bitter; Pat Blattman; Mel Brown; Jenny Browne; Sally Buchanan; Jeff Callender; Jerry Comalander; Larry Collins; George Contreras; Genie Cooper; Pat Cordova; Frederick Costa; Jim Cullum Jr.; Bob Davis; Paige Davis; Julie Domel; John Feik; Carol Fenley; Mary Fisher; Tracy Frisbie; Gary Fuller; Butch Gerfers;

Theresa Gold; John Gonzalez; Marion Green; Ken Haase; Alex Halff; Phil Hardberger; Calvin Harlos; Harry Harlos; Susan Hasslocher; Harriet Marmon Helmle; John Hornbeak; Mary Jo Houston; Charlie Hubertus; Edgar and Allene Humbertus; John Igo; Kelly Irvin; Robert Judela; Jim Kimbrough; Wayne King; Richard M. "Tres" Kleberg III; Rosemary Kowalski; Cappy Lawton; Brother Edward Loch; Rene Lynn; Bill Lyons; Cynthia Leal; Dale Meek; Bob McCullough; Jim McKinney; Marti Merkens; Jane Middleswart; Doug Miller; Palmer Moe; Dan Parman; Alfred Moursund; Amber Murray; Sallie Newman; Kelly O'Connor; Wllbur Palmer; Mike Panasenko; Alice Yturri Peña; Beth Pittman;

Sarah Reveley; Marlene Richardson; Melaine Richardson; Becky Rittiman; Letty Saavedra; Joe Schafer; Clarence Schell; Jeff Schorr; Pat Semmes; Ben Singleton; George H. Spencer Jr.; Megan Stacy; Matthew Strange; Jim Stewart; Louise Thomas; Joe Tobar; Wilson Toudouze; Chuck Toudoze; Linda Transou; Chris Trevino; Diana Barrios Trevino; Jim Uptmore; Carol VanCleave; Wayne Vick; Ted Walker; Dean Weirtz; Fred Wendt; and Charles Wiseman.

The last two editions of *Place Names* have also been enhanced by the encyclopedic knowledge and recollection powers of Tom Shelton, whose photographic files at the Institute of Texan Cultures are a treasure trove of San Antonio history. Each time I get ready to publish a new edition I give him my "wish list" of photos, not knowing if such a picture even exists, and he manages to find most of what I am looking for.

And of course I continue to be grateful to my publisher, Lewis F. Fisher, who has given me the opportunity to pursue my odd hobby of tracking down trivia, and who has preserved much of our city's history in his own impressive collections of writings.

PHOTO CREDITS

Air Education and Training Command 51, 185; Richard O. Arneson 85; Audi Murphy VA Hospital 173; Chris Avery 167; Gayle and Tom Benson 134; Nell Bueher 102 (above); Howard E. Butt Jr. family 166; George Bush Presidential Library 101 (right); Casa Navarro State Historic Park 16; Chris Cheever 23; Juanita Herff Chipman 13; Cole High School 187; Jerry Comalander 107 (bottom), 108 (top); Jim Cullum 87(above); Josh Davis 108 (below); First Presbyterian Church 28; Fort Sam Houston Museum 31, 59, 63 (below), 101 (left), 104, 106 (below), 115, 186; Lewis F. Fisher 1, 8 (below), 9–10, 15, 17, 21–23, 36, 70, 80, 103, 121, 137 (above), 149; Congressman Charles Gonzalez 153; Bill Greehey 177; David P. Green 5, 47, 79, 86; C.H. Guenther & Son Inc. 11; Valerie Guenther 174, 182; Carl Gufstafson 118; Ellen Gunn 61 (top); Mary McDermott Gwin 64 (below); Ewing Halsell Foundation 176 (above); Susan Hasslocher 168; Frost Bank 152; Hall and Pat Hammond 58 (center), 61 (below); Phil Hardberger 83; Harlandale ISD 98; Corbett Holmgreen 180 (above); John Igo 138 (above); Jessie Mathis Kardys 157; Mary Kurio 176 (below); Gen. Douglas MacArthur Foundation 105; McCombs Enterprises 151; John Hornbeak 180 (below); Catherine Meaney 150; Menger Hotel 156 (above); Marty Merkens 41; Nancy Wood Moorman 107 (center); Alfred Moursund 58 (below); NASA 100, 107 (top), 128, 129; University of New Mexico, Stinson-Otero Collection, Center for Southwest Research 160; Admiral Nimitz Foundation 106 (above); 143 (above); Northside ISD 113; Linda Pace Foundation 164; Linda and Paul Pace 73; Ann Pressly 201; Randolph Air Force Base 188; Bobbi Kallison Ravicz 76; C. Mills Reeves Jr. 181; Marion Rowland 195; Rudder Middle School 114; St. Mary's University 102 (below); Thomas R. Semmes 138 (below), 143 (below); Ben Singleton 210; Marvin Smith 179; Sunshine Cottage School for the Deaf 130; Emeline Judson Synodis 98 (below); Texas State Library 11, 19, 211 (below); Tobin Theater Arts Fund 88 (below); Wilson Toudouze 18; Trinity University 103, 131, 132; Tom E. Turner Jr. 171; University of Texas at San Antonio Institute of Texan Cultures 8 (above), 26, 48, 53, 58 (top), 62, 63 (above), 64 (above), 71, 79 (top two), 82, 87 (below), 88 (above), 95, 96, 110, 121, 131, 137 (below), 139, 142, 143 (above), 145, 147 (above), 154, 161, 205, 208; University of Texas at Austin Center for American History 211 (above); Wagner High School 99; Jack Willome 55; Barbee Winn 196; Charles Wiseman 56; Witte Museum 21, 76 (above), 147 (below); Nelson Wolff 125; Zachry Construction Corp. 117; Roger Zeller 175.

BIBLIOGRAPHY

Alexander, Thomas E. *The Stars Were Big and Bright: The United States Army Air Forces and Texas During World War II*. Austin: Eakin Press, 2000.

Allen, Paula. *San Antonio Then and Now*. San Diego: Thunder Bay Press, 2005.

Anderson-Lindemann, Brenda. *Spring Branch & Western Comal County, Texas*. San Antonio: Omni Publishers, 1998.

Alexander, Thomas E. *The Stars Were Big and Bright: The United States Army Air Forces and Texas During World War II*. Austin: Eakin Press, 2000.

Atascosa History Committee. *Atascosa County History*. Dallas: Taylor Publishing, 1984.

Bailey, Valerie Martin, ed. *Bexar County Medical Dinosaurs Remember the Way It Was*. San Antonio: Rhyme or Reason Word Design Studio, 1999.

Bandera County History Book Committee. *History of Bandera County, Texas*. Dallas: Curtis Media Corporation, 1986.

Barrett, S. M. *Geronimo's Story of His Life*. Williamstown, MS.: Corner House Publishers, 1973.

Bennett, John M. *The Wednesday Lunch Club: A Brief History of a Group of Men from San Antonio*. San Antonio: n.p., 1991.

_____. *Those Who Made It: The story of the men and women of National Bank of Commerce of San Antonio*. San Antonio: N.p., 1978.

Berg, A. Scott. *Lindbergh*. New York: G. P. Putnam's Sons, 1998.

Biesele, Rudolph Leopold. *The History of the German Settlements in Texas, 1831–1861*. San Marcos: German-Texas Heritage Society, 1930.

Bowser, David. *Mysterious San Antonio*. San Antonio: N.p., 1990.

Brandon, Jay. *Law and Liberty. A History of the Legal Profession in San Antonio*. Dallas: Taylor Publishing Co., 1996.

Brown, Mel. *San Antonio in Vintage Postcards*. Charleston: Arcadia, 2000.

Burkhalter, Lois Wood. *Marion Koogler McNay: A Biography, 1883–1950*. San Antonio: McNay Art Institute, 1968.

Burkholder, Mary V. *Down the Acequia Madre in the King William Historic District*. San Antonio: N.p., 1976.

_____. *The King William Area: A History and Guide to the Houses*. San Antonio: The King William Association, 1973.

Bushick, Frank H. *Glamorous Days*. San Antonio: The Naylor Company, 1934.

Butterfield, Jack C. *The Free State of Bejar*. San Antonio: Daughters of the Republic of Texas at the Alamo, 1963.

Cameron, Rebecca Hancock. *Training to Fly: Military Flight Training 1907–1945*. Air Force History and Museums Program, 1999.

Carter, Wanda Bassett. *Elmendorf and Related Families*. Luling: June Publications, 1990.

Castaneda, Carlos. *Our Catholic Heritage in Texas. The Mission Era: The Winning of Texas 1693–1731*. Austin: Von Boeckmann-Jones Company, 1936.

Castro Colonies Heritage Association. *The History of Medina County, Texas*. Dallas: National ShareGraphics, n.d.

Chabot, Frederick C. *With the Makers of San Antonio*. San Antonio: Artes Graficas, 1937.

Corner, William. *San Antonio De Bexar: A Guide and History*. San Antonio: Bainbridge & Corner, 1890.

Crisp, James E. *Sleuthing the Alamo*. New York: Oxford University Press, 2005.

Crook, Cornelia. *San Pedro Springs Park: Texas' Oldest Recreation Area*. N.p., 1967.

Crutchfield, James A. *It Happened in Texas*. Helena, MT: Twodot, 1996.

Curtis, Albert. *Fabulous San Antonio*. San Antonio: The Naylor Company, 1955.

Davis, Ellis A. and Edwin H. Grobe. *The New Encyclopedia of Texas*. Dallas: Texas Development Bureau, 1930.

Diehl, Kemper. *Saint Mary's Hall: First Century*. San Antonio: N.p., 1979.

Dillon, David. *The Architecture of O'Neil Ford: Celebrating Place*. Austin: University of Texas Press, 1999.

Dixon, Jeanne, and Marlene Richardson. The Settlement of Leon Springs, from Prussia to Persia. San Antonio: Passing Memories, 2008.

Dingus, Anne. *The Book of Texas Lists*. Austin: Texas Monthly Press, 1981.

_____. *The Truth about Texas*. Houston: Gulf Publishing Company, 1995.

Du Gard, Rene Coulet. *Dictionary of Spanish Place Names: Texas and Arizona, vol. 4*. Editions des Deux Mondes, 1983.

Dunn, Edward C. *USAA: Life Story of a Business Cooperative*. New York: McGraw-Hill Book Company, 1970.

Everett, Donald E. *San Antonio: The Flavor of Its Past, 1845–1898*. San Antonio: Trinity University Press, 1975.

_____. *San Antonio's Monte Vista: Architecture and Society in a Gilded Age, 1890–1930*. San Antonio: Maverick Publishing Company, 1999.

Fehrenbach, T.R. *Fire and Blood: A History of Mexico*. New York: Macmillan Publishing Co., 1973.

Fisher, Lewis F. *Balcones Heights: A Crossroads of San Antonio*. San Antonio: Maverick Publishing Company, 1999.

_____. *River Walk: The Epic Story of San Antonio's River*. San Antonio: Maverick Publishing Company, 2007.

_____. *San Antonio: Outpost of Empires*. San Antonio: Maverick Publishing Company, 1997.

_____. *Saving San Antonio: The Precarious Preservation of a Heritage*. Lubbock: Texas Tech University Press, 1996.

_____. *The Spanish Missions of San Antonio*. San Antonio: Maverick Publishing Company, 1988.

Fort Sam Houston Museum Division. *Surrounded by History: How Fort Sam Houston's Built Environment Embodies the Values of Distinguished Soldiers*. San Antonio: N.p., 1999.

Gambrell, Herbert, and Virginia Gambrell. *A Pictorial History of Texas*. New York: E. P. Dutton & Co., 1960.

George, Mary Carolyn Hollers. *O'Neil Ford, Architect*. College Station: Texas A & M University Press, 1992.

Gesick, E. John. *Under the Live Oak Tree: A History of Seguin*. Seguin: N.p., n.d.

Gille, Frank H., ed. *Encyclopedia of Texas*. St. Clairs Shores, MI: Somerset Publishers, 1985.

Gillis, JoAnn Kester. *Helotes Happenings*. Austin: Nortex Press, 1998.

Graham, Henry. *History of the Texas Cavaliers*. San Antonio: N.p., 1976.

Groneman, Bill. *Alamo Defenders, A Genealogy: The People and Their Words*. Austin: Eakin Press, 1990.

_____. *Eyewitness to the Alamo*. Plano, TX: Republic of Texas Press, 1996.

Guerra, Henry. *Henry Guerra's San Antonio: A Unique History and Pictorial Guide*. San Antonio: Alamo Press, 1998.

Haas, Oscar. *History of New Braunfels and Comal County, Texas 1844–1946*. Austin: N.p., 1968.

Hafertepe, Kenneth. "The Texas Homes of Sam and Mary Maverick," *Southwestern Historical Quarterly* 109 No. 1, July 2005.

Hagner, Lillie May. *Alluring San Antonio, Through the Eyes of an Artist*. San Antonio: Clemens Printing Co., 1947.

Handy, Mary Olivia. *History of Fort Sam Houston*. San Antonio: The Naylor Company, 1951.

Harlandale Independent School District. *The Harlandale Story: Celebrating 100 Years of Education*. San Antonio: Harlandale ISD, 1994.

Hendricks, Frances Kellam. *A History of Southwest Texas Methodist Hospital, 1955–1980*. San Antonio: N.p., 1983.

Henson, Margaret Swett. *Lorenzo de Zavala, the Pragmatic Idealist*. Fort Worth: Texas Christian University Press, 1996.

Herff, Ferdinand Peter. *The Doctors Herff: A Three-Generation Memoir*. San Antonio: Trinity University Press, 1973.

Heusinger, Edward W. *A Chronology of Events in San Antonio*. San Antonio: Standard Printing Company, 1951.

Hills, William J. *Stories of the Nix Hospital: A 75-Year Anniversary Celebration*, San Antonio: N.p., 2005.

House, Boyce. *San Antonio. City of Flaming Adventure*, 2nd ed. San Antonio: The Naylor Company, 1968.

Jennings, Frank W. *San Antonio: The Story of an Enchanted City*. San Antonio: San Antonio Express-News, 1998.

Jimenez, Diane, and George Southern, Consultants. *Wilson County History*. Dallas: Taylor Publishing Company, 1990.

Johnson, Edgar D., Waynne I. Cox, and C. Britt Bousman. *HemisFair Park, San Antonio, Texas: An Archival Study for the Convention Center Expansion*. San Antonio: University of Texas at San Antonio, 1997.

Johnston, Leah Carter. *San Antonio: St. Anthony's Town*. San Antonio: The Naylor Company, 1976.

Katz, Susanna R., and Anne A. Fox. *Archaeological and Historical Assessment of Brackenridge Park, City of San Antonio, Texas*. San Antonio: University of Texas at San Antonio, 1979.

Kendall County Historical Commission. *A History of Kendall County, Texas*. Dallas: Taylor Publishing Company, 1984.

Kownslar, Allan O. *The European Texans*. College Station: Texas A & M University Press, 2004.

Krause, Cathe, ed. *Alamo Heights Golden Anniversary*. San Antonio: City of Alamo Heights, 1972.

Kunhardt, Philip B., Jr., Phillip B. Kunhardt III, and Peter W. Kunhardt. *The American President*. New York: Riverhead Books, 1999.

Lair, Gerald, and Susanna Nawrocki. *San Antonio: The Soul of Texas*. Atlanta: Longstreet Press, 1993.

Leal, John Ogden. *Journey of the Canary Island Families to Texas, 1731*. San Antonio: N.p., 1991.

Lich, Glen E. *The German Texans*. San Antonio: University of Texas Institute of Texan Cultures, 1981.

Livingston, Mary E. *San Antonio in the 1920s and 1930s*. Charleston, SC: Arcadia Publishing, 2000.

Lochbaum, Jerry, ed. *Old San Antonio: History in Pictures*. San Antonio: Express Publishing Co., 1968.

Lynn, Rene. "Austin Highway Then and Now." Supplement to *The North San Antonio Times*, April 2, 1987.

MacArthur, Douglas. *Reminiscences*. New York: McGraw-Hill, 1964.

Manchester, William. *American Caesar: Douglas MacArthur, 1880–1964*. Boston: Little, Brown, and Company, 1978.

Manguso, John. Hospitals at Fort Sam Houston. San Antonio: Fort Sam Houston Museum, 2006.

Martinello, Marian L., and Thomas H. Robinson. *San Antonio, The First Civil Settlement in Texas. A Guide for Teachers, K–12*. San Antonio: N.p., 1981.

Matthews, Wilbur L. *History of San Antonio Medical Foundation and South Texas Medical Center*. San Antonio: N.p., 1983. Rev. 1988.

McComb, David G. *Texas: An Illustrated History*. New York: Oxford University Press, 1995.

McCullough, William Wallace, Jr. *John McCullough: Pioneer Presbyterian Missionary and Teacher in the Republic of Texas*. Austin: Pemberton Press, 1966.

Michener, James A. *The Eagle and the Raven*. Austin: State House Press, 1990.

Miller, Char, and Heywood T. Sanders, eds. *Urban Texas: Politics and Development*. College Station: Texas A & M University Press, 1990.

Miller, Ray. *The Eyes of Texas Travel Guide, San Antonio/Border Edition*. Houston: Cordovan Corp., 1979.

Morrison, Andrew. *San Antonio, Texas*. St. Louis: Geo. W. Englehardt and Co., 1895.

Nep, Johnny. The Early Years of Military Aviation in San Antonio, 1910–1947. San Antonio: Air Education and Training Command History Office, 2006.

Newcomb, Pearson. *The Alamo City*. San Antonio: Standard Printing Company, 1926.

Newton, Pauline T. *Around San Antonio*. Charleston: Arcadia Publishing, 1999.

Nimitz, Chester W. *Some Thoughts to Live By*. Fredericksburg, TX: The Admiral Nimitz Foundation, 1985.

Nixon, Pat Ireland. *A Century of Medicine in San Antonio*. San Antonio: N.p., 1936.

Noonan Guerra, Mary Ann. *The History of San Antonio's Market Square*. San Antonio: Alamo Press, 1988.

_____. *The Story of the San Antonio River*. San Antonio: San Antonio River Authority, 1978.

Norton, Charles G., ed. *Men of Affairs of San Antonio*. San Antonio: San Antonio Newspaper Artists' Association, 1912.

Odom, Marianne, and Gaylon Finklea Young. *The Businesses That Built San Antonio.* San Antonio, Living Legacies, 1985.

Ornish, Natalie. *Pioneer Jewish Texans: Their Impact on Texas and American History for Four Hundred Years, 1590–1990.* Dallas: Texas Heritage Press, 1989.

Perry, Garland A. *Historic Images of Boerne, Texas.* Boerne: Perry Enterprises, 1982.

Pfeiffer, Maria Watson. *School by the River: Ursuline Academy to Southwest School of Art and Craft, 1851–2001.* San Antonio: Maverick Publishing Company, 2001.

Rahe, Alton J. *History of Sattler and Mountain Valley School in Comal County, Texas, 1846–1964.* New Braunfels. N.p., 1999.

Ramsdell, Charles. *San Antonio: A Historical and Pictorial Guide.* Austin: University of Texas Press, 1959.

Ransleben, Guido E. *A Hundred Years of Comfort in Texas.* San Antonio: The Naylor Company, 1954.

Robinson-Zwahr, Robert R. *The Bremers and Their Kin in Germany and in Texas.* Burnet, TX: Nortex Press, 1979.

Rybczyk, Mark Louis. *San Antonio Uncovered.* Plano, TX: Wordware Publishing, 1992.

Salazar, Veronica. *Dedication Rewarded: Prominent Mexican Americans.* San Antonio: Express-News Corp., n.d.

_____. *Dedication Rewarded,. vol. 2.* San Antonio: Munguia Printers, 1981.

San Antonio Board of Realtors. *San Antonio: Reflections of the Last Two Hundred Years.* San Antonio: American Printers, 1976.

Sibley, Marilyn McAdams. *George W. Brackenridge, Maverick Philanthropist.* Austin: University of Texas Press, 1973.

Steinfeldt, Cecilia. *San Antonio Was: Seen through a Magic Lantern.* San Antonio: San Antonio Museum Association, 1978.

Steves, Albert IV. *The Tobins of Texas: The First 150 Years.* N.p., 2000.

Tarpley, Fred. *1001 Texas Place Names.* Austin: University of Texas Press, 1980.

Thurston, Herbert, and Donald Attwater. *Butler's Lives of the Saints.* Westminster, MD: Christian Classics, 1956.

Tolbert, Frank X. *An Informal History of Texas.* New York: Harper & Bros., 1951.

Thompson, Frank. *Texas Hollywood: Filmmaking in San Antonio since 1910.* San Antonio: Maverick Publishing Company, 2002.

Tyler, Ron, et. al., eds. *The New Handbook of Texas.* Austin: Texas State Historical Association, 1996.

Underwood, John. *The Stinsons: A Pictorial History.* Glendale, CA: Heritage Press, 1983.

Walker, Tom. Banking on Tradition: The 130-Year History of Frost National Bank. San Antonio: Frost National Bank, 2000.

Whisenhunt, Donald W. *Chronology of Texas History.* Burnet, TX: Eakin Press, 1982.

Williams, Docia Schultz. *Best Tales of Texas Ghosts.* Plano, TX: Republic of Texas Press, 1998.

Wolff, Nelson W. *Mayor: An Inside View of San Antonio Politics, 1981–1995.* San

Antonio: San Antonio Express-News, 1997.

Woolford, Bess Carroll, and Ellen Schulz Quillin. *The Story of the Witte Memorial Museum, 1922–1960*. San Antonio: N.p., 1966.

Woolford, Sam. *San Antonio: A History for Tomorrow*. San Antonio: n.p., 1963.

Zunker, Vernon G. *A Dream Come True: Robert Hugman and San Antonio's River Walk*. San Antonio: N.p., 1983.

SELECTED INTERNET RESOURCES*

Catholic Encyclopedia   www.newadvent.org

City of San Antonio   www.ci.sat.tx.us

Daughters of the Republic of Texas Library   www.drtl.org

Encyclopedia Britannica   www.britannica.com

The New Handbook of Texas On-line   www.tsha.utexas.edu

Northside Independent School District   www.nisd.net

Old maps of San Antonio   www.texasfreeway.com

San Antonio Express-News Archives   www.mysanantonio.com

San Antonio Public Library   www.sat.lib.tx.us

Texas Historic Sites Atlas   www.atlas.thc.state.tx.us

* All school districts have Websites, which are marvelous sources of school names and histories.

INDEX

Biering Lane 49
Bill Greehey Arena 120
Bill Miller Bar-B-Q 165
Billa, Bob 58
Billa, Jeanne 141
Billie Jean King Drive 198
Billy Mitchell Boulevard 57–58
Binz-Engleman Road 46
Bitter, John A. 35
Bitters Road 35
Black, Claude 142
Blake, Gordon A. 25
Block, George 118
Blossom, Virgil T. 107–08
Blossom Athletic Center 107–08
Bluemel, Richard 35
Bluemel Road 35
Bob and Jeanne Billa Learning
    and Leadership Development
    Center 141
Bob Billa Road 58
Boerne 209
Boerne, Ludwig 209
Bogart Drive 198
Bolívar, Simón 77
Bolivar Hall 77
Bonham, James B. 7
Bonham Street 7
Bonnie Conners Park 69–70
Booker, Pat 30
Bordelon, William J. 65–66
Borg Drive 198
Bowen, John 85–86
Bowen's Island 85–86
Bowers, Ruth M. 175
Bowie, James 7
Bowie Street 7
Brackenridge, George W. 70, 121, 132
Brackenridge High School 121
Brackenridge Park 70–72
Bradley, Omar 101
Bradley Middle School 101
Brady, Lady B. 150
Brady, Thomas F. 149–50
Brady Building 149–50
Brady-Green Clinic 150
Brandeis, Louis D. 109
Brandeis High School 109
Braun, Philip 35
Braun Road 35–36
Braunig, Victor 162
Brees, Herbert J. 21–22
Brees Boulevard 21–22
Brenan, Walter 133
Brenda Lane 198

Brennan, William J. 109–10
Brennan High School 109–10
Brentwood Middle School 95
Briscoe, Dolph Jr. 175
Brooke, Roger 184
Brooke Army Medical Center
    (BAMC) 184
Brooks, Sidney 185
Brooks City Base 185
Brooks Field 185
Bryan McClain Park 72
Bryant, Frank 143–44
Budge Street 198
Buena Vista Street 7
Bull Run Drive 197
Bullis, John H. 185–86
Bulverde 204
Bulverde, Lorenzo de 204
Burbank, Luther 121
Burbank High School 121
Burton and Miriam Grossman
    Cancer Treatment Center 173
Bush, Barbara 101
Bush Middle School 101
Bushnell, Alen R. 22
Bushnell Avenue 22
Butt, Howard E. 167

Cadena, Carlos C. 150–51
Cadena-Reeves Justice Center 150–51
Calla Real 9
Callaghan, Alfred 36
Callaghan, Bryan Jr. 7–8
Callaghan Avenue 7–8
Callaghan Road 36
Calle de Alamdea 9
Calle del Potreto 9
Callies, R. A. 67
Camargo, Mateo 80
Camaron Street
Cambell, Neil 94
Camp Bullis 185–86
Camp Funston 186
Camp Kelly 187
Camp Stanley 186
Campbell, John F. 200
Campbell, Jourdan 201
Campbellton 200
Can't Stop Street 46
Cappy's 164
Cardenas, José A. 96–97
Carter, Henry C. 155
Carver, George W, 94, 136, 141–42
Carver Academy 93–94
Carver Branch Library 136

Dan Parman Auditorium 174
Dana Bible Drive 198
Danny Kaye Drive 198
Dashiell, Jeremiah Y. 78
Dashiell House 78
David Edwards Street 24
Davis, Jefferson 121
Davis, Josh 108
Davis, Odie Jr. 143
Davis, S. J. 121–22
Davis Middle School 121–22
Davis-Scott YMCA 143
Dawson, Robert A. 73–74
Dawson Park 73–74
De Zavala, Adina 36
De Zavala, Augustin 36
De Zavala, Lorenzo 36
De Zavala Road 36
Dean Martin Drive 198
Defenders Parkway 197
Delavan, George 46, 130
Delavan Tennis Stadium 130
Dellcrest 46
Desilu Drive 198
Devine 211
Devine, Thomas J. 133, 211
Devlin Point 198
Dewees 213
Dewees, Thomas 213
Dignowity, Anthony M. 74
Dignowity Hill 74
Dignowity Park 74
Dobie, J. Frank 126–27
Dolorosa Street 10
Dolph Briscoe Jr. Library 175
Don Hardin Athletic
    Complex 117–18
Don Rafael Gonzales
    Elementary School 126
Don Strange Ranch 210
Dona Anna Cove 198
Donaldson, Arthur 50
Donaldson, David 50
Donaldson Avenue 50
Dorie Miller Community Center 143
Dove, Marion 207
Dr. Frank Bryant Health
    Center 143–44
Dr. Hector P. Garcia Middle
    School 110–11
Dreeben, Alan 134
Dreeben, Barbara B. 134
Dreeben School of Education 134
Driscoll, Clara 102
Driscoll Middle School 102

Dub Farris Athletic Complex 117
Dullnig, George 151
Dullnig Building 151
Duncan, Thomas 50
Duncan Drive 50
Duncan Field 50
Dunlay 212
Dunlay, Jerry 212
Dwight Avenue 62
Dwight Middle School 128
Dwyer, Edward 11
Dwyer Avenue 11

E. M. Stevens Stadium 131
Earl Abel's 165–66
East Central High School 94
East Central ISD 94
Eckert, Gus 38
Eckhert Road 37
Ed Wiseman Trace 56
Edgewood Communications
    and Fine Arts Academy 97
Edgewood ISD 95
Edie Adams Drive 198
Edison, Thomas A. 122
Edison High School 122
Edmunds, Ernest B. 148
Edward Ximenes Avenue 132
Edwards, David 24
Edwards, Hayden 166
Edwards Aquifer 166
Eisenhauer, Paul 24
Eisenhauer, William 24
Eisenhauer Road 24
Eisenhower, Dwight D. 74, 102, 128
Eisenhower Middle School 102
Eisenhower Park 74
Elizabeth Road 24
Ella Austin Community Center 144
Ellison, Ray 54–55
Elmendorf 191
Elmendorf, Carl A. 191
Emerson Middle School 125
Emile and Albert Friedrich
    Wilderness Park 74
Emily Morgan Hotel 151–52
Enchanted Drive 197
Englemann, Ferdinand B. 46
Englemann, H. 46
Enrique M. Barrera Community
    Center 144
Epler Drive 43
Errol Flynn Drive 198
Espada, Mission 4
Espanola Drive 198